MULTI-AGENT SYSTEMS

Edited by **Jorge Rocha**

Multi-agent Systems
http://dx.doi.org/10.5772/66595
Edited by Jorge Rocha

Contributors

Fábio Januário, Alberto Cardoso, Paulo Gil, Joaquim Leitão, Seungyeol Lee, Jeon-Il Moon, Maddgedara Lalith, Leonel Aguilar, Muneo Hori, Danilo Saft, Volker Nissen, Nicksson Ckayo Arrais De Freitas, Marcelino Silva, Jorge Rocha, Inês Boavida-Portugal, Eduardo Gomes, Maricela Bravo, Alejandro Reyes, Leonardo Sánchez, Roberto Alcántara-Ramírez, Jesús Santiaguillo-Salinas, Eduardo Aranda-Bricaire, Muhammad Nasiruddin Mahyuddin, Ali Safaei, Raul Campos-Rodriguez, Luis Gonzalez-Jimenez, Francisco Cervantes Alvarez, Francisco Amezcua Garcia, Miguel Fernandez Garcia

Published by InTech
Janeza Trdine 9, 51000 Rijeka, Croatia

Publishing Process Manager Nina Kalinic
Technical Editor SPi Global
Cover InTech Design team

First published September, 2017
Printed in Croatia
Legal deposit, Croatia: National and University Library in Zagreb

Additional hard copies can be obtained from orders@intechopen.com

Multi-agent Systems, Edited by Jorge Rocha
p. cm.
Print ISBN 978-953-51-3535-7
Online ISBN 978-953-51-3536-4

For EU product safety concerns:
IN TECH d.o.o., Prolaz Marije Krucifikse Kozulić 3, 51000 Rijeka, Croatia,
info@intechopen.com or visit our website at intechopen.com.

Meet the editor

Jorge Rocha, a geographer, was born in Lisbon in 1970. He is an MSc degree holder in Geographic Information Systems (2003) and in Territorial Management (2013) and a PhD degree holder in Geographic Information Science (2012). Currently, he is an assistant professor of the Institute of Geography and Spatial Planning and a member of the Modelling, Urban and Regional Planning and Environmental Hazard and Risk Assessment and Management research groups of the Centre for Geographical Studies, all from the University of Lisbon. His fields of expertise are geosimulation and geocomputation involving artificial neural networks, graphs theory, cellular automata and multi-agent systems. Jorge's works are quite diverse, focusing mainly on, but not exclusively, urban morphology, remote sensing, epidemiology, health geography, smart cities and big data (geomarketing and tourism).

Contents

Preface

Multi-agent systems (MAS) is an expanding field in science and engineering. It merges classical fields like game theory (gamification) and decentralized control with modern ones like machine learning and computer science. This book provides a succinct introduction to the subject, covering the theoretical fundamentals as well as the latter developments in a coherent and clear manner. The incentive for going into MAS often arises from interest in artificial agents. Such agents can be, but not limited to, trading agents, e.g. interface agents, game-playing agents or autonomous robots in a multi-robot situation.

MAS spans disciplines as diverse as biology, ecology, computer simulation, business, economic science, policy, social sciences, political science, military studies and many others. The technical material includes logic, probability theory, game theory, and optimization. Each of these topics can easily become an independent book, and this book does not aim to replace them. Rather, the aim has been to gather elements from several disciplines and put them together into a balanced and accurate approach to this broad field.

As the umbrella of MAS is so broad, the decision of what to include in a book on the topic and how to organize the designated content is crucial. To begin with, this book concentrates on practical applications rather than introductory topics. Although occasionally makes reference to the concepts involved, it will do so primarily to clarify real-world applications. The intention is to analyse each topic in detail so readers can be able to tackle some technical material and then point possible directions for further research topics.

The chapters in this book cover a wide spectrum of issues related to MAS applications. The book is organized in sections: the first one, with the cover designation, is the introductory chapter that explains the basic concepts underlying MAS. This is followed by application chapters which deal with specific MAS and empirical applications. The empirical chapters are organized in five sections, covering issues so diverse as Traffic and Transportation Systems, Crowds and Evacuation Modelling, Processes Control in Industrial Applications, Data Mining and Image processing, and Emergence, Cognition and Context Awareness

Finally, the range of author affiliations covers a significant fraction of the organizations that are currently working in MAS, and powerfully proves the universal nature of this relatively new field of research. In the end, acknowledgements are due to the contributing authors, because without them it would not have been possible to make this book true.

Ph.D. Jorge Rocha
Institute of Geography and Spatial Planning
University of Lisbon

Section 1

Introductory: Multi-Agent Systems

Chapter 1

Introductory Chapter: Multi-Agent Systems

Jorge Rocha, Inês Boavida-Portugal and
Eduardo Gomes

Additional information is available at the end of the chapter

http://dx.doi.org/10.5772/intechopen.70241

1. Introduction

Agents, or more precisely intelligent agents, are a novel paradigm for software applications development, supporting the simulation of complex individual interactions. Moreover, agent-based computing has been welcomed as the latest paradigm shift in software development as well as the new software revolution. Presently, agents are one of the main fields of interest in computer science, artificial intelligence (AI), and complex system theory.

Intelligent (or rational) agents are used in a wide multiplicity of applications, ranging from relatively small systems, e.g. email filters, to large complex systems, such as air traffic control, bird flocking, or human social behaviour. Apparently, it may look that such particularly unlike types of system cannot have much in common. Still, nothing can be more deceitful, as in both the key concept is the agent.

Before addressing the issue of agent-based systems (ABS) development, one should try to define what terms 'agent' and ABS mean. Regrettably, there is a lack of commonly accepted definitions about key concepts in agent-based computing. Actually, there is no genuine agreement on the definition of the term agent.

As Russell and Norvig [1] stated an agent is anything that can be considered able to perceive its environment through sensors and act on this environment through actuators. To Macal [2], an agent shall have the following characteristics: (i) be identifiable—a discrete individual with a set of features and rules (mathematical or logic) that govern behaviour and decision-making capacity; (ii) be located—settled in an environment with which it interacts and also in which interacts with other agents; (iii) be goal-driven; (iv) be self-contained; and (v) be flexible, and have the ability to learn and adapt its behaviour through time-based experiences.

Most authors agree that although there are multiple definitions of the term 'agent', several attributes can be pointed out such as heterogeneity, autonomy, capacity to process and exchange information, follow if-then rules, goal-driven, and deductive code-based units, with boundary and state. There are also core behaviours: mobility, interaction, adaptation, and bounded rationality [3].

Agents are not aggregated into homogeneous pools. Rather, agents are heterogeneous with different attributes, behaviours and rules, which may differ in multiple ways (e.g. social network, individual preferences), and over time. For instance, one can model groups of residents in a specific neighbourhood but these individuals can have heterogeneous characteristics such as age, gender, income, and living preferences, although associating with the same group.

Agents are autonomous entities that are not subjected to the influence of external direction. They are developed over a bottom-up approach and have the capacity for processing information, while sharing it with other agents, through individual-based interaction that does not suffer top-down control. However, when a new agent enters the simulation, its actions can be conditioned by pre-existing norms that have been instituted through earlier agent interactions and persisted through time steps. These interactions can be expressed by the interchange of data from one agent to another. In such a way, micro and macro level will typically coevolve without pre-defined upper level controllers (i.e., bottom-up approach).

An agent may be goal-driven and takes independent actions to reach its goals. Thus, agents compare behaviour outcomes to its goals and adapt responses in the future. An agent's behaviour can be described by simple if-then rules that used to describe the theoretical assumptions of agent behaviour, in the form of computational procedures that lead to goal achievement. These procedures constitute a plan for achieving agents' objectives.

ABS is one where an agent is used as key abstraction. Theoretically, an ABS could be conceptualized in terms of agents and still be implemented without using any software consistent to agents. There is an obvious parallelism with object-oriented software, where it is fully conceivable to design a system based on objects, and implement it without getting use of object-oriented software. Nevertheless, this would be counterproductive or, at least, unusual. The same happens with ABS, where users expect agents to be designed and implemented using agent paradigm (e.g., using specific agent based software).

One should note that an ABS may have any non-zero amount of agents. A multi-agent system (MAS), designed and implemented by means of several interacting agents, is more general and pointedly more complex than the unitary (single case) agent. In real world, there are various number of situations where the single-agent case is suitable. A good example is the expert assistant, where an agent acts like an expert assistant to a user attempting to fulfil some task on a computer.

MAS is a computer-based environment made of multiple interacting intelligent agents. MAS are preferably used in solving problems that are difficult (or impossible) for an individual agent. As with agents, there is no categorical definition of MAS so let us focus on one that is relatively consensual. In Stone and Veloso [4], MAS is defined as 'a loosely coupled network of problem-solving entities (agents) that work together to find answers to problems that are beyond the individual capabilities or knowledge of each entity (agent)'.

As in MAS, agent-based model (ABM) also consists of interacting agents within a specific environment. ABM is known by different names due to its wide variety of applications, which could refer to entirely diverse methodologies. It can also be called a multi-agent system (MAS) or agent-based system (ABS).

In a computer science (e.g. AI), ABM usually states a computer-based method for studying the (inter)actions of a set of autonomous entities. In non-computing–related scientific domains as in social sciences, ABM could refer to an actor in the social world and be called agent-based social simulation (ABSS). Davidsson [5], using different combinations of focus areas (e.g. agent-based computing, computer simulation, and social sciences), further subdivides ABSS into three categories: (i) social aspects of agent systems (SAAS); (ii) multi-agent based simulation (MABS); and (iii) social simulation (SocSim).

In other domains (e.g. transportation ecological science or life science), ABM mostly refer to an individual-based model or a self-sufficient computing method. Although ABM is a wide ranging paradigm applied in totally different manners in all types of scientific domains, eventually all its subtle differences meet together under the domain of agent-based computing [6].

Even though there is a significant overlay, MAS not necessarily means the same as ABM. The objective of an ABM is to search for descriptive insights into the agents' (not necessarily intelligent) collective behaviour following simple rules (typical of natural systems) rather than solving particular engineering problems. ABM is more often used in the sciences, whereas MAS is frequently applied in engineering- and technology-related issues [6]. Hereafter the designation MAS will be use as a general term covering all agent related semantics discussed in previous paragraphs.

2. MAS characteristics

An agent could refer to different components as applications have different objectives and lay down in different paradigms [7]. One can see an agent as being part of a program (e.g. model, system, or subsystem) or any type of independent entity (e.g. organization or individuals). Each agent is programmed to react to other agents and to its computational environment, with respect to behaviour rules from primitive reaction decisions to complex adaptive AI. However, one may believe that the majority of researchers should be in general agreement with Wooldridge and Jennings [8] who defined an agent as a piece of hardware or a software-based computer system that entail the following properties:

- Reactivity, in the sense agents have the perception of their environment and respond quickly to changes that may occur.
- Pro-activity, not being limited to acting in response to the environment, agents are able to take the initiative and show behaviour driven by objectives.
- Social skills. The agents are able to interact/communicate (cognitive model) with other agents (and possibly humans) through a given Agent Communication Language (ACL) and establishing connections between their autonomous objectives and the spatial context.

These properties are somewhat difficult to identify than it may seem at first sight. Autonomy, although consensual in the agents' community and essential in Wooldridge and Jennings agent definition, can never be fully achieved. It is clear that the agent has to be created and put into operation by a human (or another agent). The assumption that the agent action will not have an end is also not entirely valid. Of course, under the aegis of current science, the agent will have a limited lifetime and a final action. On the other hand, although autonomy (i.e., actions are carried out without human interference) is essential to the agent, usually human-agent interaction is desirable or even essential. It is usual to build agents that behave autonomously but are also able to take orders or instructions from humans.

To build purely reactive agents can be a simple task, but is not entirely desirable. A purely reactive agent would react to changes in environment consecutively without seeking to achieve its medium or long-term objectives, i.e. display goal-oriented behaviour. One should define agents capable of balancing reactive with proactive behaviour. Nonetheless, the difficulty in balancing these two types of behaviour is very high [9].

The pro-activeness is simple to get in functional systems. Still, this simplicity only applies if a static environment is considered, i.e. it does not change during the accomplishment of a given procedure or function. In addition, the agent should have all the information it needs to run that procedure or function, without any uncertainty in the environment. However, these assumptions are not valid for most environments. For dynamic and not fully accessible environments, the agents must be able to react to changes in the environment and reason if the original objectives are still valid, due to the changes in the environment while performing a given procedure. This means that the agents have to be reactive and therefore able to quickly adapt to phase-shifts in the environment.

The social capacity of an agent is related to its ability to exchange high-level messages (and not only data-bytes without an associated meaning) and carry out processes of social interaction with other agents (and/or humans) similar to those used by humans in their daily lives, establishing collective behaviours. These processes include the coordination, cooperation, and negotiation. In order to conduct them, it is necessary to reason about the objectives of the other agents (if any) present in the environment or, at least, have notion of their existence.

It is also necessary to understand that they are also autonomous agents and do not necessarily share common goals. In this way, it may be necessary to negotiate and cooperate with other agents, eventually exchanging information and/or goods. For example, in order to convince an agent to cooperate, it might be necessary to make a payment or offer a particular good or service. In several cases, agents have opposite objectives and, therefore, are not able to carry out any cooperative process that includes them.

The equilibrium between social capacity and proactive or reactive capabilities is also of great importance. This importance is even greater in a scheme of cooperative work set by a group of agents who share a common goal. In these situations, each agent has to adapt his reaction to the events that occur in the modeling environment, both with the free will needed to perform individual tasks and with the social behaviors necessary to perform collective tasks [9].

Some researchers highlight other aspects of agency (e.g. mobility and adaptability). Indeed, agents may have supplementary features, and in specific uses, some features can be more significant than others. Yet, is the conjugation of the three main properties (reactivity, pro-activity and social skills) in a single entity that gives importance to the agent paradigm and makes the difference between agent systems and related software paradigms, e.g. object-oriented systems, distributed systems, and expert systems [10].

Franklin and Graesser [7] discuss about various definitions of agents and list some behaviours displayed by them: (i) reactive; (ii) autonomous; (iii) guided by objective(s)/pro-active; (iv) temporally continuous; (v) social/communicative; (vi) have ability to learn/adapt; (vii) mobile; (viii) flexible; and (ix) have personality. There are still other agents classification schemes based, for example, on the type of task they are running or in their architecture.

The very definition of agent satisfies only the first four identified features, as Franklin and Graesser [7] state 'an agent is a system located in an environment and is part of it. An agent understands the environment and acts on it over time. An agent has its own agenda in order to reflect its perceptions of future'. But even so, this definition is generic enough to cover from a thermostat, containing one or two sensors and extremely simple control structure, to human beings with multiple and conflicting guidelines, various sensors, various possibilities of actions, and structures of extremely complex and sophisticated control.

The concept of agent is related to rationality. According to Russel and Norvig [1], rationality is associated with four factors: (i) the performance measure that defines success criteria; (ii) the prior knowledge of the agent about the environment; (iii) the actions that the agent is capable to perform; and (iv) the sequence of agent's perceptions. These lead to the definition that 'for each possible perceptions, a rational agent must select an action that is expected to maximize its performance measure, given the evidence provided by the sequence of perceptions and any prior internal knowledge of the agent' [1].

3. MAS classification

Due to the wide range of applications, the difficulty in defining what is truly an 'intelligent agent' and to the enormous momentum that this area of research has had over the past few years, there are several synonyms of the term 'intelligent agent' created by different researchers in an attempt to better characterize their own work. Thus, it is usually found in the specialized agent literature designations such as robots, software agents (or softbots), knowbots, taskbots or userbots, personal assistants, virtual characters, and so on. Although the existence of these synonyms is perfectly understandable, sometimes obscures the concept itself making it harder to define the object in MAS research.

In order to better characterize the agents' scientific area, it is useful to divide agents into classes analysing the different typologies of agents proposed in the literature. The high number of attributes previously discussed allows to realize how difficult it is to implement an agent that incorporates all those attributes. This is also related to the fact that the characteristics of an agent are ideally application-type dependents. The analysis of agents' attributes has been used by researchers to sort and categorize them in types. A typology is a classification by types of agents that have attributes in common.

Nwana [11] proposes a typology of agents, identifying seven distinct classification dimensions:

1. **Mobility**. Static or mobile agents. Mobile agents can be resident in the source machine or temporarily in another one.
2. **Reasoning model**. Presence or not of a type of symbolic reasoning, i.e. an agent may be reactive or purely deliberative.
3. **Agent function**. The main function assumed by the agent, such as an information search agent (looking for information for a given user on the Internet) or interface (which facilitates the interaction man-machine of a given application).
4. **Autonomy**. Agents operate without any direct human or other agents intervention, they have some kind of control over their actions and internal state, and they are able to exchange information with other agents. Agents are not subjected to the influence of external direction.
5. **Cooperation**. Realization of cooperative actions with other agents.
6. **Learning**. Inclusion or not of learning capabilities in the agent (individual, evolutionary, and social).
7. **Hybrid features**. These combine two or more different behaviour philosophies in the same agent.

Combining the characteristics of autonomy, cooperation, and learning, Nwana [11] derives four types of agents: (i) collaborative agents; (ii) collaborative agents with learning (memory) ability; (iii) interface agents; and (iv) truly intelligent agents (**Figure 1**). It is important to note that the bounds of this classification should not be interpreted as a strict and well-defined fact.

After establishing a typology, Nwana [11] defined seven categories of agents according to their architecture and function: (i) collaborative agents; (ii) interface agents; (iii) mobile agents, (iv) information agents, (v) reactive agents, (vi) hybrid agents, and (vii) intelligent agents. Franklin and Graesser [7] believe that an agent, by definition, must be a continuous process execution and presented the taxonomy represented diagrammatically in **Figure 2**, which divides the autonomous agents into three main groups: biological, robotic, and computational agents.

Agent-based applications can be classified through many orthogonal dimensions. They can be classified by the type of the agent, by the technology used to implement the agent, or by the application domain itself. We will focus on the latest one since it is the one that fits best the objectives and structure of this book. The aim of this classification scheme is simply to give a visual understanding of the scale and variety of agent applications.

These include, among others, information research, personal assistants, e-mail management, control of electrical energy, telecommunications network management, traffic management,

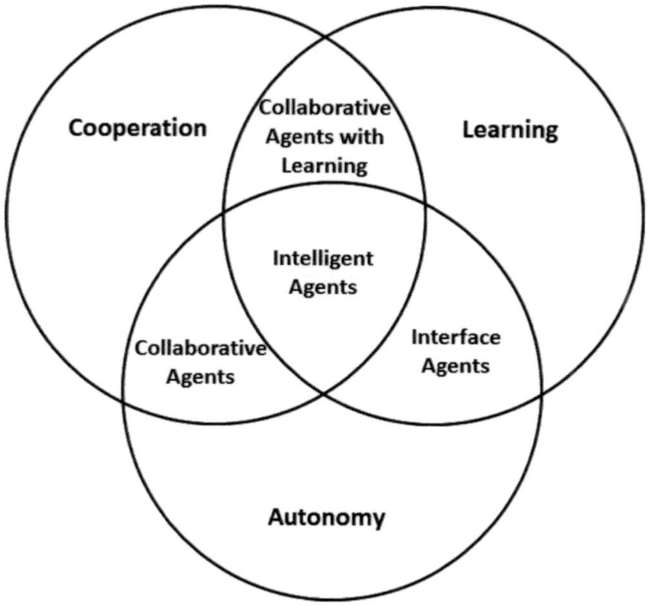

Figure 1. Agents' categories defined by Nwana [11].

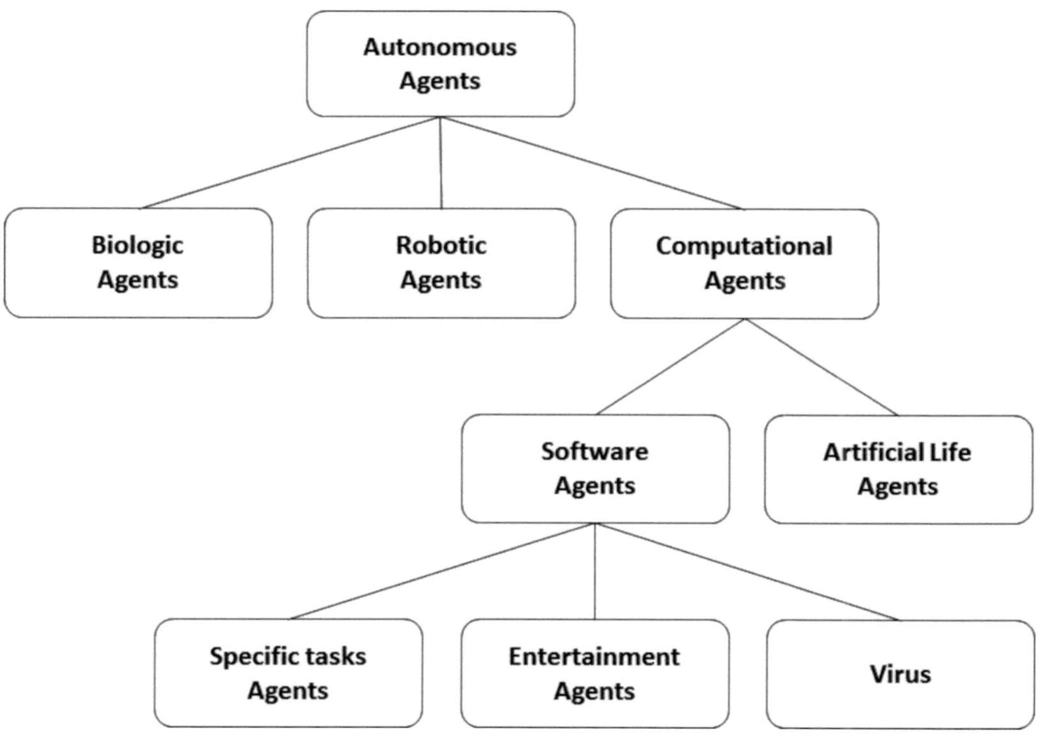

Figure 2. Agents' categories defined by Franklin and Graesser [7].

underwater exploration, control of vehicles and spacecraft, computer-integrated manufacturing, air traffic management, transport management, trading, e-commerce, financial transactions and exchanges, training of teams, games, entertainment, and virtual characters. Wooldridge and Jennings [8] draw one of the first attempts to classify agents in such a way (**Table 1**).

Actual MAS are dynamically being applied in various fields of knowledge. Practical cases of uses include [12] the modelling of organizational behaviour, team working, supply chain, consumer behaviour, social networks, distributed computing, transportation, and environmental studies. MAS have also been applied [13] to several social and society fields, comprising population dynamics, epidemics outbreaks, biological applications, civilization development, and military applications.

Macal and North [3] categorized all of these MAS applications into two types:

1. **Minimalist models**—Based on a set of idealized assumptions, it is designed to capture only the most salient features of a system. These are exploratory electronic laboratories, involving resources at computer modelling level, in which a wide range of assumptions can be varied over a large number of experimental simulations.
2. **Decision support systems (DSS)**—Tend to be large-scale applications, it is designed to answer a broad range of real-world policy questions, making efforts to support stakeholders in their decision-making activities. These models are distinguished by including real data and having passed some degree of validation to establish credibility in their results.

Table 2 summarizes a list of MAS applications drawn by Macal and North [3].

Industrial applications	**Commercial applications**
• Process control	• Information management
• Manufacturing	• Electronic commerce
• Traffic and transportation systems	• Business process management
Medical applications	**Entertainment**
• Patient monitoring	• Games
• Health care	• Interactive theatre and cinema

Table 1. MAS applications according to Wooldridge and Jennings [8].

Business and organizations	Society and culture
• Manufacturing operations	• Ancient civilizations
• Supply chains	• Civil disobedience
• Consumer markets	• Social determinants of terrorism
• Insurance industry	• Organizational networks
Economics	**Military**
• Artificial financial markets	• Command and control
• Trade networks	• Force-on-force
Infrastructure	**Biology**
• Electric power markets	• Population dynamics
• Transportation	• Ecological networks
• Hydrogen infrastructure	• Animal group behaviour
	• Cell behaviour and subcellular processes
Crowds	
• Pedestrian movement	
• Evacuation modelling	

Table 2. MAS applications according to Macal and North [3].

4. Conclusions

It is our strong belief that the concept of an agent as an independent rational decision maker has great value, not only in AI but also for conventional computer science. Likewise, the recent developments in MAS research, enabling agents to cooperate and negotiate, will surely be of vital importance in the future. The cognition and knowledge of MAS and the recognition of its applications continue to expand in line with its quick advances.

Yet, one can say that MAS are an overvalued technology of the last decades. Indeed, the current interest in agents carries with it the drawback of trying to label everything as an agent. Despite this fact, the technology has much to offer and it is imperative not to oversell it. MAS are likely to be most useful for a specific class of applications, which exhibit the kind of properties listed in Section 2. MAS has been broadly applied in a range of disciplines that include, but not limited to biology, ecology, computer simulation, business, economic science, policy, social sciences, political science, and military studies.

This book reviews several MAS applications and depicts the concept of MAS as scoped in the literature. Those applications fall mainly into two operational fields: individual-based models that study personal transportation-related activities and behaviour and system and computational methods to study collaborative and reactive autonomous decision making.

The chapters in this book cover a wide spectrum of issues related to the applications of intelligent agents and MAS. The introductory chapter explains the basic concepts underlying MAS, followed by experience chapters that deal with specific MAS and empirical applications. Application MAS domains include: collision avoidance, automotive applications, evacuation simulation, emergence analyses, cooperative control, context awareness, data (image) mining, resilience enhancement, and the management of a single-user multi-robot. The range of author affiliations covers a significant proportion of the organizations that are currently working in MAS and powerfully proves the universal nature of this relatively new field of research.

Author details

Jorge Rocha[1*], Inês Boavida-Portugal[2] and Eduardo Gomes[3]

*Address all correspondence to: jorge.rocha@campus.ul.pt

1 Institute of Geography and Spatial Planning, Universidade de Lisboa, Portugal

2 Department of Spatial Planning and Environment, University of Groningen, The Netherlands

3 Géographie-cités, UMR 8504, Université Paris 1 Panthéon-Sorbonne, France

References

[1] Russel S, Norvig P. Artificial Intelligence—A Modern Approach. 3rd ed. England: Pearson Education Limited; 2014. p. 1079

[2] Macal CM. Everything you need to know about agent-based modelling and simulation. Journal of Simulation. 2016;**10**(2):144-156

[3] Macal CM, North MJ. Tutorial on agent-based modelling and simulation. Journal of Simulation. 2010;**4**(3):151-162. DOI: 10.1057/jos.2010.3

[4] Stone P, Veloso M. Multiagent systems: A survey from a machine learning perspective. Autonomous Robots. 2000;**8**(3):345-383

[5] Davidsson P. Agent-based social simulation: A computer science view. Journal of Artificial Societies and Social Simulation. 2002;**5**(1):1-7

[6] Niazi M, Hussain A. Agent-based computing from multi-agent systems to agent-based models: A visual survey. Scientometrics. 2011;**89**(2):479-499

[7] Franklin S, Graesser A. Is it an agent, or just a program?: A taxonomy for autonomous agents In: Intelligent Agents III. Agent Theories, Architectures, and Languages, Proceedings of ECAI'96 Workshop (ATAL), Budapest, Hungary, August 12-13, 1996, Müller, J., Wooldridge, M.J., Jennings, N.R. (Eds.), Lecture Notes in Computer Science, Springer, 1997;**1193**:21-35

[8] Wooldridge M, Jennings NR. Intelligent agents: theory and practice. The Knowledge Engineering Review. 1995;**10**(2):115-152

[9] Reis L, Paulo L, Nuno O, Eugénio C. Situation based strategic positioning for coordinating a team of homogeneous agents. In: Hannenbauer M, Wendler J, Pagello E, editors. Balancing Reactivity and Social Deliberation in Multi-Agent System—From RoboCup to Real-World Applications. Lecture Notes in Artificial Intelligence, Berlin: Springer; 2001;**2013**:175-197

[10] Wooldridge M. An Introduction to Multi-Agent Systems. 2nd ed. England: John Wiley & Sons; 2009. p. 453

[11] Nwana H. Software agents: An overview. Knowledge Engineering Review. 1996;**11**(3):1-40

[12] Hughes HPN, Clegg CW, Robinson MA, Crowder RM. Agent-based modelling and simulation: The potential contribution to organizational psychology. Journal of Occupational and Organizational Psychology. 2012;**85**(3):487-502

[13] Aschwanden G, Wullschleger T, Muller H, Schmitt G. Agent-based evaluation of dynamic city models: A combination of human decision processes and an emission model for transportation based on acceleration and instantaneous speed. Automation in Construction. 2012;**22**:81-89

Section 2

Traffic and Transportation Systems

Chapter 2

Motion Coordination Problems with Collision Avoidance for Multi-Agent Systems

Jesús Santiaguillo-Salinas and
Eduardo Aranda-Bricaire

Additional information is available at the end of the chapter

http://dx.doi.org/10.5772/intechopen.69845

Abstract

This chapter studies the collision avoidance problem in the motion coordination control strategies for multi-agent systems. The proposed control strategies are decentralised, since agents have no global knowledge of the goal to achieve, knowing only the position and velocity of some agents. These control strategies allow a set of mobile agents achieve formations, formation tracking and containment. For the collision avoidance, we add a repulsive vector field of the unstable focus type to the motion coordination control strategies. We use formation graphs to represent interactions between agents. The results are presented for the front points of differential-drive mobile robots. The theoretical results are verified by numerical simulation.

Keywords: motion coordination, formation control, formation tracking control, containment control, time-varying formations, collision avoidance, repulsive vector fields, multi-agent systems, differential-drive mobile robots

1. Introduction

Multi-agent systems are defined as bundles of multiple autonomous robots coordinated to accomplish cooperative tasks. In recent years, the study of multi-agent systems has gained special interest, because these systems can achieve tasks that would be hard or impossible to achieve by agents working individually. Multiple agents can solve tasks working cooperatively, making them more reliable, faster and cheaper than it is possible with a single agent [1].

The main applications of multi-agent systems include the transport and manipulation of objects, localization, exploration and motion coordination [1, 2]. The main idea of motion coordination is the strategic navigation of a group of agents. Some of the main areas of research in the motion coordination are the formation control, where the goal is to achieve a desired pattern defined by relative position vectors, the time-varying formation tracking control, where the goal is to track a pre-established trajectory while the agents maintain a time-varying desired formation and the time-varying containment control, which consists in a group of mobile agents (called leaders) that track a predetermined trajectory, while another group of agents (called followers) remain within the region determined by the leaders [3].

The time-varying formation problem has been scarcely studied and some examples can be found in [4–7]. The time-varying formation control can be applied as the solution to complex motion coordination problems. In our case, the time-varying formation allows trajectory tracking with formations oriented to the heading angle of a leader robot, as well as changes in the physical dimensions of the formations. More specifically, the time-varying formation is composed of a predefined static formation which is transformed by a rotation matrix, which depends on the orientation of a specific leader robot and a scaling matrix, which depends on a factor that varies with respect to time. This time-varying formation allows the group of agents to behave as a rigid body which can be translated, rotated and scaled in the plane.

Another ubiquitous problem in all areas of motion coordination is the possible collision between agents when they try to achieve a desired position into a formation or during the trajectory tracking. In the literature, we can find different methods to predict/avoid collisions. In Ref. [8], a mechanism for collision avoidance under central control mode (traffic control type) is presented. In Refs. [9–11], navigation functions and artificial potential functions are used to avoid collisions between agents. These non-collision strategies are developed based on a combination of attractive potential functions (APFs) and repulsive potential functions (RPFs). Works [12–15] address the formation control problem without collisions using discontinuous vector fields.

The interaction topology between agents is modelled by formation graphs, where each agent is represented by a vertex, and the sharing of information between agents is represented by an edge. The control strategies designed in this work are presented for differential-drive mobile robots. This kind of mobile robots is commonly chosen as test bed because of simplicity and commercial availability. Differential-drive mobile robots present interesting challenges because they possess non-holonomic restrictions and even though have a simple kinematic model, it presents singularities. For this reason, the stabilization of such kind of mobile robots has been studied for several years by researches from diverse viewpoints.

The goal of this chapter is to design decentralised control strategies that allow motion coordination for multi-agent systems avoiding collisions between agents. The non-collision strategy is based on previous works [16, 17]. We use bounded control strategies based on sigmoid functions adding a repulsive vector field.

2. Preliminaries

2.1. Differential-drive mobile robots

Let $N = \{R_1, \ldots, R_n\}$ be a set of differential-drive mobile robots moving on the plane with positions $\xi_i = [x_i, y_i]^T, i = 1, \ldots, n$. The kinematic model for each robot according to **Figure 1**, is given by

$$\begin{bmatrix} \dot{x}_i \\ \dot{y}_i \\ \dot{\theta}_i \end{bmatrix} = \begin{bmatrix} \cos\theta_i & 0 \\ \sin\theta_i & 0 \\ 0 & 1 \end{bmatrix} \begin{bmatrix} v_i \\ w_i \end{bmatrix}, \quad i = 1, \ldots, n \tag{1}$$

where v_i is the longitudinal velocity of the middle point of wheels axis of the ith robot, w_i its angular velocity and θ_i the orientation with respect to the X axis. It is known that systems like Eq. (1) cannot be stabilised by any continuous and time-invariant control law [18]. Moreover, if the position ξ_i is taken as output of the system Eq. (1), the so-called decoupling matrix becomes singular. For this reason, to avoid singularities in the control law, it is common to study the kinematics of a point α_i off the wheels axis. The coordinates of point α_i are given by

$$\alpha_i = \begin{bmatrix} \alpha_{xi} \\ \alpha_{yi} \end{bmatrix} = \begin{bmatrix} x_i + \ell\cos\theta_i \\ y_i + \ell\sin\theta_i \end{bmatrix} \tag{2}$$

The kinematics of point α_i is given by

$$\begin{bmatrix} \dot{\alpha}_{xi} \\ \dot{\alpha}_{yi} \end{bmatrix} = \begin{bmatrix} \cos\theta_i & -\ell\sin\theta_i \\ \sin\theta_i & \ell\cos\theta_i \end{bmatrix} \begin{bmatrix} v_i \\ w_i \end{bmatrix} = A_i(\theta_i) \begin{bmatrix} v_i \\ w_i \end{bmatrix} \tag{3}$$

where $A_i(\theta_i)$ is the decoupling matrix for each robot R_i. The decoupling matrix is non-singular since $\det\left(A_i(\theta_i)\right) = \ell \neq 0$.

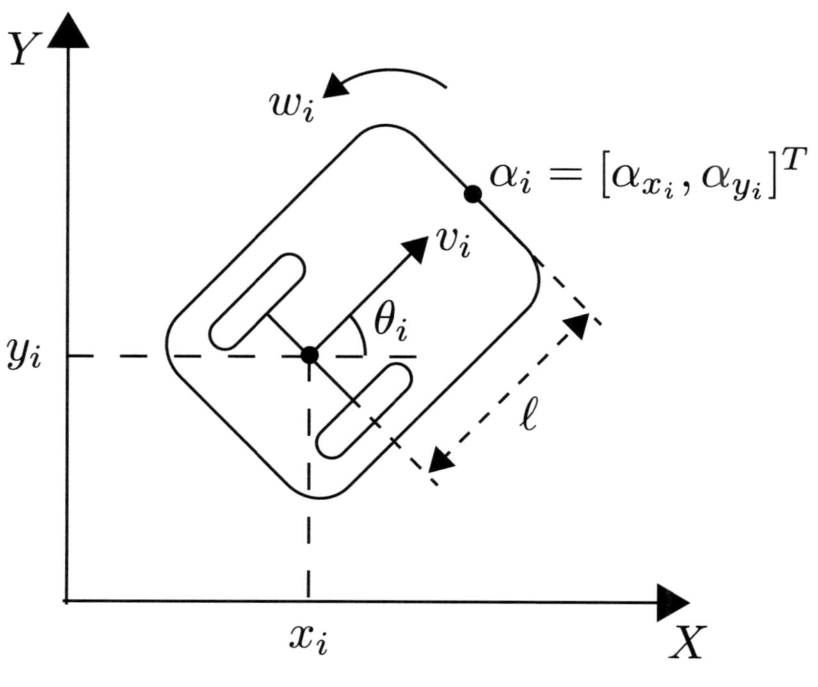

Figure 1. Kinematic model of the differential-drive mobile robot.

2.2. Algebraic graph theory

Definition 1. *(Formation Graph). Let* $N = \{R_1, \ldots, R_n\}$ *be a set of mobile agents and* N_i *be the subset of agents which have a flow of information towards the ith agent. A formation graph* $G = \{V, E, C\}$ *consists of*

- *A set of vertices* $V = \{R_1, \ldots, R_n\}$ *corresponding to the n agents of the system.*
- *A set of edges* $E = \{(R_j, R_i) \in V \times V | j \in N_i\}$ *where each edge represents a flow of information that goes from agent* R_j *towards agent* R_i*.*
- *A set of labels* $C = \{c_{ji} = R_i - R_j\}$ *with* $(R_j\, R_i) \in E$*,* $c_{ji} \in \mathbb{R}^2$*, with* c_{ji} *being a vector specifying a desired relative position between the agents* R_j *and* R_i*.*

Definition 2. (Laplacian*). Let us have a formation graph G, the Laplacian associated with G is given by*

$$\mathcal{L}(G) = \Delta - \mathcal{A}_d \tag{4}$$

With Δ *the degree matrix defined by*

$$\Delta = \operatorname{diag}\{g_1, \ldots, g_n\} \tag{5}$$

where $g_i = \operatorname{card}\{N_i\}, i = 1, \ldots, n$ *and* $\mathcal{A}_d$ *is the adjacency matrix of G defined by*

$$a_{ij} = \begin{cases} 1, & \text{if } (R_j, R_i) \in E \\ 0, & \text{otherwise.} \end{cases} \tag{6}$$

Given a formation graph G, there exist a *path* in this graph if between the vertices R_i and R_j, there is a sequence of edges $(R_i, R_{m_1}), (R_{m_1}, R_{m_2}), \ldots, (R_{m_r}, R_j)$ with $i \neq j$. We call *cycle* to a path that begins and ends at the same vertex.

For further details about formation graphs, Laplacian and its properties and algebraic graph theory, the reader is referred to Refs. [19–21].

2.3. Mathematical miscellaneous

Definition 3. [22, 23] *Let* $A = (a_{ij}) \in \mathbb{R}^{n \times n}$ *that satisfies* $a_{ij} \leq 0$ *whenever* $i \neq j$ *and* $a_{ii} > 0$ *for each i. The matrix A is called an M-matrix if it satisfies any one of the following equivalent conditions*

- $A = \eta I - M$ *for some non-negative matrix M and some* $\eta > \rho(M)$*, where* $\rho(M)$ *is the spectral radius of M.*
- *The real part of each eigenvalue of A is positive.*
- *All principal minors of A are positive.*
- A^{-1} *exists and the elements of* A^{-1} *are non-negative.*

Definition 4. [24] *The convex hull of a set of vectors* $Z = \{z_1, \ldots, z_p\} \subset \mathbb{R}^n$*, denoted by* co(Z)*, is defined by*

http://dx.doi.org/10.5772/intechopen.69845

$$\mathrm{co}(Z) = \left\{ \sum_{j=1}^{p} \mu_j z_j \mid \mu_j \in \mathbb{R}, \mu_j \geq 0, \sum_{j=i}^{p} \mu_j = 1 \right\}. \tag{7}$$

Definition 5. *Given a point* $z_q = [x, y]^T$ *and a set* $Z = \{z_1, \ldots, z_p\}$*, the distance between* z_q *and* $\mathrm{co}(Z)$ *is defined by* $\mathrm{dist}(z_q, \mathrm{co}(Z)) = \inf(\mathrm{dist}(z_q, z)), z \in Z$.

Definition 6. *Given a vector* $z = [z_1, \ldots, z_p]^T$*, we define*

$$\tanh(z) = [\tanh(z_1), \ldots, \tanh(z_p)]^T. \tag{8}$$

Definition 7. *Given a matrix* $A \in \mathbb{C}^{n \times n}$ *with eigenvalues* $\lambda_1, \ldots, \lambda_n$*, then its spectral radius* $\rho(X)$ *is defined as* $\rho(X) = \max\{|\lambda_1|, \ldots, |\lambda_n|\}$.

Definition 8. *Let* $H \in \mathbb{R}^{n \times n}$ *be a block triangular matrix*

$$H = \begin{bmatrix} A & B \\ 0 & C \end{bmatrix} \tag{9}$$

With $A \in \mathbb{R}^{k \times k}$ *and* $C \in \mathbb{R}^{(n-k) \times (n-k)}$*. Then, the eigenvalues of the matrix H are the eigenvalues of the submatrices A and C.*

Definition 9. [17] *Consider the dynamical system* $\dot{x} = Ax$ *with* $x = [x_1, \ldots, x_n]^T$ *and* $A \in \mathbb{R}^{n \times n}$ *Hurwitz. Then, the normalised system* $\dot{x} = AD(x)x$ *with* $D(x) = \mathrm{diag}\{1/\|x_1\|, \ldots, 1/\|x_n\|\}$ *is stable with finite time convergence.*

2.4. Repulsive vector fields

Let $N = \{R_1, \ldots, R_n\}$ be a set of first order agents moving on the plane. The distance between two agents is given by $\|\xi_i - \xi_j\|, \forall i, j \in N, i \neq j$. Then, the agents R_j that are in risk of collision with agent R_i belong to the set

$$M_i = \{R_j \in N \big| \|\xi_i - \xi_j\| \leq d\}, \quad i = 1, 2, \ldots, n \tag{10}$$

where d is the minimum allowed distance between the agents. To avoid collisions between agents, we propose repulsive vector fields given by

$$\beta_i = \epsilon \sum_{j \in M_i} \delta_{ij} \begin{bmatrix} (x_i - x_j) - (y_i - y_j) \\ (x_i - x_j) + (y_i - y_j) \end{bmatrix} \tag{11}$$

where $\epsilon > 0$ and the parameter δ_{ij} is given as follows

$$\delta_{ij} = \begin{cases} 1, & \text{if } \|\xi_i - \xi_j\| \leq d \\ 0, & \text{if } \|\xi_i - \xi_j\| > d \end{cases} \tag{12}$$

The repulsive vector fields are proposed in such a way that there is an unstable focus that rotates anticlockwise as shown in **Figure 2**, centred on the position of the other agents that are in risk of collision.

For the control strategies designed in this chapter, we will take into account the following assumptions:

Assumption 1. *The initial conditions of all agents satisfy* $\|\alpha_i(0) - \alpha_j(0)\| \geq d, \forall i, j \in N$, *with* $i \neq j$. *That is, there is no risk of collision between any agents at* $t = 0$.

Assumption 2. *The ith agent, besides knowing the position of the agents of the set* N_i, *it can detect the presence of any other agent that is within the circle of radius* d.

Also, consider the following:

Remark 1. *It should be clear that the minimum allowed distance between agents d must be less than the minimum distance between agents within a desired formation, i.e.* $d < \min\{|c_{ij}|\}$.

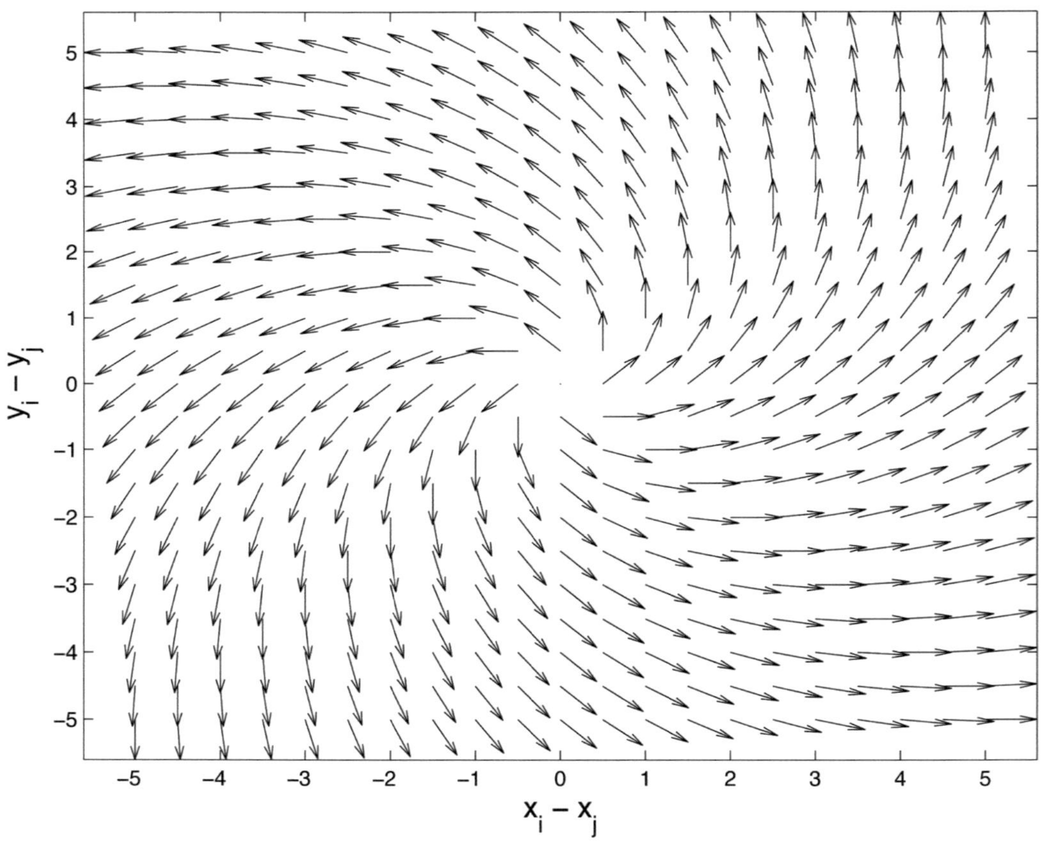

Figure 2. Phase plane of the repulsive vector field β_{ij}.

http://dx.doi.org/10.5772/intechopen.69845

2.5. Case of study: Formation with collision avoidance

The desired relative position of the ith agent in a desired formation is given by

$$\alpha_i^* = \frac{1}{g_i} \sum_{k \in N_i} (\alpha_k + c_{ki}) \tag{13}$$

where c_{ki} is the position vector between agents R_i and R_k. The goal is to design a decentralised control law $[v_i, w_i]^T = f_i(\alpha_i, N_i),\ i = 1,\ldots,n$ such that

- The agents achieve a desired formation, i.e.

$$\lim_{t \to \infty} \left(\alpha_i(t) - \alpha_i^*(t) \right) = 0 \tag{14}$$

- Collision avoidance among agents is achieved. In addition, for all time t, the agents remain at a distance greater than or equal to a predefined minimum distance d between them, i.e.

$$\|\alpha_i(t) - \alpha_j(t)\| \geq d, \forall t \geq 0, i \neq j \tag{15}$$

A control law to achieve a desired formation is given by

$$\gamma_i = -ke_i, \quad i = 1, \ldots, n \tag{16}$$

where $e_i = \alpha_i - \alpha_i^*$ is the position error and $k > 0$ the control gain. For differential-drive mobile robots, we have

$$\begin{bmatrix} v_i \\ w_i \end{bmatrix} = A_i^{-1}(\theta_i)\gamma_i, \quad i = 1, \ldots, n \tag{17}$$

where $A_i^{-1}(\theta_i)$ is the inverse of the decoupling matrix. We consider a normalised version of Eq. (10) to deal with a system where all agents move at the same velocity, given by

$$\gamma_i = \begin{cases} -\mu \dfrac{e_i}{\|e_i\|}, & e_i \neq 0 \\ 0, & e_i = 0 \end{cases} \quad i = 1, \ldots, n \tag{18}$$

where μ is the constant velocity of all agents.

Proposition 1. *Consider the system Eq. (3) and the control law Eq. (17) with γ_i given by (18) and a connected formation graph composed entirety by the superposition of different cycles. Then, in the closed-loop system Eqs. (3)–(17), we have finite time convergence of the agents to the desired formation.*

Proof. The proof of this Proposition is detailed in [17]. ■

To achieve formation with collision avoidance between agents, we propose a control law given by

$$\begin{bmatrix} v_i \\ w_i \end{bmatrix} = A_i^{-1}(\theta_i)(\gamma_i + \beta_i), \quad i = 1, \ldots, n \tag{19}$$

With γ_i given by Eq. (18) and β_i the repulsive vector field given by Eq. (11).

Proposition 2. *Consider the system Eq. (3) and the control law Eq. (19) with Eqs. (18) and (11). Also consider a connected formation graph composed entirety by the superposition of different cycles. Suppose that there exist risk of collision between n agents at time instant t and* $\epsilon > 6(\mu/d)$. *Then, in the closed-loop system Eqs. (3)–(19), the agents reach their desired position in finite time and remain at a distance greater than or equal to a predefined minimum distance d between them for all* $t \geq 0$.

Proof. For the proof of this Proposition, mathematical induction is performed, first showing the cases of risk of collision between two agents and between three agents, applying induction to arrive at the general solution of n agents. This proof is detailed in Ref. [17]. It is worth mentioning that, geometrically, the worst case occurs when an agent is surrounded by other six agents. Also, the value of $\epsilon > 6(\mu/d)$ is very conservative, so it is possible that with a lower ϵ, collision avoidance is achieved. ■

The results obtained from a numerical simulation using the control strategy given by Eq. (19) are shown below. For the simulation, three differential-drive mobile robots are considered, where the point α_i to be controlled is located at 0.045 m in front of the mid-point of wheels axis. The formation graph using in the simulation is shown in **Figure 3**.

The parameters used in the simulation are $d = 0.2, \mu = 0.1, \epsilon = 2(\mu/d)$. The position vectors are given by $c_{32} = [-0.3, 0]^T, c_{21} = [0.3\cos(\pi/3), 0.3\sin(\pi/3)]^T$ and $c_{13} = [0.3\sin(\pi/6), -0.3\cos(\pi/6)]^T$. The desired formation is an equilateral triangle of 0.3 m. The agents were placed in initial positions in such a way that in the trajectories towards their desired positions risk of collision between them exits.

Figure 4 shows the motion of the agents in the plane. It is observed how the agents achieve the desired formation avoiding collisions. The effect of the repulsive vector fields can be seen when modified the trajectories of the agents to avoid collisions. In **Figure 5**, the distances between agents are shown, we can see that the minimum distance between agents is always greater

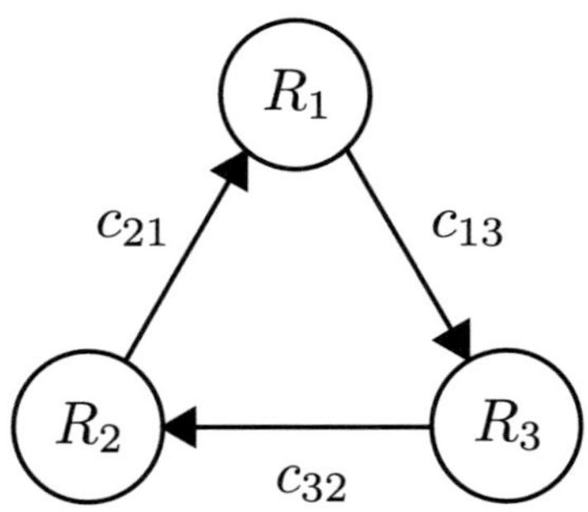

Figure 3. Formation graph for the simulation (formation with collision avoidance problem).

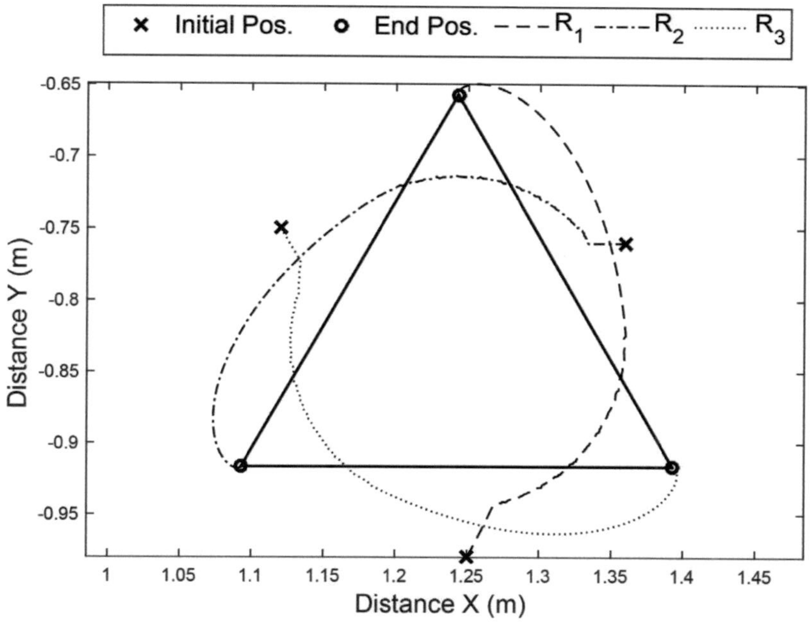

Figure 4. Trajectories of the agents in the plane (formation with collision avoidance problem).

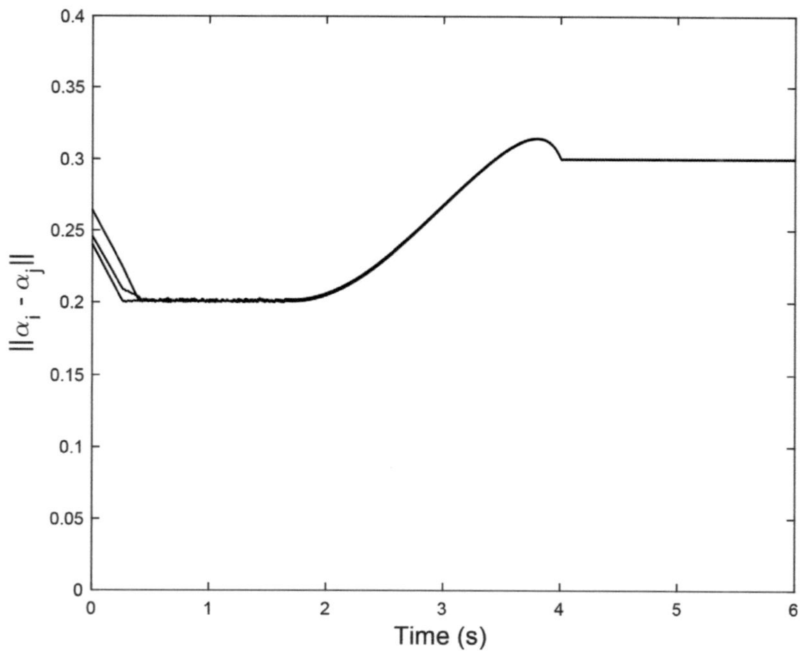

Figure 5. Distances between agents (formation with collision avoidance problem).

than or equal to the predefined distance d = 0.2. **Figure 6** shows the position errors of the agents. Such errors converge to zero.

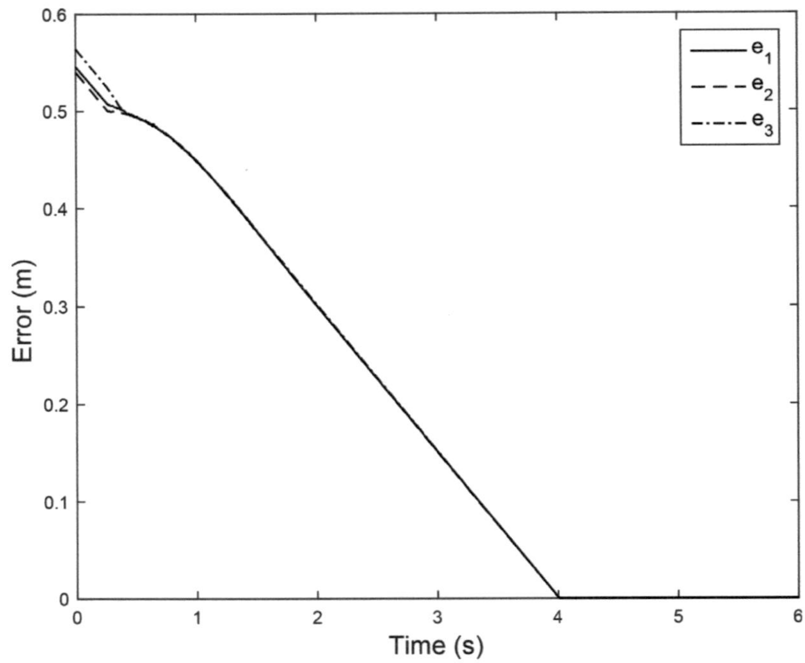

Figure 6. Position errors of the agents (formation with collision avoidance problem).

3. Motion coordination control strategies

3.1. Time-varying position vector

In order to maintain a formation oriented to the direction of a leader agent R_n and resize the formation, we use a time-varying position vector given by

$$C_{ji}(t) = \delta(t)R(\theta_n)c_{ji} \tag{20}$$

where c_{ji} is a position vector corresponding to the static desired formation, $R(\theta_n)$ is a rotation matrix given by

$$R(\theta_n) = \begin{bmatrix} \cos\theta_n & -\sin\theta_n \\ \sin\theta_n & \cos\theta_n \end{bmatrix} \tag{21}$$

and $\delta(t)$ is a scaling factor. The time derivative of Eq. (14) is given by

$$\dot{C}_{ji}(t) = \dot{\delta}(t)R(\theta_n)c_{ji} + \delta(t)\dot{R}(\theta_n)c_{ji} \tag{22}$$

where

$$\dot{R}(\theta_n) = \begin{bmatrix} -\sin\theta_n & -\cos\theta_n \\ \cos\theta_n & -\sin\theta_n \end{bmatrix} w_n \tag{23}$$

3.2. Time-varying formation tracking with collision avoidance

In the time-varying formation tracking problem presented in this subsection, the agent R_n is the leader, responsible for tracking a desired trajectory. The n–1 remaining agents are follower, responsible for performing a time-varying formation with respect to the leader. The leader agent does not know the position and velocities of the followers agents but only knows the desired trajectory and velocity. The followers do not know the desired trajectory and velocity but only knows the positions and velocities of others agents in the system.

We make the following standing assumption

Assumption 3. *For each follower agent, there is a path to the leader agent, i.e., for all R_i, $i = 1, \ldots, n-1$, there are edges (R_n, R_{m_1}), (R_{m_1}, R_{m_2}), …, $(R_{m_r}, R_i) \in E$.*

Let $m(t) = [m_p(t), m_q(t)]^T$ be a continuously differentiable pre-established navigation trajectory, where $\|\dot{m}(t)\| \leq \eta_m$, $\forall t \geq 0$.

The desired relative position of the ith follower within the desired time-varying formation is given by

$$\alpha_i^*(t) = \frac{1}{g_i} \sum_{j \in N_i} \left(\alpha_j(t) + C_{ji}(t)\right), \quad i = 1, \ldots, n-1, \tag{24}$$

where $C_{ji}(t)$ is a time-varying position vector between the agents R_i and R_j. The time derivative of $C_{ji}(t)$ satisfies $\|\dot{C}_{ji}(t)\| \leq \eta_c$, $\forall t \geq 0$.

The goal is to design a decentralised control law $[v_i, w_i]^T = f_i(\alpha_i, N_i)$, $i = 1, \ldots, n$ that achieves

- Asymptotic tracking of a prescribed trajectory by the leader agent, i.e.

$$\lim_{t\to\infty}\left(\alpha_n(t) - m(t)\right) = 0. \tag{25}$$

- Asymptotic time-varying formation by the follower agents, i.e. for $i = 1, \ldots, n-1$

$$\lim_{t\to\infty}\left(\alpha_i(t) - \alpha_i^*(t)\right) = 0. \tag{26}$$

- Collision avoidance between agents, that is, all agents in the system remain at some distance greater than or equal to a predefined minimum distance d from each other, i.e.

$$\|\alpha_i(t) - \alpha_j(t)\| \geq d, \quad i, j = 1, \ldots, n, i \neq j, \forall t \geq 0. \tag{27}$$

To achieve time-varying formation tracking, we propose a control law defined by

$$\begin{bmatrix} v_n \\ w_n \end{bmatrix} = A_n^{-1}(\theta_n)\Big(- k_m \tanh\Big(\alpha_n - m(t)\Big) + \dot{m}(t)\Big)$$
$$\begin{bmatrix} v_i \\ w_i \end{bmatrix} = A_i^{-1}(\theta_i)\Big(- k_f \tanh(\alpha_i - \alpha_i^*) + \dot{\alpha}_i^*\Big), i = 1, \ldots, n-1 \tag{28}$$

where $A_i^{-1}(\theta_i)$ is the inverse of the decoupling matrix, $m(t)$ is the desired trajectory, $\dot{m}(t)$ is the navigation velocity, k_m and k_f are the control gains.

The first main result of this subsection is the following:

Proposition 3. *Consider the system Eq. (3) and the control law Eq. (28). Suppose that $k_m, k_f > 0$. Then, in the closed-loop system defined by Eqs. (3)–(28), it follows that the leader agent R_n converge to the desired trajectory, i.e.$\lim_{t\to\infty}\Big(\alpha_n(t) - m(t)\Big) = 0$, whereas the follower agents converge to the desired formation, i.e. $\lim_{t\to\infty}\Big(\alpha_i(t) - \alpha_i^*(t)\Big) = 0$, for $i = 1, \ldots, n-1$.*

Proof. The closed-loop system Eqs. (3)–(28) is given by

$$\dot{\alpha} \quad = (A \otimes I_2)^{-1}[-(K \otimes I_2)\tanh((A \otimes I_2)\alpha - C) + M] \tag{29}$$

where $\alpha = [\alpha_1, \ldots, \alpha_n]^T, K = \text{diag}\{k_f, \ldots, k_f, k_m\}$, $\otimes$ denote the Kronecker product, I_2 is the 2×2 identity matrix,

$$C = \left[\frac{1}{g_1}\sum_{j\in N_1} C_{ji}(t), \ldots, \frac{1}{g_{n-1}}\sum_{j\in N_{n-1}} C_{ji}(t), m(t)\right]^T \tag{30}$$

$$M = \left[\frac{1}{g_1}\sum_{j\in N_1} \dot{C}_{ji}(t), \ldots, \frac{1}{g_{n-1}}\sum_{j\in N_{n-1}} \dot{C}_{ji}(t), \dot{m}(t)\right]^T$$

$A = \Lambda\mathcal{L}(G) + \Gamma$, where $\mathcal{L}(G)$ is the Laplacian of the formation graph G,$\Lambda = \text{diag}\{1/g_1, \ldots, 1/g_{n-1}, 0\}$ and

$$\Gamma = \begin{bmatrix} 0 & \cdots & 0 \\ \vdots & \ddots & \vdots \\ 0 & \cdots & 1 \end{bmatrix}. \tag{31}$$

At this point, we have to show that $(A \otimes I_2)$ is invertible. From the properties of the Kronecker product, we have $(A \otimes I_2)^{-1} = A^{-1} \otimes I_2^{-1}$. Since I_2 is the identity matrix, then I_2^{-1} exits and we address in the matrix $A = \Lambda\mathcal{L}(G) + \Gamma$. From the properties of the Laplacian, we know that the matrix $\Lambda\mathcal{L}(G)$ is positive semidefinite and singular, that is, it has no inverse. This since the vector of ones $X = [1, \ldots, 1]^T$ is solution of the system $\Lambda\mathcal{L}(G)X = 0$. When matrix Γ is added to $\Lambda\mathcal{L}(G)$, the resulting matrix A is no singular and positive definite, since taking into consideration the Assumption 3, the system $\Lambda\mathcal{L}(G)X = 0$ has the unique solution $X = [0, \ldots, 0]^T$.

http://dx.doi.org/10.5772/intechopen.69845

Now define the errors of the system as

$$\begin{aligned} e_n &= \alpha_n - m(t) \\ e_i &= \alpha_i - \alpha_i^*, i = 1, \ldots, n-1 \end{aligned} \quad (32)$$

The system errors in matrix form are given by

$$e = (A \otimes I_2)\alpha - C \quad (33)$$

where $e = [e_1, \ldots, e_n]^T$. The dynamics of the error coordinates are given by

$$\dot{e} = -(K \otimes I_2)\tanh(e) \quad (34)$$

We propose a Lyapunov function candidate given by

$$V = \frac{1}{2} e^T (K \otimes I_2)^{-1} e \quad (35)$$

and evaluating its time derivative along the trajectories of the system, we have

$$\dot{V} = e^T (K \otimes I_2)^{-1} (K \otimes I_2)\tanh(e) = -e^T \tanh(e) < 0, \forall e \text{ with } e \neq 0 \quad (36)$$

then the errors converge asymptotically to zero. ■

Modifying the previous control law Eq. (28) by adding the repulsive vector field Eq. (11), finally, we have the strategy to achieve time-varying formation tracking with collision avoidance given by

$$\begin{aligned} \begin{bmatrix} v_n \\ w_n \end{bmatrix} &= A_n^{-1}(\theta_n)\Big(-k_m \tanh(\alpha_n - m(t)) + \dot{m}(t) + \beta_n \Big) \\ \begin{bmatrix} v_i \\ w_i \end{bmatrix} &= A_i^{-1}(\theta_i)\Big(-k_f \tanh(\alpha_i - \alpha_i^*) + \dot{\alpha}_i^* + \beta_i \Big), i = 1, \ldots, n-1 \end{aligned} \quad (37)$$

To analyse the relative distance among the jth and ith agents, we define the variables $p_{ji} = \alpha_{xi} - \alpha_{xj}$ and $q_{ji} = \alpha_{yi} - \alpha_{yj}, j, i = 1, \ldots, n, j \neq i$ which correspond to the horizontal and vertical distances between agents. In the plane $p_{ji} - q_{ji}$, we identify the origin as the point where collision between the jth and ith agents occurs and a circle of radius d, centred at the origin, as the influence region between the two agents. Outside the circle, only the time-varying formation tracking control law acts, while inside the circle, the repulsive vector fields appear.

In order to present our second main result, we need to establish the following Technical Lemma.

Lemma 1. *Consider the system Eq. (3) and the control law Eq. (28) along with definitions* $k^* = \max(k_f, k_m)$ *and* $\eta^* = \max(\eta_m, \eta_c)$. *Then in the closed-loop system Eqs. (3)–(28), the velocities of the agents are bounded by* $\hat{\eta} = \sqrt{\rho(A^{-1})}(k^*\sqrt{2n} + \eta^*\sqrt{n})$.

Proof. Taking the norm of the system Eq. (29), we get

$$\begin{aligned}\|\dot{\alpha}\| &\leq \|(A\otimes I_2)^{-1}[-(K\otimes I_2)\tanh((A\otimes I_2)\alpha - C) + M]\| \\ \|\dot{\alpha}\| &\leq \|(A\otimes I_2)^{-1}\|\|-(K\otimes I_2)\|\|\tanh((A\otimes I_2)\alpha - C)\| + \|M\|\end{aligned} \tag{38}$$

where $\|\tanh((A\otimes I_2)\alpha - C)\| \leq \sqrt{2n}$, $\|M\| \leq \eta^*\sqrt{n}$, with $\|-(K\otimes I_2)\| = \rho(K\otimes I_2)$ and $\|(A\otimes I_2)^{-1}\| = \sqrt{\rho\left([(A\otimes I_2)^{-1}]\right)}$, but since I_2 is the identity matrix with two eigenvalues 1 and from the spectrum properties of the Kronecker product, we have $\|-(K\otimes I_2)\| = \rho(K) = \max(k_f, k_m) = k^*$ and $\|(A\otimes I_2)^{-1}\| = \sqrt{\rho\left([(A)^{-1}]\right)}$. Finally, we have

$$\|\dot{\alpha}\| \leq \sqrt{\rho(A^{-1})}(k^*\sqrt{2n} + \eta^*\sqrt{n}) = \hat{\eta}. \tag{39}$$

This concludes the proof. ■

Now, we can state our second main result. First, we consider the case when only two agents are in risk of collision. From this simplest case, we state a series of theorems leading to the general case.

Proposition 4. *Consider the system Eq. (3) and the control law Eq. (37). Suppose that there exists risk of collision between only two agents at time instant t and the parameter ϵ satisfies $\epsilon > \hat{\eta}/d$. Then, in the closed-loop system Eqs. (3)–(37), the agents tend asymptotically to their desired positions, and they stay at a distance greater than or equal to d, $\forall t \geq 0$.*

Proof. We show that the rth and sth agents will avoid collision between them, and they stay at some minimum distance from each other. Define a surface given by

$$\sigma_{rs} = p_{rs}^2 + q_{rs}^2 - d^2 = 0 \tag{40}$$

To determine the behaviour under the action of the repulsive vector fields, we use the positive definite function $V = \frac{1}{2}\sigma_{rs}^2$ which time derivative is given by $\dot{V} = \sigma_{rs}\dot{\sigma}_{rs}$. The time derivative of Eq. (40) along the trajectories of the closed-loop system is given by

$$\begin{aligned}\dot{\sigma}_{rs} &= 2[p_{rs} \quad q_{rs}]\begin{bmatrix}\dot{p}_{rs} \\ \dot{q}_{rs}\end{bmatrix} = 4\epsilon(p_{rs}^2 + q_{rs}^2) \\ &-2[p_{rs} \quad q_{rs}]\left((\dot{\alpha}_s^* - k_s\tanh(\alpha_s - \alpha_s^*)) - (\dot{\alpha}_r^* - k_r\tanh(\alpha_r - \alpha_r^*))\right)\end{aligned} \tag{41}$$

Therefore, $\dot{V} \leq 0$ is achieved if $\sigma_{rs}\dot{\sigma}_{rs} \leq 0$. When there exists risk of collision, (p_{rs}, q_{rs}) lies in the inner region of $\sigma_{rs} = 0$, that is $\sigma_{rs} \leq 0$, then the analysis reduces to show that $\dot{\sigma}_{rs} \geq 0$. That means the resulting vector fields inside the circle point outwards, that is, to the region free of collision. Using the definition of the cross product, we have

$$\dot{\sigma}_{rs} = 4\epsilon(p_{rs}^2 + q_{rs}^2) + 4\sqrt{p_{rs}^2 + q_{rs}^2}\hat{\eta}\cos\theta_{rs} \geq 4\epsilon(p_{rs}^2 + q_{rs}^2) - 4\sqrt{p_{rs}^2 + q_{rs}^2}\hat{\eta} > 0. \tag{42}$$

Solving for ϵ, we have that, if $\epsilon > \hat{\eta}/d$, then $\dot{\sigma}_{rs} > 0$. This implies that the rth and sth agents move away from each other until they reach a distance d. Since $\|\alpha_s(0) - \alpha_r(0)\| \geq d$, then the agents not only avoid collision but also satisfy $\|\alpha_s(t) - \alpha_r(t)\| \geq d$ for all time.

Now, we consider the case when three agents are in risk of collision, that is, agent R_r is in risk of collision against agents R_{s1} and R_{s2}. ■

Proposition 5. *Consider the system Eq. (3) and the control law Eq. (37). Suppose that there exists risk of collision between three agents and the parameter* ϵ *satisfies* $\epsilon > 2(\hat{\eta}/d)$. *Then, in the closed-loop system, Eqs. (3)–(37), the agents converge asymptotically to their desired positions, and they stay at a distance greater than or equal to d,* $\forall t \geq 0$.

Proof. We define a surface composed of two components given by

$$\sigma = \begin{bmatrix} \sigma_{rs1} \\ \sigma_{rs2} \end{bmatrix} = \begin{bmatrix} p_{rs1}^2 + q_{rs1}^2 - d^2 \\ p_{rs2}^2 + q_{rs2}^2 - d^2 \end{bmatrix} = 0. \tag{43}$$

We use the positive definite function $V = \frac{1}{2}\sigma^T\sigma$ which time derivative is given by $\dot{V} = \sigma^T\dot{\sigma} = \sigma_{rs1}\dot{\sigma}_{rs1} + \sigma_{rs2}\dot{\sigma}_{rs2} \leq \sigma^*(\dot{\sigma}_{rs1} + \dot{\sigma}_{rs2})$ where $\sigma^* = \max\{\sigma_{rs1}, \sigma_{rs2}\}$. Evaluating $\dot{V}$ and considering that the trajectories lie in the inner region of $\sigma = 0$, that is, $\sigma_{rs1}, \sigma_{rs2} < 0$ then the analysis reduces to show that $\dot{\sigma}_{rs1} + \dot{\sigma}_{rs2} > 0$. Hence,

$$\begin{aligned} \dot{\sigma}_{rs1} + \dot{\sigma}_{rs2} = {} & 4\epsilon(p_{rs1}^2 + q_{rs1}^2) + 2[p_{rs1} \quad q_{rs1}]\Big((-k_{s1}\tanh(\alpha_{s1} - \alpha_{s1}^*) + \dot{\alpha}_{s1}^*) \\ & - (-k_r\tanh(\alpha_r - \alpha_r^*) + \dot{\alpha}_r^*)\Big) + 4\epsilon(p_{rs2}^2 + q_{rs2}^2) \\ & + 2[p_{rs2} \quad q_{rs2}]\Big((-k_{s2}\tanh(\alpha_{s2} - \alpha_{s2}^*) + \dot{\alpha}_{s2}^*) \\ & - (-k_r\tanh(\alpha_r - \alpha_r^*) + \dot{\alpha}_r^*)\Big) + 4\epsilon[p_{rs1} \quad q_{rs1}]\begin{bmatrix} p_{rs2} \\ q_{rs2} \end{bmatrix} \\ & \geq 4\epsilon(p_{rs1}^2 + q_{rs1}^2) - 4\sqrt{p_{rs1}^2 + q_{rs1}^2}\hat{\eta} + 4\epsilon(p_{rs2}^2 + q_{rs2}^2) \\ & - 4\sqrt{p_{rs2}^2 + q_{rs2}^2}\hat{\eta} + 4\epsilon\sqrt{p_{rs1}^2 + q_{rs1}^2}\sqrt{p_{rs2}^2 + q_{rs2}^2}\cos\theta_{rs1,rs2} \\ & > 0. \end{aligned} \tag{44}$$

In this scenario, agents R_{s1} and R_{s2} can be positioned at any point of the circumference of radius d around the agent R_r, considering that, from Proposition 4, they must remain at a distance greater than or equal to d between them. The worst case occurs when the agents R_{s1} and R_{s2} are uniformly distributed over the circumference of radius d. Thus, $\cos\theta_{rs1,rs2} = -1$ and solving for ϵ, we have that, if $\epsilon > 2(\hat{\eta}/d)$, then $\dot{\sigma}_{rs1} + \dot{\sigma}_{rs2} > 0$. This implies that agents R_{s1}, R_{s2} and R_r avoid collision between them.

Geometrically, the most general case occurs when the rth agent is surrounded by six agents, i.e. seven agents are in danger of collision.

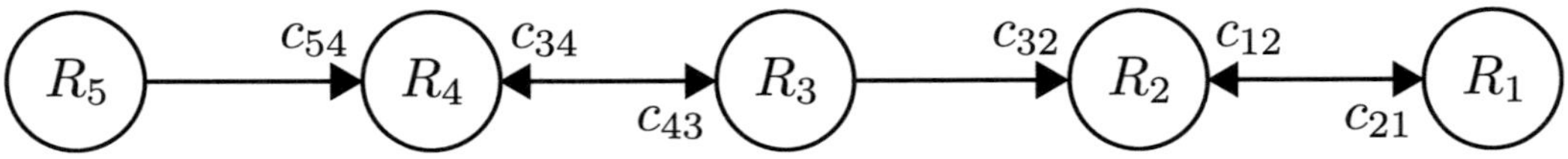

Figure 7. Formation graph for the simulation (formation tracking with collision avoidance problem).

Proposition 6. Consider the system Eq. (3) and the control law Eq. (37). Suppose that there exists risk of collision between $n \geq 3$ agents and the parameter ϵ satisfies $\epsilon > 2(\hat{\eta}/d)$. Then, in the closed-loop system Eqs. (3)–(37), the agents converge asymptotically to their desired positions, and they stay at a distance greater than or equal to d, $\forall t \geq 0$.

Proof. We follow a similar procedure to that presented in the proof of Proposition 5, considering a surface with $n - 1$ components and showing that, if $\sigma_{rs1} + \ldots + \dot{\sigma}_{r(n-1)} > 0$, then $\dot{V} < 0$, taking into account that the worst case is presented when the $n - 1$ agents are uniformly distributed over the circumference of radio d around the agent R_r, so the agents avoid collision between them. ■

The results of a numerical simulation using the control strategy given by Eq. (37) are shown below. For the simulation, we considered five differential-drive mobile robots, where the point α_i to control is located 0.15 m ahead the mid-point of the wheel axis. The formation graph employed in the simulation is shown in **Figure 7**.

The control gains used in the simulation are $k_m = 2$ and $k_f = 3$. The desired marching trajectory is a quadrifolium curve given by $m(t) = [4\sin(2\omega t)\cos(\omega t), 4\sin(2\omega t)\sin(\omega t)]^T$ where $\omega = 2\pi/T$ with a period of $T = 80$s. The static position vectors are given by $c_{12} = [0, 0.6]^T$, $c_{21} = [0, -0.6]^T$, $c_{32} = [-0.6\cos(\pi/10), -0.6\sin(\pi/10)]^T$, $c_{34} = [0, -0.97]^T$, $c_{43} = [0, 0.97]^T$, and $c_{54} = [-0.6\cos(3\pi/10), -0.6\sin(3\pi/10)]^T$. The scaling factor is given by $\delta(t) = 1 + 0.2\sin(\omega t)$.

The minimum allowed distance between agents is $d = 0.3$ m and the parameter ϵ was set to $\epsilon = 1.5(2(\hat{\eta}/d))$ to ensure the minimum distance condition will not be violated.

Figure 8 shows the motion of the agents in the plane. The initial position of the agents is indicated with an 'x' and positions in different time instants are represented with a circle 'o'. Is observed how the leader follows the desired trajectory while the followers achieve a time-varying formation. Furthermore, the minimum distance requirement is satisfied as shown in **Figure 9**, which depicts all the possible distances between agents. The distances between any pair of agents are always greater than or equal to the predefined distance $d = 0.3$. **Figure 10** shows the position errors of the agents. Such errors converge to zero.

3.3. Time-varying containment problem with collision avoidance

Let $N = \{R_1, \ldots, R_n\}$ be a set of mobile robots. The set N is composed of two disjoint subsets, so that $N = N_F \cup N_L$, where $N_F = \{R_1, \ldots, R_{n_F}\}$, with n_F agents, is the subset of followers, and $N_L = \{R_{n_F+1}, \ldots, R_n\}$, with n_L agents, is the subset of leaders. The agent R_n is the main leader, responsible for tracking a desired trajectory. The $n_L - 1$ remaining agents are secondary leaders, responsible for performing a time-varying formation with respect to the main leader.

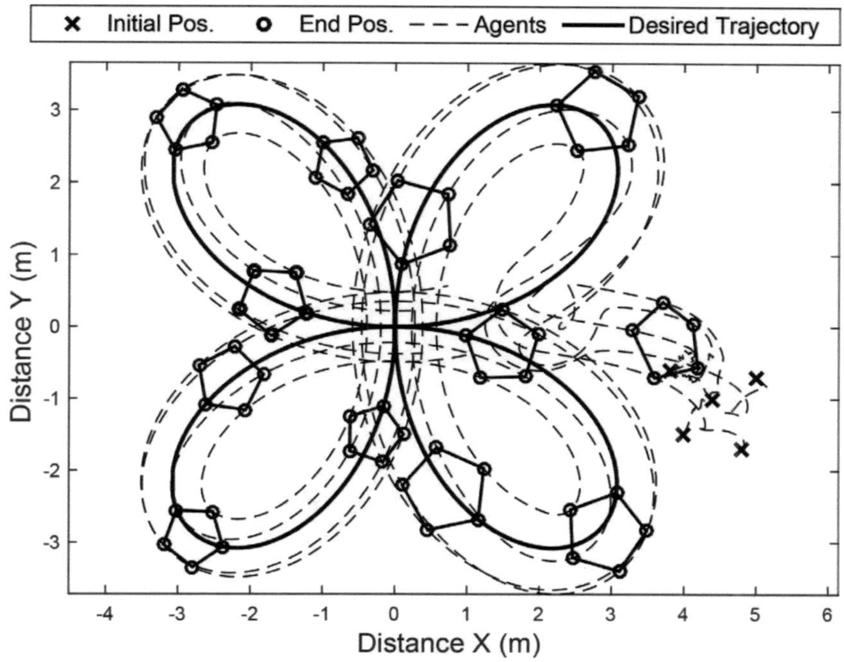

Figure 8. Trajectories of the agents in the plane (formation tracking with collision avoidance problem).

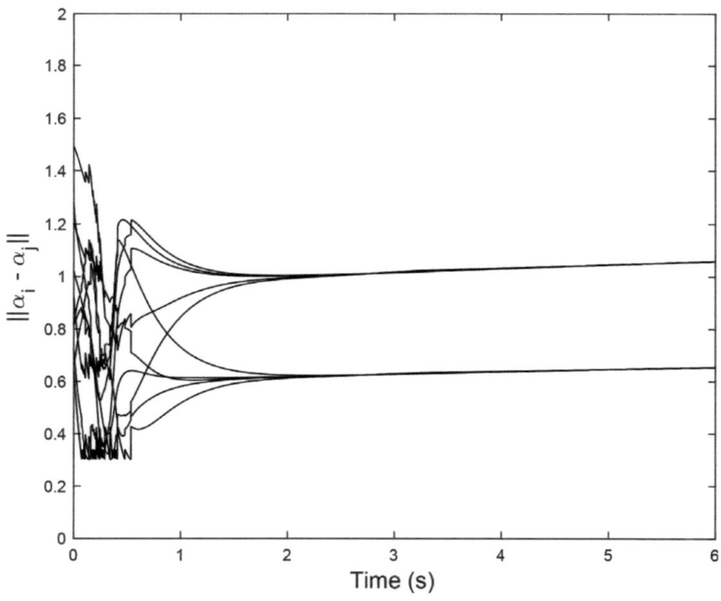

Figure 9. Distances among agents (formation tracking with collision avoidance problem).

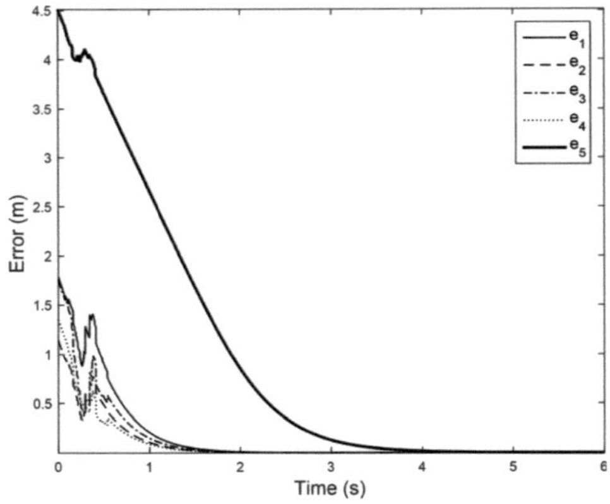

Figure 10. Position Errors of the agents (formation tracking with collision avoidance problem).

In this subsection, we make the following standings assumptions

Assumption 4. *For each follower, there is a path to at least one leader agent, i.e. for all* $R_j \in N_F$*, there are edges* $(R_i, R_{m_1}), (R_{m_1}, R_{m_2}), \ldots, (R_{m_r}, R_j) \in E$ *with* $R_i \in N_L$.

Assumption 5. *For each secondary leader, there is a path to the main leader, i.e. for all* $R_i \in N_L$*,* $i = n_F + 1, \ldots, n-1$*, there are edges* $(R_n, R_{m_1}), (R_{m_1}, R_{m_2}), \ldots, (R_{m_r}, R_i) \in E$.

In order to define the problem statement, let us introduce some notation. Let $m(t) = [m_p(t), m_q(t)]^T$ be a continuously differentiable pre-established trajectory, where $\|\dot{m}(t)\| \leq \eta_m, \forall t \geq 0$. The desired relative position of the ith secondary leader within the desired time-varying formation is given by

$$\alpha_i^*(t) = \frac{1}{g_i} \sum_{k \in N_i} \Big(\alpha_k(t) + C_{ki}(t) \Big), \quad i = n_F + 1, \ldots, n-1, \tag{45}$$

where $C_{ji}(t)$ is a time-varying position vector between the agents R_i and R_j where $\|\dot{C}_{ji}(t)\| \leq \eta_c, \forall t \geq 0$. The desired relative position of the jth follower is given by

$$\alpha_j^* = \frac{1}{g_j} \sum_{k \in N_j} \alpha_k, \quad j = 1, \ldots, n_F. \tag{46}$$

The goal of this work is to design a decentralised control law $[v_i, w_i]^T = (\alpha_i, N_i), i = 1, \ldots, n$ that ensures

- Asymptotic tracking of a prescribed trajectory by the main leader agent, i.e.

$$\lim_{t \to \infty} \Big(\alpha_n(t) - m(t) \Big) = 0. \tag{47}$$

- Asymptotic time-varying formation by the secondary leader agents, i.e.

$$\lim_{t \to \infty} \Big(\alpha_i(t) - \alpha_i^*(t) \Big) = 0, \quad i = n_F + 1, \ldots, n-1. \tag{48}$$

- Convergence of the follower agents to the convex hull formed by the leaders, i.e.

$$\lim_{t\to\infty} \text{dist}\Big(\alpha_i(t), \text{co}(\alpha_L(t))\Big) = 0, \quad i = 1, \ldots, n_F. \tag{49}$$

- Collision avoidance among all agents, that is, all agents in the system remain at a distance greater than or equal to a predefined minimum distance d from each other, i.e.

$$\|\alpha_r(t) - \alpha_s(t) \geq d\|, \quad r, s = 1, \ldots, n, r \neq s, \forall t \geq 0. \tag{50}$$

To achieve time-varying containment, we propose a bounded control law given by

$$\begin{aligned}
\begin{bmatrix} v_n \\ w_n \end{bmatrix} &= A_n^{-1}(\theta_n)\Big(-k_m \tanh\Big(\alpha_n - m(t)\Big) + \dot{m}(t)\Big) \\
\begin{bmatrix} v_i \\ w_i \end{bmatrix} &= A_i^{-1}(\theta_i)\Big(-k_f \tanh(\alpha_i - \alpha_i^*) + \dot{\alpha}_i^*\Big), \quad i = n_F + 1, \ldots, n-1 \\
\begin{bmatrix} v_j \\ w_j \end{bmatrix} &= A_j^{-1}(\theta_j)\Big(-k_c \tanh(\alpha_j - \alpha_j^*) + \dot{\alpha}_j^*\Big), \quad j = 1, \ldots, n_F
\end{aligned} \tag{51}$$

where k_m, k_f and k_c are control gains. Note that for each secondary leader and each follower, the control input depends on the position and velocity of the agents with which has a communication. In practical implementations, these velocities can be calculated by numerical differentiation.

The first main result of this subsection is the following.

Proposition 7. *Consider the system Eq. (3) and the control law Eq. (51). Suppose that* $k_m, k_f, k_c > 0$. *Then, in the closed-loop system defined by Eqs. (3)–(51), it follows that:*

1. *The main leader* R_n *converges to the desired marching trajectory, i.e.* $\lim_{t\to\infty}\Big(\alpha_n(t) - m(t)\Big) = 0$, *whereas the secondary leaders converge to the desired formation, i.e.* $\lim_{t\to\infty}\Big(\alpha_i(t) - \alpha_i^*(t)\Big) = 0$, *for* $i = n_F + 1, \ldots, n-1$.
2. *The followers converge to the convex hull formed by the leaders, i.e.* $\lim_{t\to\infty} \text{dist}\Big(\alpha_j(t), \text{co}(\alpha_L(t))\Big) = 0$, *for* $j = n_1, \ldots, n_F$.

Proof. For part 1, the proof has a procedure similar to that performed in the Proposition 3.

For part 2, the system errors are given by

$$\begin{bmatrix} e_F \\ e_L \end{bmatrix} = \left(\begin{bmatrix} P_{FF} & P_{FL} \\ 0 & P_{LL} \end{bmatrix} \otimes I_2 \right) \begin{bmatrix} \alpha_F \\ \alpha_L \end{bmatrix} - \begin{bmatrix} 0 \\ \tilde{C}_L \end{bmatrix} \tag{52}$$

where $e_F = [e_1^T, \ldots, e_{n_F}^T]^T$, $e_L = [e_{n_F+1}^T, \ldots, e_n^T]^T$, $\alpha_F = [\alpha_1^T, \ldots, \alpha_{n_F}^T]^T$, $\alpha_L = [\alpha_{n_F+1}^T, \ldots, \alpha_n^T]^T$,

$$\tilde{C}_L = \left[\frac{1}{g_{n_F+1}} \sum_{k \in N_{n_F+1}} C^T_{k(n_F+1)}(t), \dots, \frac{1}{g_{n-1}} \sum_{k \in N_{n-1}} C^T_{k(n-1)}(t), m^T(t) \right]^T, \tag{53}$$

$$P_{FF} = \left[\frac{1}{g_1} \mathcal{L}^T_{FF_1}, \dots, \frac{1}{g_{n_F}} \mathcal{L}^T_{FF_{n_F}} \right]^T, P_{FL} = \left[\frac{1}{g_1} \mathcal{L}^T_{FL_1}, \dots, \frac{1}{g_{n_F}} \mathcal{L}^T_{FL_{n_F}} \right]^T,$$

$$P_{LL} = \left[\frac{1}{g_{n_F+1}} \mathcal{L}^T_{LL_1}, \dots, \frac{1}{g_{n-1}} \mathcal{L}^T_{LL_{n_L-1}}, ([0 \quad \cdots \quad 0 \quad 1]_{1 \times n_L})^T \right]^T,$$

where $\mathcal{L}_{FF_i}$, $\mathcal{L}_{FL_i}$, and $\mathcal{L}_{LL_i}$ are the ith row of the submatrices $\mathcal{L}_{FF}$, $\mathcal{L}_{FL}$, and $\mathcal{L}_{LL}$, respectively.

Solving for the position of follower agents $\alpha_F(t)$ of Eq. (52), we have

$$\alpha_F(t) = P^{-1}_{FF} e_F(t) - P^{-1}_{FF} P_{FL} \alpha_L(t). \tag{54}$$

Since $e_F(t) \to 0$ as $t \to \infty$, then $\alpha_F(t) \to -P^{-1}_{FF} P_{FL} \alpha_L(t)$. To verify that P^{-1}_{FF} exist, we have to analyse the submatrix P_{FF}. Making a similar analysis to [25], we can rewrite P_{FF} as

$$P_{FF} = \eta I_{FF_{n_F \times n_F}} - M_{FF_{n_F \times n_F}}, \tag{55}$$

where $\eta = 1$, $M_{FF_{n_F \times n_F}}$ is a non-negative matrix and according to Assumption 4, it holds that $\rho(M_{FF_{n_F \times n_F}}) < \eta$. Therefore, P_{FF} is an M-matrix, which is non-singular, thus P^{-1}_{FF} exists, and the elements of P^{-1}_{FF} are non-negative. Since the elements of P_{FL} are negative or zero, then the elements of $-P^{-1}_{FF} P_{FL}$ are non-negative. Since the sum of the elements of each row of $[P_{FF} \quad P_{FL}]$ is 0, we have that the sum of the elements of each row of $-P^{-1}_{FF} P_{FL}$ is 1 and according to Definition 4, when $t \to \infty$, the follower positions are within the convex hull formed by the leaders.

Modifying the previous control law Eq. (51) by adding the repulsive vector field Eq. (11), finally, we have the strategy to achieve time-varying containment with collision avoidance given by

$$\begin{aligned}
\begin{bmatrix} v_n \\ w_n \end{bmatrix} &= A^{-1}_n(\theta_n)\Big(- k_m \tanh(\alpha_n - m(t)) + \dot{m}(t) + \beta_n \Big) \\
\begin{bmatrix} v_i \\ w_i \end{bmatrix} &= A^{-1}_i(\theta_i)\Big(- k_f \tanh(\alpha_i - \alpha^*_i) + \dot{\alpha}^*_i + \beta_i \Big), \quad i = n_F + 1, \dots, n-1 \\
\begin{bmatrix} v_j \\ w_j \end{bmatrix} &= A^{-1}_j(\theta_j)\Big(- k_c \tanh(\alpha_j - \alpha^*_j) + \dot{\alpha}^*_j + \beta_j \Big), \quad j = 1, \dots, n_F
\end{aligned} \tag{56}$$

The second main result in this subsection is very similar to the second presented in the previous subsection, which consists of a series of three propositions, considering the simplest case, when there is risk of collision between two agents, then the case when there is risk of collision between three agents and, finally, the general case.

The results of a numerical simulation using the control strategy given by (56) are shown below. For the simulation, we considered eight differential-drive mobile robots, where the point α_i to control is located 0.15 m ahead the mid-point of the wheels axis. The formation graph employed in the simulation is shown in **Figure 11**.

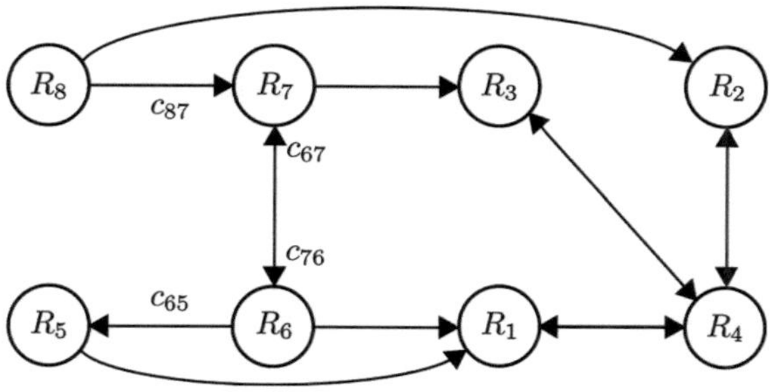

Figure 11. Formation graph (time-varying containment with collision avoidance problem).

The parameters used in the simulation are $k_m = 1$, $k_f = k_c = 2$. The desired marching trajectory is a Lissajous curve given by$m(t) = \left[4.5\sin\left(\omega_x t + (\pi/2)\right), 1.5\sin\left(\omega_{yt}\right)\right]^T$ where $\omega_x = 2\pi/T$ and $\omega_y = 6\pi/T$ with a period of T = 80s. The static position vectors are $c_{87} = [-1.2, -0.6]^T$, $c_{76} = [0, 1.2]^T$, $c_{67} = [0, -1.2]^T$ and $c_{65} = [-0.6, -0.6]^T$. The scaling factor is given by $\delta(t) = 1 + 0.2\sin(\omega_x t)$.

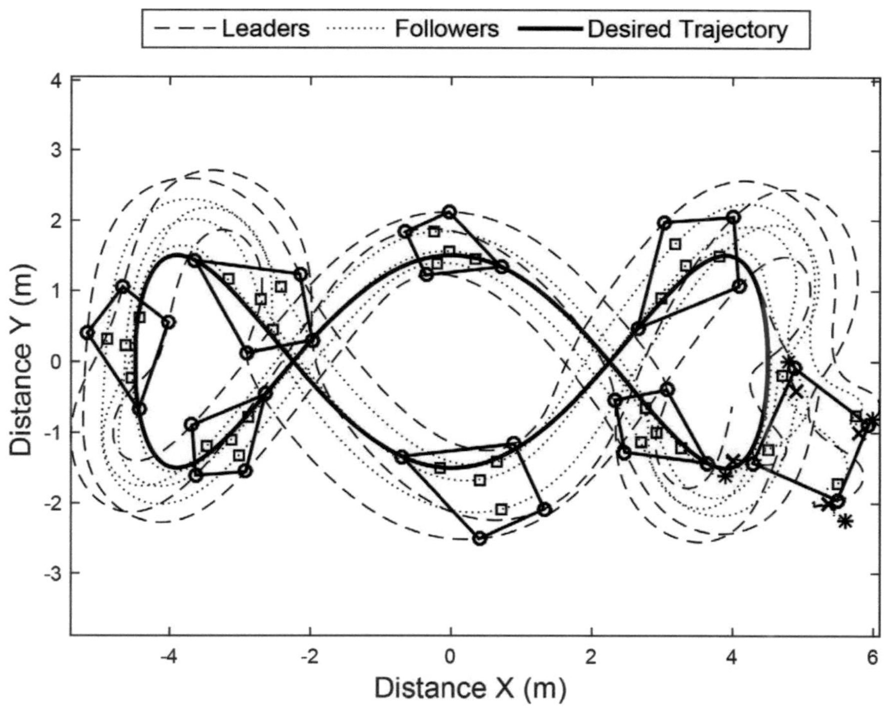

Figure 12. Trajectories of the agents (time-varying containment with collision avoidance problem).

The minimum allowed distance between agents is d = 0.2 m, and the parameter ϵ was set to $\epsilon = 1.5(2(\hat{\eta}/d))$ to ensure the minimum distance condition will not be violated.

Figure 12 shows the motion of the agents in the plane. The initial positions of leader and follower agents are indicated with an 'x' '*' and positions in times $t = 0.38, 12, 22, 32, 42, 52, 62$ and 72 s are represented with a circle 'o' □. It is observed how the main leader follows the desired trajectory while the secondary leaders achieve a time-varying formation and the followers converge to the convex hull formed by the leaders. Furthermore, there is no collision between agents as shown in **Figure 13**, which depicts all the possible distances between agents. The distances between any

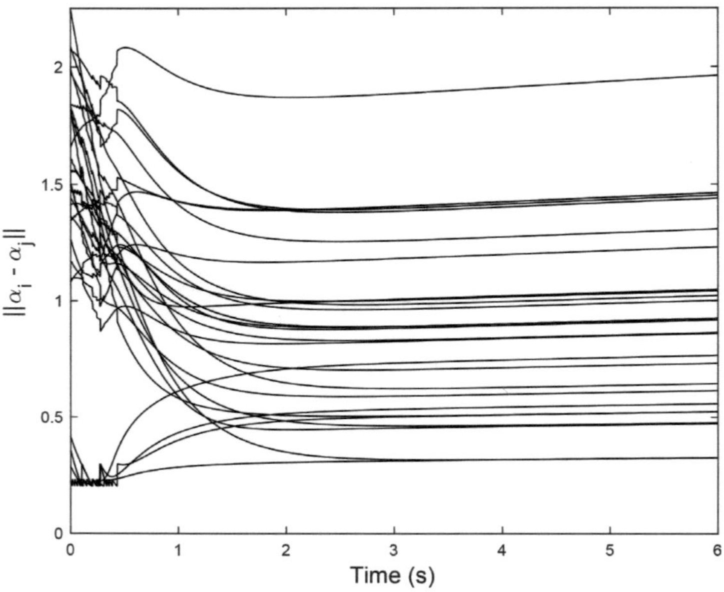

Figure 13. Distances among agents (time-varying containment with collision avoidance problem).

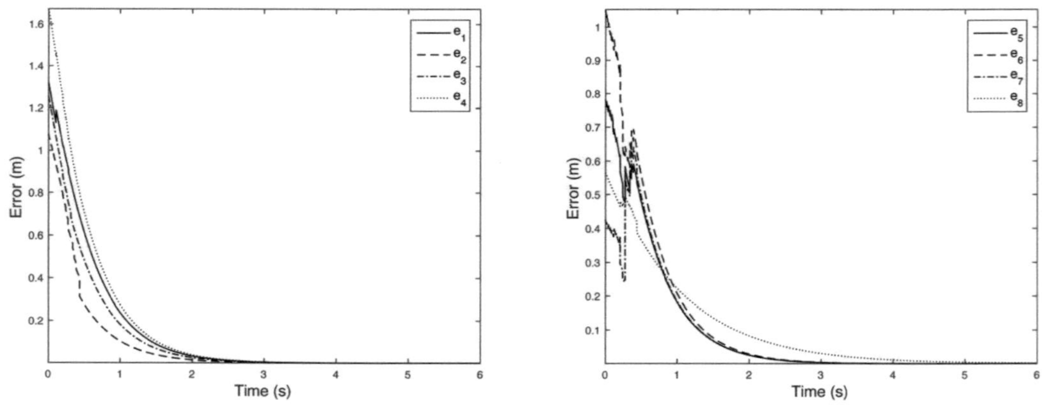

Figure 14. Position errors of the agents (time-varying containment with collision avoidance problem).

http://dx.doi.org/10.5772/intechopen.69845

pair of agents are always greater than or equal to the predefined distance $d = 0.2$. **Figure 14** shows the position errors of the follower and the leaders. Such errors converge to zero.

4. Conclusions and outlooks

This chapter presents motion coordination problems with collision avoidance for multi-agent systems, where the agents are differential-drive mobile robots. We propose decentralised control strategies which ensure formation, time-varying formation tracking and time-varying containment. Furthermore, collision avoidance between agents is achieved. We use formation graphs to represent interactions between agents. As shown in numerical simulations, the goals are achieved and system errors converge to zero.

As future work, it is proposed to control the mid-point of wheel axis of the differential-drive mobile robots and include a strategy for obstacle avoidance. It is also intended to validate the theoretical results obtained through real-time experiments.

Author details

Jesús Santiaguillo-Salinas* and Eduardo Aranda-Bricaire

*Address all correspondence to: jsantiaguillo@cinvestav.mx

Department of Electrical Engineering, Mechatronics Section, CINVESTAV, México City, México

References

[1] Cao YU, Fukunaga AS, Kahng AB. Cooperative mobile robotics: Antecedents and directions. Autonomous Robots. 1997;**4**:226–234

[2] Arai T, Pagello E, Parker LE. Guest editorial advances in multirobot systems. IEEE Transactions on Robotics and Automation. 2002;**18**:655–661

[3] Ji M, Ferrari-Trecate G, Egerstedt M, Buffa A. Containment control in mobile networks. IEEE Transactions on Automatic Control. 2008;**53**(8):1972–1975

[4] Briñon-Arranz L, Seuret A, Canudas-de-Wit C. Cooperative control design for time-varying formations of multi-agent systems. IEEE Transactions on Automatic Control. 2014;**59**(8):2283–2288

[5] González-Sierra J, Aranda-Bricaire E. Design of a virtual mechanism for trajectory tracking of convoys of mobile robots. In: Proceedings of the 10th International Conference on

Electrical Engineering, Computing Science and Automatic Control (CCE '13); 2013. 30 September–4, October 2013, Mexico City, Mexico: IEEE. pp. 364–368

[6] Peñaloza-Mendoza GR, Hernández-Mendoza DE, Aranda-Bricaire E. Time-varying formation control for multi-agent systems applied to n-trailer configuration. In: Proceedings of the 8th International Conference on Electrical Engineering, Computing Science and Automatic Control (CCE '11); 26–28 October 2011, Mérida City, México, IEEE. 2011. pp. 1–6

[7] Rendón-Benitez F, Santiaguillo-Salinas J, González-Sierra J, Aranda-Bricaire E. Marching control of multi-agent systems with orientation to the marching angle of the leader (in Spanish). In: Proceedings of the XV Congreso Latinoamericano de Control Automático (CLCA '12); 23–26 October 2012, Lima, Perú. 2012

[8] Qianwei H, Hongxu M, Hui Z. Collision-avoidance mechanism of multi agent system. In: Proceedings of the 2003 IEEE International Conference on Robotics, Intelligent Systems and Signal Processing; 8–13 October 2, Changsha, China: IEEE. 2003. pp. 1036–1040

[9] De Gennaro MC, Jadbabaie A. Formation control for a cooperative multi-agent system using decentralized navigation functions. In: Proceedings of the American Control Conference (ACC '06); 14–16 June, Minneapolis, Minnesota, USA: IEEE. 2006. pp. 1346–1351

[10] Dimarogonas DV, Kyriakopoulos KJ. Distributed cooperative control and collision avoidance for multiple kinematic agents. In: Proceedings of the 45th IEEE Conference on Decision and Control (CDC '06); 13–15 December, San Diego, CA, USA: IEEE. 2006. pp. 721–726

[11] Dimarogonas DV, Loizou SG, Kyriakopoulos KJ, Zavlanos MM. A feedback stabilization and collision avoidance scheme for multiple independent non-point agents. Automatica. 2006;**42**:229–243

[12] Hernández-Martínez E, Aranda-Bricaire E. Multi-agent formation control with collision avoidance based on discontinuous vector fields. In: Proceedings of the 35th Annual Conference of IEEE Industrial Electronics (IECON '09); 3–5 November, Porto, Portugal, IEEE. 2009. pp. 2283–2288

[13] Hernández-Martínez E, Aranda-Bricaire E. Collision avoidance in formation control using discontinuous vector fields. In: Proceeding of the 9th IFAC Symposium on Nonlinear Control Systems (NOLCOS '13); 4–6 September, Toulouse, France: IFAC. 2013. pp. 797–802

[14] Loizou SG, Tannert HG, Kumar V, kyriakopoulos KJ. Closed loop navigation for mobile agents in dynamic environments. In: Procedings of the 2003 IEEE/RSJ International Conference on Intelligent Robots and Systems (IROS '03); 27–31 October, 4, Las Vegas, Nevada: IEEE. 2003. pp. 3769–3774

[15] Yao J, Ordoez R, Gazi V. Swarm tracking using artificial potentials and sliding mode control. In: Proceedings of the 45th IEEE Conference on Decision and Control (CDC '06); 13–15 December, San Diego, CA, USA: IEEE. 2006. pp. 4670–4675

[16] Flores-Resendiz JF, Aranda-Bricaire E. Cyclic pursuit formation control without collisions in multi-agent systems using discontinuous vector fields. In: Proceedings of the XVI Congreso Latinoamericano de Control Automático (CLCA '14); 14–17 October, Cancún Quintana Roo, México. 2014. pp. 941–946

[17] Flores-Resendiz JF, Aranda-Bricaire E, González-Sierra J, Santiaguillo-Salinas J. Finite-time formation control without collisions for multiagent systems with communication graphs composed of cyclic paths. Mathematical Problems in Engineering. 2015;**1**:17

[18] Brockett RW. Asymptotic stability and feedback stabilization. In: Millman RS, Brockett RW, Sussmann HJ, editors. Differential Geometric Control Theory. Boston, Birkhauser; 1983. pp. 181–191

[19] Fax JA, Murray RM. Graph laplacians and stabilization of vehicle formations. In: Proceedings of the 15th IFAC World Congress; 2002: 21–26 July, Barcelona, Spain: Elsevier Science. 2002. p. 15

[20] Desai JP. A graph theoretic approach for modeling mobile robot team formations. Journal of Robotic Systems. 2002;**19**(11):511–525

[21] Lafferriere G, Caughman J, Williams A. Graph theoretic methods in the stability of vehicle formations. In: Proceedings of the American Control Conference (ACC '04); 2004. 30 June–2 July, Boston, Massachusetts: IEEE. 2004. pp. 3729–3734

[22] Horn RA, Johnson CR. Topics in Matrix Analysis (Online publication). Cambridge University Press; United Kingdom. 2011

[23] Poole GD. Generalized M-matrices and applications. Mathematics of Computation. 1975;**29**(131):903–910

[24] Rockafellar RT. Convex Analysis. Princeton University Press; New Jersey. 1997

[25] Cai Y, Liu H, Xie G. Finite-time containment control for multi-agent systems with single-integrator dynamics. In: Proceedings of the 31st Chinese Control Conference (CCC '12); 2012. 25–27 July, Hefei, China: IEEE. 2012. pp. 6433–6438

Chapter 3

Multiagent Systems in Automotive Applications

Raul Campos-Rodriguez, Luis Gonzalez-Jimenez,
Francisco Cervantes-Alvarez,
Francisco Amezcua-Garcia and
Miguel Fernandez-Garcia

Additional information is available at the end of the chapter

http://dx.doi.org/10.5772/intechopen.69687

Abstract

The multiagent systems have proved to be a useful tool in the design of solutions to problems of distributed nature. In a distributed system, it is possible that the data, the control actions or even both, be distributed. The concept of agent is a suitable notion for capturing situations where the global knowledge about the status of a system is complex or even impossible to acquire in a single entity. In automotive applications, there exist a great number of scenarios of distributed nature, such as the traffic coordination, routes load balancing problems, traffic negotiation among the infrastructure and cars, to mention a few. Even more, the autonomous driving features of the new generation of cars will require the new methods of car to car communication, car to infrastructure negotiation, and even infrastructure to infrastructure communication. This chapter proposes the application of multiagent system techniques to some problems in the automotive field.

Keywords: multiagent systems, automotive applications, traffic coordination, automobile negotiation, car-2-X communication

1. Introduction

One of the primary goals of the artificial intelligence field remains open; this is the development of autonomous systems capable of performing self-directed tasks in a similar way that humans do. Challenges and issues involved in the development of autonomous systems deployable in dynamic and open environments have led to fields as multiagent systems [1]. It is a discipline that forms a profound interdisciplinary study of fundamentals such as autonomy, agency, negotiation, communication, interaction, and cooperation. The major objective of this field is to develop autonomous systems capable of coexisting and cooperating with people and other systems in the real world. The principal motivation of this effort to develop autonomous systems is related to how people live in a digital and interconnected world, where new challenges and opportunities are arising (e.g., Internet of Things (IoT), smart cities, and big data [2]) as consequence of technology is strongly embedded in our daily life. Thus, we are near to see in our local environment, autonomous systems like smart environments (rural and urban scenarios), humanoid robots, unmanned vehicles (aerial and ground), among other autonomous systems capable of supporting people in their daily life. An important feature of these systems is the autonomy because they must be capable of embodying self-governance and decision-making. In this sense, to ensure that the autonomous systems are useful, they should be endowed with the ability to exhibit a smart negotiation to achieve its goals through the cooperation. It is supposed that these properties enable distributed systems to improve their performance.

Negotiation enables multiagent systems to achieve their goals. Although there are several research achievements that concern to strategies and protocols in the field of negotiation nowadays, its implementation in applications in real world scenarios is still far to reach. In a general sense, the multiagent system (MAS) is a paradigm in the computer sciences and related areas where a system of interest is conceived as a set of autonomous entities called agents, as well as its interaction mechanisms. The agent is an autonomous entity with the ability to "sense" the environment through a set of physical or logical sensors and to "interact" or "modify" such an environment by a set of physical or logical actuators, as well. A kind of "intelligence" or "inference" mechanism is also conferred to an agent. Thus, actions to the environment are based on the sensors and the inference machinery.

1.1. Multiagent systems

The MAS approach has proved to be a suitable solution for problems of distributed nature, where the information, the control, the processing, or all of them are not centralized but rather distributed. Thus, a set of problems has been well studied and useful solutions have been obtained. The interaction among agents is generally considered as message passing based on a well-structured interaction protocols. The content of the message is "information" that may lay in a context called ontology. **Figure 1** depicts a general layout of a MAS accordingly Foundation for Intelligent Physical Agents (FIPA) [3, 4].

The Foundation for Intelligent Physical Agents (FIPA) is an IEEE organization promoting the technology and standardization of multiagent systems. FIPA defines a set of specifications in the basic layer for the agent communication, management, and message transportation, as well as specification for the abstract architecture and applications layers. The interaction protocols, communicative acts, and the content of the messages interchanged between the agents are covered by the specifications defined by FIPA. For example, the auction and call for proposal mechanisms among a set of agents are defined as interaction protocols in the FIPA specifications [5].

1.2. Automobile applications

The automotive industry is moving toward the automated mobility. To achieve the goal of making mobility safer and having an optimized system for moving people in the world, a visionary technology is needed. The approach followed in this chapter is based on MAS

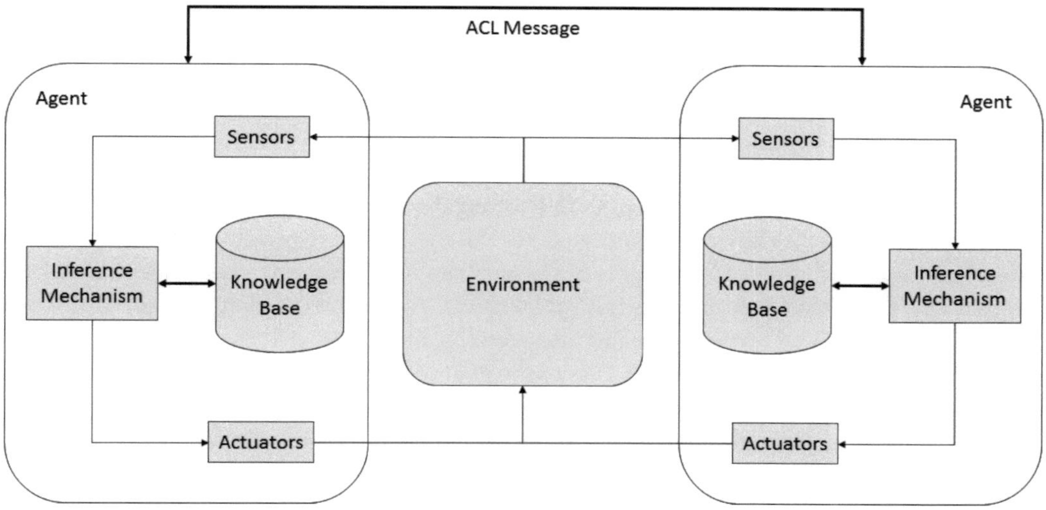

Figure 1. General layout of a multiagent system.

applied to the automotive scenarios [6]. The internet of things (IoT) is part of the design, as it is a trending technology for the connected cars and smart cities.

The applications of MAS to automotive applications, like traffic management and load balancing problem, include multiple possibilities, since the agents could represent different actors in the implementation of the solution. For example, in [6], the authors identify five types of agents: pedestrians, vehicles, traffic lights, streets, and parking lots. In this chapter, we consider the use of coordinators, route agents and traffic light cycles (phases), as an extension to the entities involved in the traffic manipulation.

The use of pedestrians as agents suffers from the problem to manage the communication with other agents. For example, other agents like vehicles and traffic lights can be incorporated with electric source and wireless link that helps power sensor systems or technology to help them accomplish that purpose of communication. Though, pedestrians normally do not have the facilities to perform those functions, however, the benefits to consider pedestrians as agents can be substantial due to obvious reasons. An approach to incorporate pedestrians into the system is to use a mobile device, such as the smart phones. By using these devices to identify pedestrians, its sensors may allow to monitor the position of the pedestrians, among other cases.

Other examples of vehicles as agents are reported in [7] and [8]. These works consider the communication between vehicles to coordinate the routes, every vehicle should take to reach its destiny. Within this approach, every vehicle has information that helps them to accomplish their goal, which deals with moving from point A to point B in the shortest time possible. The agents or cars can share or keep this information according to its heuristics which are the rules they use to make any decision that push them closer to complete their goal. Making local individual decisions based on information gathered by themselves or cooperating with other agents help they accomplish a global goal of coordination between vehicles in such a way that every agent can reach their destiny in less time than picking the common fast routes, and sometimes creating bottlenecks on those streets or avenues.

Another popular approach is to focus on traffic lights since they are typically the most common points where traffic loads are introduced into the system. There are several papers focusing on intersections like [9–12]. These works focus on coordination of phases between different intersections. The hypothesis is that creating local solutions in each intersection will produce a better performance overall in the system as a whole.

In [13] the authors propose using a set of Q-learning iterations to approach the optimal solution of load balancing. They also mentioned several methods to control the traffic lights and intersections using different techniques of the artificial intelligence, such as fuzzy rules, predefined rule-based systems, and centralized methods. An important feature of this approach is that when controlling traffic lights and intersections, the phases that control traffic in different roads are a key element for the success of the goal of the system. Indeed, the coordination between changes of lights and what streets have preference before others are crucial to get a good traffic flow in the right direction. This feature is considered in this chapter.

Other important example that implements multiple agents as a solution to automotive scenarios is [14]. In this work, the focus is to make buses arrive on time to their stops. The system uses four agents: the bus vehicle, the bus route, the intersections, and the stages. The bus vehicle drives through the route informing the route agent their times, the route agent checks the time between the buses in the same route and if the buses are late or early, it communicates with the main agent, the intersection. The intersections analyze what to do; if the bus is to early then the stages where the bus is not currently transiting have priority to be set in the traffic light. On the contrary, if the bus is too late, the stages where the bus is going should have more probability of appearing in the traffic light. One important aspect to notice is the priority, having a greater priority does not mean that automatically that stage will be next. It only gives to the agent more tools to coordinate with other stages to be the one at the top, which is a goal. The stages need to coordinate and from that process, the next stage in the traffic light is selected. The coordination is selected by multiple factors, the number of buses in the lane, the green time required by the stage, the velocity of the vehicles in the lane, etc.

1.3. Technology used

Based on the specifications defined by FIPA, several implementations provide frameworks for the development of MAS. For example, the JAVA Agent Development (JADE) Framework is a platform for the development of agent-based applications. JADE is fully compliant with the FIPA specifications and provides a basic class for agent instantiation, communication protocols, ontology implementation, and graphical management tools. **Figure 2** provides a reference model for the management of agents within the platform [15].

When working with automotive traffic, it is difficult to find a real environment for testing. For example, closing a group of intersections and sending vehicles in a predefine pattern, are desired features for the experimentation process in MAS applied to automotive scenarios. Fortunately, there are some computer traffic simulators that, with some sort of work, could be coupled to MAS development frameworks such as JADE, which is one of the target environments of this chapter.

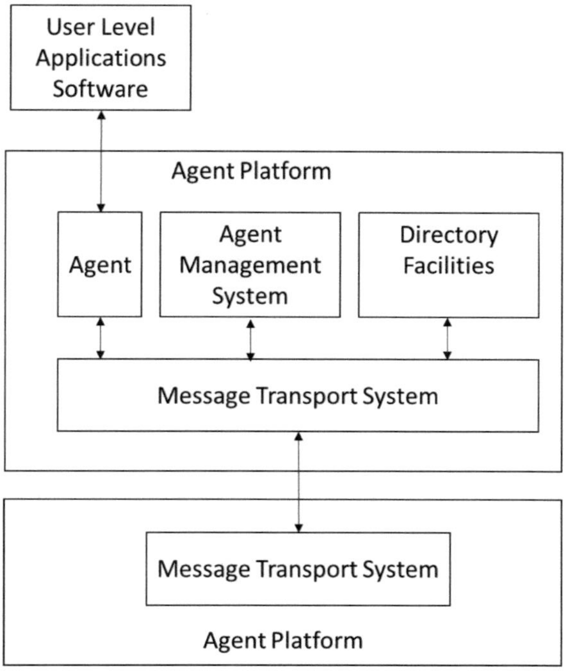

Figure 2. Agent management reference model in JADE.

To mention some simulators, consider for example VISSIM, Paramics, Aimsun, Dynameq, MITSIMLab, Simulation Urban Mobility (SUMO), DRACULA, DynaMIT, MEANET, and MATSim [14]. The simulators provide different characteristics that made them ideal for multiple scenarios. However, SUMO [18] seems to be used more often because it is microscopic, free, and easy to use. This chapter will focus on SUMO to simulate required traffic patterns and to interconnect these results with the JADE development framework in the section devoted to the negotiation and coordination applied to traffic load balancing with the use of intuitive ideas and common sense decisions [19].

SUMO stands for Simulation Urban Mobility, and is an open source project to create a portable traffic simulator. This simulator provides a lot of characteristics that made it ideal for the experiments of the last scenario considered in this chapter. First, the interfaces are visual and easy to use, the way to create routes and export them to be used is very much like a city simulation game. In the interface, multiple lanes can be created for a single street, intersections can be configured to set the phases of the traffic light, and the behaviors that vehicles can perform. SUMO provides an API to manipulate the simulation and obtain information about the same, making it ideal to work with other systems like the JADE framework, which was successfully used in the construction of Multiagent systems [20].

SUMO provides the user with tools to easily represent real streets and roads, then insert into the simulation elements like vehicles, which try to behave as their counter parts in the real world. In this way, the simulations are quicker and cheaper than the real-time events and allow to test the same rules in different environments in a practical way.

Within the SUMO simulator, some designs have been taken to fit with the scenarios required in this chapter. Basically, there are two kinds of simulation processes, macroscopic and microscopic. The macroscopic simulation focuses on the system as a whole. It considers the state of the system at every moment, density, speed, and volume of vehicles. On the other hand, the microscopic simulation focuses on the actions of individual members of the systems. Thus, the approach followed in this chapter is the microscopic simulations, since the actions of the agents can be easily applied to members of the simulation, and within the approach proposed in this chapter, it corresponds to vehicle and infrastructure actions.

The most common simulation scenarios of interaction between agents considered in this chapter are the intersections. Among the two most common intersections where vehicles interact are the crossroad and the T, as depicted in **Figure 3**.

A simulation is composed by several elements but mainly defined by two principal configurations, the network configuration and the traffic demand configuration [11, 12]. This configuration is done through xml files. The network configuration contains multiple components starting with the nodes and edges. A node represents a joint point between edges, while edges represent the roads through which traffic will be circulating. A node is simply a representation of a point in the map that only requires three elements, an identifier and a pair (x, y) of coordinates.

1.4. Contributions of this chapter

This work presents application scenarios that take advantage of the MAS in the automotive field. In this work, the cars and infrastructure devices, like semaphores, are considered to be agents. The agents are communicating with each other by using a wireless network, through the usage of well-structured ACL messages. The agents send messages to know the status of the system, and based on that information, they can make decisions on how to use the available resources, for example, the roads.

In the approach proposed in this chapter, the infrastructure devices have information about routes they are managing. When a vehicle agent requests information about a specific route, the infrastructure device informs the status of the variables of such a route. Once the vehicle

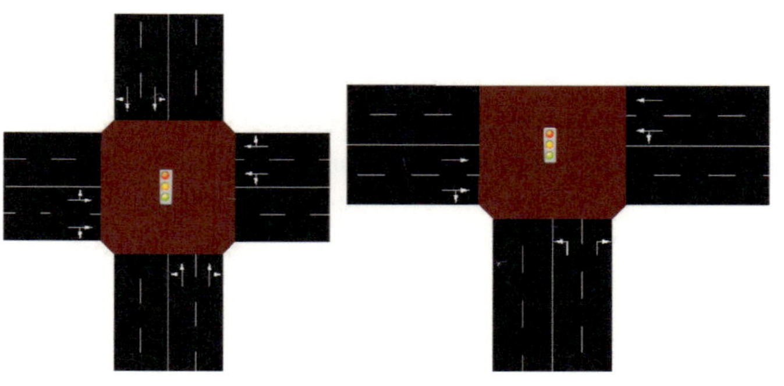

Figure 3. To the left, a crossroad and to the right, a T form intersection.

has the information, it evaluates which route is the best based on its goals and in some cases, the individual agents consider information about the preferences of other agents to get a suitable global solution.

In this way, a cooperative, distributed multiagent system can be used to improve dynamic routing and traffic management. Distributed artificial intelligence techniques, those applicable to MAS, could be used to solve decision-making problems to solve city mobility issues with the new technology cars.

2. QoS approach applied to traffic balancing

The QoS approach considers a method to calculate the best route for a vehicle based on a set of requirements, of the drivers as well of the infrastructure. It was firstly proposed in the telephony and computer network industries to measure the requirements of different users. To quantify the service of the network, several aspects of the service are considered such as the bit rate, mean of errors in the transmissions, throughout, jitter, transmission delays, or availability, among others. In QoS, a weight is assigned to each of the goals of the user, depending on the importance assigned to each aspect of the service they require. Then, a negotiation process is executed between the clients and the service network.

In the context of the automotive field, such interaction helps to find a better route for an agent, or rather the driver it represents. On one hand, as far as information of different routes is shared, the traffic management system (the network) tries to maintain a balanced traffic accordingly to its own goals. On the other hand, the vehicle agents have their own priorities. For example, it could be possible that for a specific type of driver, the distance it will travel is quite important; while for the another one, the number of turns it will make on its travel is the key parameter. Consider, the case of a big cargo truck versus a utilitarian car, for example.

In this approach, the information about traffic is currently used to decide whether to use a certain route or not. However, infrastructure typically does not take part in a system to keep the traffic balanced. It is supposed that the infrastructure could play an important role in the load balancing strategy. In this approach, the infrastructure may consider information about building constructions in certain areas. Thus, an objective of the infrastructure could be to reduce the traffic flow in those areas.

The implementation described in this chapter explains how a distributed system changes the perspective of the traffic in a city, and how important is to see it as part of a smart infrastructure where all agents play an important role. The definition of the objectives of the drivers and the infrastructure play a key role in this approach.

2.1. Goal definition by a utility function

The car agents must define in a quantitative way, the goals and preferences of the drivers they represent. Based on the received information, vehicle agents may calculate the utility as follows:

$$U^{ip} = \sum_{g} W_g^i N_g^{ip} \quad (1)$$

such that:

$$\sum_{g} W_g^i = 100 \quad (2)$$

Where i stands for the $i-th$ agent, p is the specific path, g is the specific goal, U is the overall utility function, W is the weight conferred to specific goal by $i-th$ agent, and N is the normalized score for goal g by $i-th$ agent.

The goals that a vehicle agent considers are based on the driver preferences. For example, but not limited, to the following goals:

a. Minimize Travel Time, g_1

b. Minimize Travel Distance, g_2

c. Minimize/Maximize Arterial Streets, g_3

d. Minimize Number of turns, g_4

e. Minimize/Maximize Roadway classification changes, g_5

Thus, for example, a cargo truck may confer big weight to the number of turns in the selection of its best route, as follows:

$$U^{cargoTruck} = 10\,g_1 + 10\,g_2 + 0\,g_3 + 80\,g_4 + 0\,g_5 \quad (3)$$

In a similar way, the other types of cars can define the preferences of their drivers in the negotiation of the best route based on the QoS approach. For additional information about the goal-based QoS.

2.2. Architectural design

Figure 4 provides a conceptual diagram of the agent interaction proposed in this chapter for the architecture implementing the QoS approach. In the figure, the car agents "request" information about the "status" of the infrastructure is done by asking to the proper agent. With the information of the nearby lanes, the car agents can decide which one provides the best solution for the goals of the driver they represent. The diagram is supported in the JADE framework [15].

2.3. Experimentation

In this approach, the implementation considers the following aspects:

- The number of car agents in the MAS is arbitrary. That is, it could be from two agents, i.e., one car and one infrastructure or route, to an open number of cars and routes.

- The agents of the system are implemented on an embedded board, e.g., the Intel Galileo Board Single hardware **Figure 5**, based in the JADE framework [15] where human decision of driving agents are tried to be programmed algorithmically [16, 17].
- The architecture distinguishes two types of agents: unsteady (e.g., routes) and steady (e.g., cars).
- The architecture considers a load balancing algorithm among the car agents and route agents based on QoS.
- The architecture considers that the route agents shall send their parameters of interest to all the car agents that request them. The parameters of interest are automatically updated in every 1 min.
- The car agents use the information provided by the route agents to calculate its best route.
- The distributed load balancing algorithm considers the infrastructure requirements, for example, to keep some route under some peak value of traffic density.

For illustrative purposes, **Table 1** summarizes the parameters for the experiments in the QoS approach. There are four routes available, each one known by an infrastructure agent. There are two vehicles that would receive information from such routes. According to the MAS, they will be "born" with some attributes that will receive through the arguments, which are described in **Table 1**.

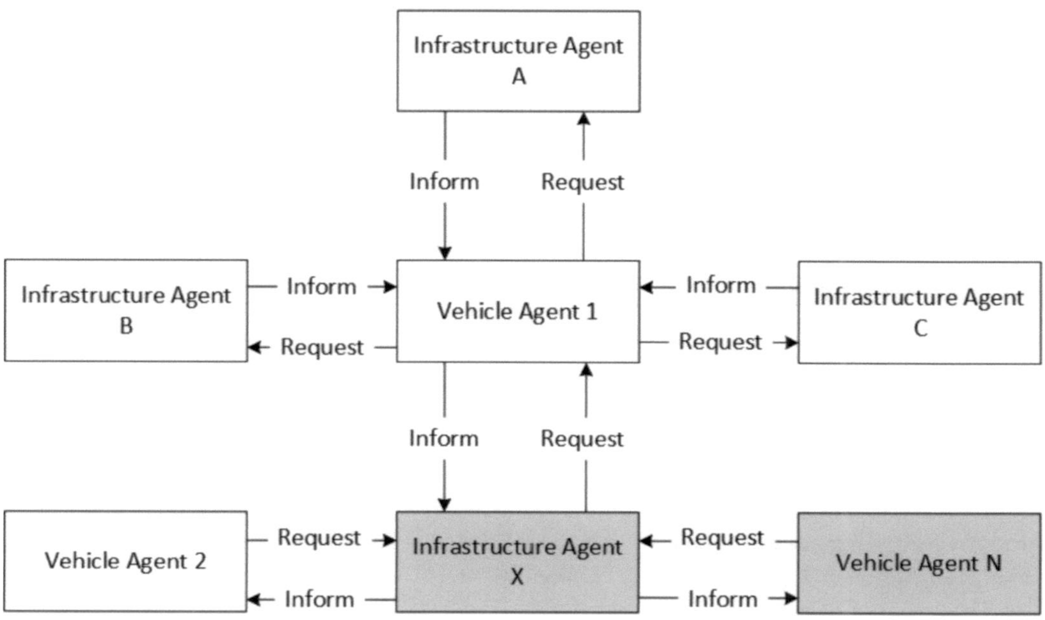

Figure 4. Conceptual diagram of the agent's interaction.

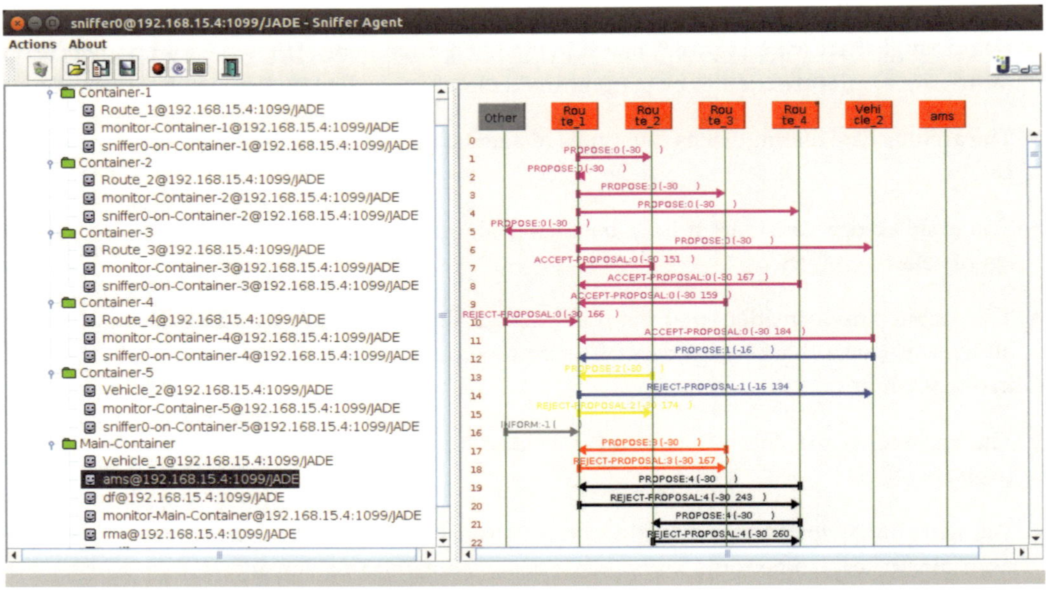

Figure 5. Example of agents' communication.

	Arguments						
Agent name	**Travel time**	**Travel distance**	**Arterial streets**	**Turns**	**Roadway changes**	**Vehicle?**	**Route number**
Route_1	0	0	0	0	0	False	1
Route_2	0	0	0	0	0	False	2
Route_3	0	0	0	0	0	False	3
Route_4	0	0	0	0	0	False	4
Vehicle_1	55	10	5	5	25	True	0
Vehicle_2	5	5	80	5	5	True	0

Table 1. Agents parameters for the scenario.

The first group of five arguments (columns) represents the weight (importance) that each agent gives to that goal. The first group of four agents (rows) represents routes. The routes have a zero value on those arguments because they do not have such goals. Rather, their job is to inform those conditions to the vehicle agents.

The sixth argument, i.e. *Vehicle?*, it is only used to indicate whether the agent is a vehicle or an infrastructure agent, since they share the same base class that the JADE framework provides for every implementation of an agent. Finally, the seventh argument indicates the route number. This value only concerns the infrastructure agents and its objective is to have a unique ID for each route.

Priorities/goals	Vehicle_1 weights (%)	Vehicle_2 weights (%)
Travel time	55	5
Travel distance	10	5
Arterial streets	5	80
Number of turns	5	5
Roadway classification changes	25	5

Table 2. Vehicle weights.

In the current implementation, the vehicle agents ask for the normalized values of each condition every 10 s. As soon as it receives the values of each route, it calculates the best route based on the weights (driver preferences) given when it was born. The vehicle has a list of routes, in case there is a new one, it will add such route to the array list *routes List*, defined as a global variable in the agent class.

The calculations were made analytically to compare against the results computed by the car agents. **Table 2** shows the weights that each agent assigns to each goal.

Tables 3–6 show the selection of the results of the utility of the routes in the experiments. These results agree with the expected values accordingly with the weights of the agents.

Route_1	Vehicle_1 utility	Vehicle_2 utility
0.11	0.0605	0.0055
0.52	0.052	0.026
0.69	0.0345	0.552
0.88	0.044	0.044
0.45	0.1125	0.0225
	0.3035	0.65

Table 3. Route_1 utilities.

Route_2	Vehicle_1 utility	Vehicle_2 utility
0.88	0.484	0.044
0.12	0.012	0.006
0.12	0.006	0.096
0.73	0.0365	0.0365
0.99	0.2475	0.0495
	0.786	0.232

Table 4. Route_2 utilities.

Route_3	Vehicle_1 utility	Vehicle_2 utility
0.23	0.1265	0.0115
0.22	0.022	0.011
0.88	0.044	0.704
0.43	0.0215	0.0215
0.25	0.0625	0.0125
	0.2765	0.7605

Table 5. Route_3 utilities.

Route_4	Vehicle_1 utility	Vehicle_2 utility
0.44	0.242	0.022
0.43	0.043	0.0215
0.19	0.0095	0.152
0.25	0.0125	0.0125
0.81	0.2025	0.0405
	0.5095	0.2485

Table 6. Route_4 utilities.

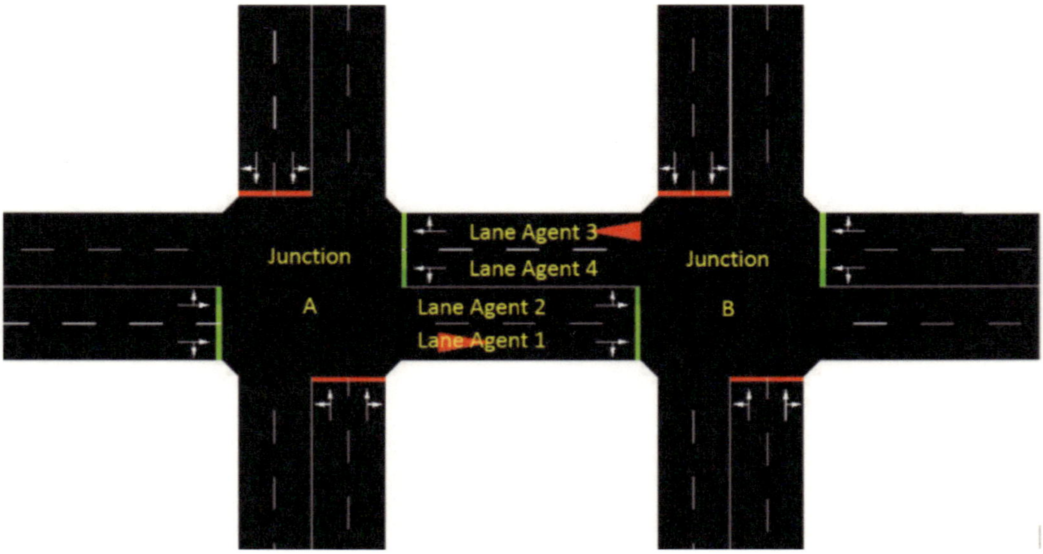

Figure 6. Lane and junctions.

The agents obtain the maximum of all the routes, the result will be the best route. In this case, Route_2 will be the best for Vehicle_1 with a total utility of 0.786 and Route_3 will be the best for Vehicle_2 with a total utility of 0.760. **Figure 6** shows a screenshot of the GUI of the Sniffer agent capturing the ACL messages of the interaction between the cars and routes. The main container with the administrative tools of the JADE platform, including the sniffer agent, is running in a laptop. The agents are running on an Intel Galileo development board.

3. Agent negotiation and coordination

The coordination of agents is a key element in the MAS field. This coordination can be accomplished by using multiple methods. For example, if the agents are competing to obtain a resource, an auction can be a good mechanism.

3.1. Design description

The approach considered in this section is like the one provided in Ref. [21]. However, instead of focusing only in the buses, we will focus on all the vehicles going through an intersection. The proposed design has three main agents: the lane agent, the junction agent, and the phase agent.

3.1.1. Lane agent

The lane agent represents one of the lanes of an edge. More precisely, let say there is a street section that goes from junction A to B, and that street goes in both directions A to B and B to A. Then, the lane agent 1 will be the lane closer to the right in the section that goes from A to B, while the lane agent 2 is the second closest to the right. A similar approach is applied to the section that goes from B to A. The lane closest to the right will be lane agent 3 and finally, the second closest lane is the lane agent 4. This approach could be followed incrementally. That is, the street can have one or more lanes going in the same direction which means that a street can have multiple lane agents assigned to them, as previously described. **Figure 7** provides an illustration of the junctions and lane agents.

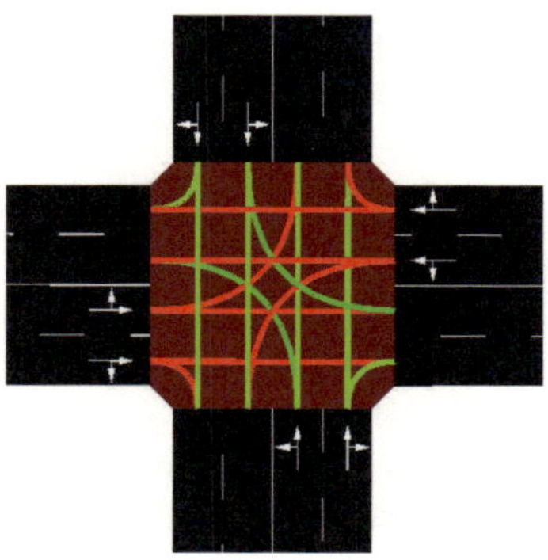

Figure 7. Connections and phase representation.

The objective for the lane agent is to keep the lowest number of automobiles in the street at any time. To accomplish that aim, the lane has a priority that is related with the capacity of the street and how close it is to reach its limit. This limit is when the lane reaches the priority 1, which means the street is almost empty. On the other hand, when the lane is at the priority 5, it means the street is at full capacity.

To calculate the lane capacity, multiple parameter are in play, for example, the length of each vehicle (C), the space between each vehicle (S), the number of vehicles (N), the length of the lane (L), and the maximum number a priority can reach (M). The following equation captures these parameters:

$$P = \frac{\sum_{i=0}^{N}\left(S_i + C_i \right)}{L} M + 1 \tag{4}$$

3.1.2. *Junction agent*

This represents an intersection in a real scenario, which is a junction between two or more streets, which also may contains a traffic light in it. The objective of this agent is to manage the traffic light cycles, which for the systems are called the phases, in such a way that the streets can allow traffic to move through the intersection. This agent is responsible for keeping the phases in a stack to inform what the current stage is and rotating the phases according to that stack.

3.1.3. *Phase agent*

This agent represents a traffic light cycle. The objective for this agent is to negotiate with other phases to go up in the stack from the junction agent. The phase has a priority to know what kind of actions it needs to negotiate with other agents and tries to stay as much time as possible at the top of the stack. To accomplish that aim, every phase agent has several seconds that can be used to negotiate with other agents.

A phase contains two arrays of elements, one with the time of the cycle and the other with a string representing the behavior that vehicles can have during that phase. These elements are represented as follows:

[31, 6]

["GGGgrrrrGGGgrrrr", "yyygrrrryyygrrrr"]

The array of string represents the behavior of the traffic lights during the cycle. For example, starting from the first lane at the top left in **Figure 6**, the vehicles can turn right in first lane and go straight, in the second lane. The same vehicles can go straight and turn right with precaution (this represents the lowercase g in the above character string). All the red lines in **Figure 7** represent connections that vehicles cannot use during this phase.

3.2. Agent coordination in QoS

This process starts when the lane agent calculates its priority. This may happen every certain quantum of time depending on the configuration of the system. The lane agent calculates its priority by checking the lane capacity with the formula seen in section describing the lane agent. That calculation returns the priority level the lane should have and if it is different from the current priority, then it sends a message to the junction agent notifying the priority change. A diagram representing this interaction by means of ACL messages is depicted in **Figure 8**. The junction agent receives the message and notifies the affected phases to calculate its priority. The phase agent will use the largest priority of the lanes that require the use of such a phase.

This simple system of three agents allows us to experiment with different methods of coordination. The proposed implementation method is to create a trade system where one phase

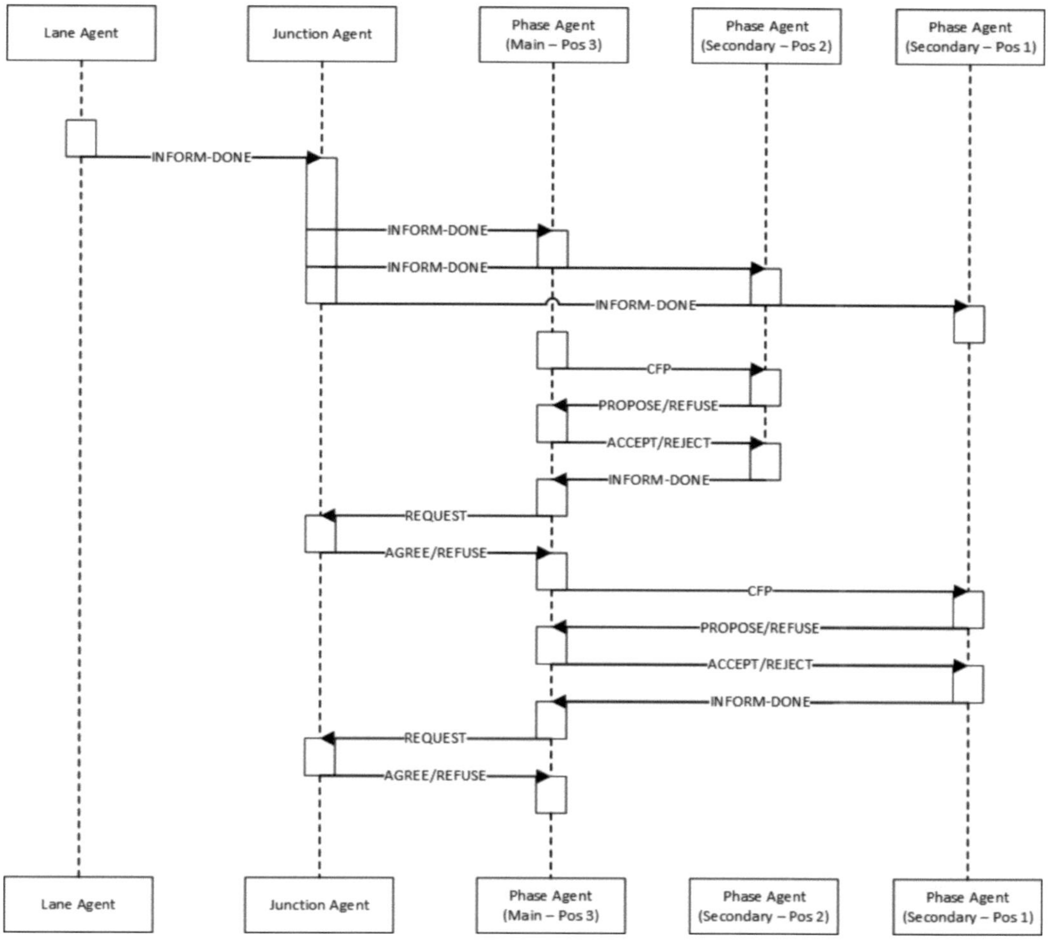

Figure 8. Diagram of negotiation process.

exchanges time for the possibility of the get up in the queue of priorities. Each phase calculates the priority as per the total number of vehicles each lane supports and the current number in the lane at a specific stage. With that information, the lane can setup a priority from one to five, where five means it is critical for that phase to be next one in the cycle.

One important aspect to consider is the fairness of the system. That is, some traffic light phases will have more seconds to negotiate than others. The rule of the tomb is a strategy for a system that can be beneficial for the phases with lower number of seconds and the phases with more seconds to spend. For this reason, instead of using the second as a raw currency, this work proposes to use the concept of a unit.

A unit may represent several seconds. However, the units may vary depending on the phase. That is, the unit will be the expected time of the phase divided by five. In this case, five is the number of columns we want our agents to work with. Thus, the expected value will be in any case that corresponds to the middle column. Accordingly, in the negotiations, any phase will have the unit value of two columns to the left to spent, and the unit value of the two columns to the right to gain. **Table 7** shows the unit values of the phase agents that it uses in the offering stage of the negotiate process.

The offer table contains the priority number as row and the number of units to gain, or lose, as columns. If the phase is at a certain priority and at a certain column, then with a simple lookup process, it is possible to determine the value that one phase agent should offer to take in the queue of another phase.

The accept table works in a similar fashion as the offer table. However, in this case when the phase receives an offer for its position in the queue, then it should check the accept table to decide whether to accept or reject the offer. The minimum value that the phase agent should accept is at the column and row of this table. Notice that there are some infinite symbols in the entries of the table. It means that for those situations, it does not matter the number of units offered, the phase will reject any offer, since that phase agent is at a situation where it is required to get into the junction cycle as soon as possible. **Table 8** shows the unit values of the phase agents that it uses in the accepting stage of the negotiate process.

For example, if the phase agent has 15 s of green time, then the unit value is 3 s (15 divided by 5).In this mechanism, the phase is not allowed to get lower than two units (6 s) and not bigger

Time (s)					
Priority	**−2**	**−1**	**0**	**+1**	**+2**
1	0	0	0	0	1
2	0	0	0	1	1
3	0	0	1	1	2
4	0	1	1	2	3
5	1	1	2	3	4

Table 7. Offer table.

http://dx.doi.org/10.5772/intechopen.69687

Time (s)					
Priority	**−2**	**−1**	**0**	**+1**	**+2**
1	2	1	1	1	8
2	3	2	1	1	8
3	4	3	2	1	8
4	4	3	2	8	8
5	8	8	8	8	8

Table 8. Accept table.

than two units (6 s again). In this case, the negotiation units are in **Table 9**. Thus, if the phase is in priority 5, for instance, and currently has 15 s, then it will offer two units to the phase at the top in the queue. If that phase does not accept the offer, then the negotiation ends. However, if the phase at the top of the queue accepts, then the offering phase will take the place of the accepting phase in the queue. Accordingly, the offering phase will lower two units of time, with 9 s of green light, but up in the queue. The phase that accepted the offer will increase its time by two units, i.e., with 21 s of green light, but lower in the queue.

3.3. Experimentation

To test the negotiation strategy described in the previous subsection, the first step is to simulate the basic scenario when coordination may occur.

Figure 10 shows a four-road intersection in the SUMO simulator, which is used to simulate the negotiation process. The implementation of the four roads needs four phases to be fully functional. To represent the states of the phases, four cardinal points, North, South, East, and West, are considered **Figure 9**.

In phase 1, the cars can move in both directions, North-South and South-North. In phase 2, the cars go from North-East and South-West. In phase 3, the cars are allowed to move from East-West and West-East. Finally, in phase 4, the vehicles can go from West-North and East-South. With these four phases, all vehicles can move from one direction to all other different

Time (s)					
Priority	**9 s**	**12 s**	**15 s**	**18 s**	**21 s**
1	0	0	0	0	1
2	0	0	0	1	1
3	0	0	1	1	2
4	0	1	1	2	3
5	1	1	2	3	4

Table 9. Offer table for green time of 15 s.

Figure 9. Four roads intersection.

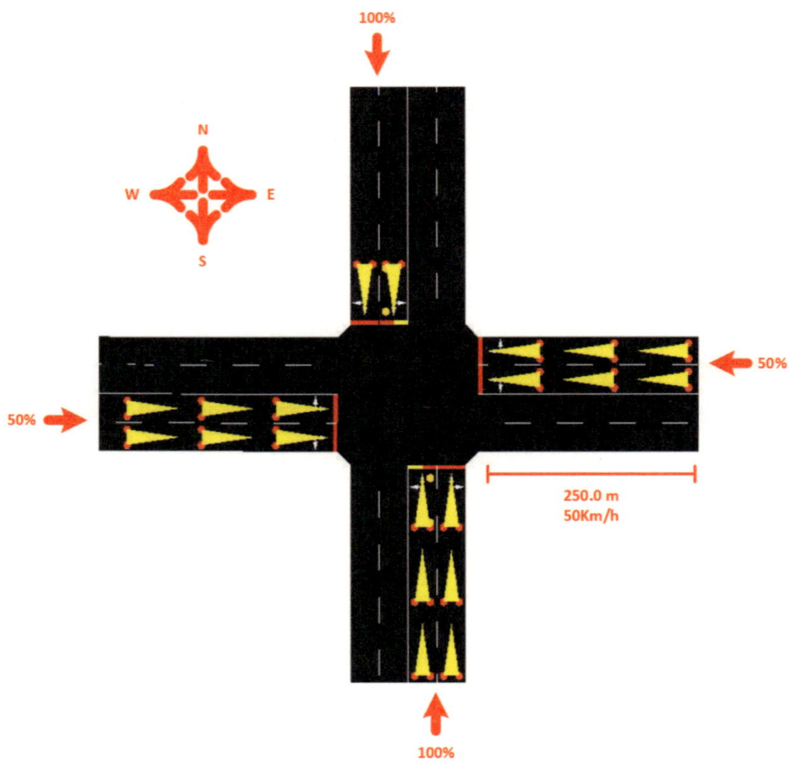

Figure 10. Simulation values.

locations they require to fully travel the intersection, even considering right turns allowed at any moment with precaution.

3.3.1. Integration of JADE agent platform and TraSMAPI

To implement the negotiation system, the SUMO simulator is interfaced with the JADE development framework. JADE requires a JVM to be executed. To execute the runtime environment, a simple command can be used to accomplish that goal:

java -cp <classpath> jade.Boot

where the classpath is the place where the jade.jar file lives in the system. However, it will create and empty the platform and the container, solely with the basic structure and no other than the default agents.

JADE provides a set of classes in the JAVA language that can be used to create the agents that implement the different pieces of the negotiation system previously described. The most important class for this purpose is the agent. The agents have a unique identifier, denoted as AID, which is used to uniquely determine a specific agent. The AID can be obtained using the method getAID. The identifiers in JADE are using a convention like an email address, i.e., <nickname>@<platform-name>; however, it is only a name and should be considered like that.

All the agents in JADE should extend the agent class. This inherits a set of methods to work in JADE framework. The two methods that require more attention are the setup and takedown.

The setup method is the place where the initialization of the agent occurs. It is used instead of the constructor method of a JAVA class. The agent class provides this different method, because it is safer to use and it can warrant that the system is up and running at that moment. This is something that cannot be possible with the traditional constructor. In the setup method, the agent parameters can be read to populate attributes by using the getArguments method.

The takedown method is invoked after the agent is terminated and this can be done by using the doDelete method in any place of the agent. The purpose of this method is to clean up any necessary objects or operations.

The communication between agents is the core functionality that needs to be implemented in JADE. To accomplish this task, JADE provides a behavior class. An agent can have different behaviors and all of them should be included using the addBehavior method. The behaviors are the mechanisms to implement the actions and methods of the agent.

There are a complete set of behaviors in JADE for different objectives. One shot behaviors, cyclic behaviors, generic behaviors, wake behaviors, and ticker behaviors, to mention some. One shot behaviors are implemented using the OneShotBehaviour class, this is meant to be executed only one time and after that delete the behavior from the agent. The cyclic behaviors use CyclicBehaviour class and they return false in the done method all the time, so this behavior repeats and keeps executing. The generic behaviors correspond to the Behaviour class, this is a vanilla class that can be extended and used as the user requires especially with communicative acts that requires several messages between agents. The waker behaviors relate to the WakerBehaviour class and will be executed after a certain condition is reached, commonly a time set like an alarm. Finally, the ticker behaviors use TickerBehaviour class and are repeated every certain interval of time.

The communication between the JADE agents with the simulator SUMO is required. For example, the lane agent requires to know the number of vehicles in the simulator lane, and the junction agent needs to modify the traffic light in the simulation according to the queue. To establish a communication between the two frameworks, this chapter uses the traSMAPI middleware.

TraSMAPI is a project from the University of Porto, which is an API to communicate with microscopic traffic simulator (like SUMO). This allows to get information and manipulate the different elements of the simulation like vehicles, traffic light, etc. One of the most important aspects is that it is written in JAVA, the same language as JADE allowing to easily integrate the multiagent environment with the Simulation [12].

The way TraSMAPI manipulates the simulation is through an interface created in SUMO, which is called TraCI (Traffic Control Interface) [22]. The interface can be accessed by enabling a remote port in SUMO. By using the command line, this can be done by adding the parameter—remote-port [portNumber] or in the sumocfg gile adding the traci_server section like this:

<traci_server>

<remote-port value="portNumber"/>

</traci_server>

With this, a series of bytes can be sent through that port to the SUMO simulation, the bytes correspond to the values of the instructions required to interact, first byte reserved for the command and the following, for parameters required to get data or modify any characteristics of the running simulation.

3.4. Experimentation

To test the implementation, two types of traffic light scenarios will be used. One with the traditional static, or fix, times for the lights in the semaphores, and one with dynamic phases negotiation that use agents.

The vehicles will be generated using a fix number per hour. Two combinations will be used to simulate more traffic flowing from north-south lines. In north to south lines, the flow will be a complete load of vehicles and in east to west lines, 50% of the full load. The full load will have values of 500, 750, 1000, and 1250 vehicles per hour. The details of the intersection are depicted in **Figure 11**. For the traffic, light phases, we will be using four phases as described in **Table 10**.

The results using static (s) traffic lights and using dynamic (d) traffic lights are shown in **Figure 11**.

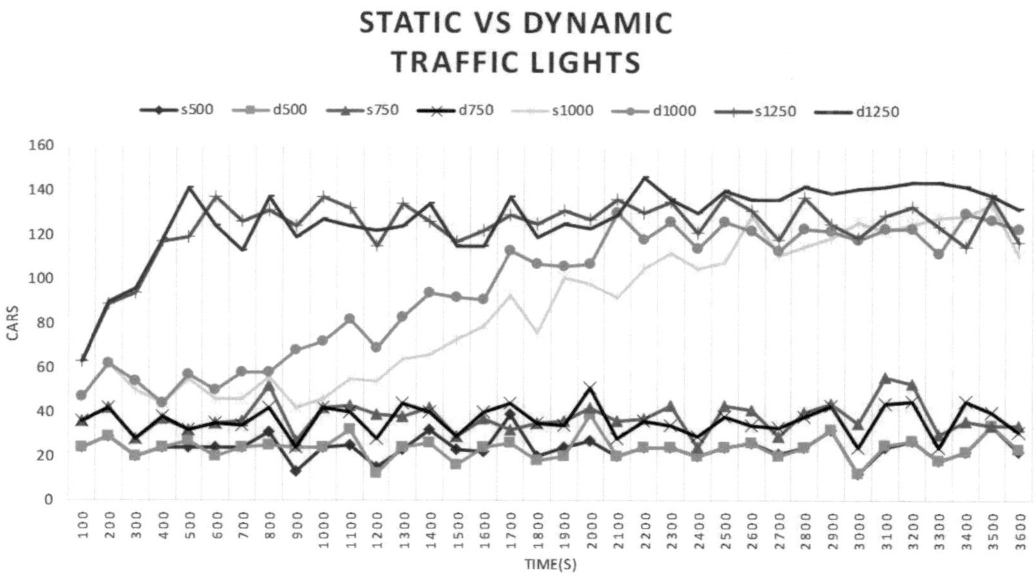

Figure 11. Static versus dynamic results.

Phase	Direction	Green time (s)	Yellow time (s)
1	NS-SN	15	4
2	NE-SW	6	4
3	WE-EW	15	4
4	WN-ES	6	4

Table 10. Configuration of the phase.

The result shows a similar behavior in the static traffic light and the dynamic ones using the negotiation mechanism with agents. At 1250 veh/h, both systems have difficulties to manage the vehicles load. Further experimentation is encouraged with different phases and times in the traffic light. It is clear that other coordination tables may be constructed to improve the balancing of vehicles under different load conditions and street configurations.

4. Conclusions

This chapter proposed the application of the MAS technology and concepts to the solution of problems in the automotive field. The MAS has provided suitable solution to problems of distributed nature, such as those present in the automotive field. The vehicles (both, cargo and utilitarian), the infrastructure (lane, semaphores, etc.), and even the pedestrian are suitable to be modeled as agents. This simplifies the modeling and simulation, and thus the construction of solution to problems of smart traffic systems. The communication mechanisms of the MAS are well suited to implement with simplicity, complex interaction protocols for the car-2-X communication. In particular, this chapter proposed the application of two mechanisms of the MAS to the automotive field. One the one hand, it proposed the utilization of QoS mechanism to the coordination between the cars and the infrastructure. On the other hand, it proposed the utilization of an auction-based mechanism for the negotiation between faces in lane intersections.

By using the set of tools and techniques described in this chapter, solutions to intelligent traffic systems may be approached from the MAS field. The experimentation with the traffic simulators and the framework for the agent implementation seem to be a new way to design solutions that may be quite complex to implement with other approaches.

Author details

Raul Campos-Rodriguez*, Luis Gonzalez-Jimenez, Francisco Cervantes-Alvarez, Francisco Amezcua-Garcia and Miguel Fernandez-Garcia

*Address all correspondence to: rcampos@iteso.mx

Electronics, Systems and Informatics Department, ITESO University, Tlaquepaque, Jalisco, Mexico

References

[1] Rogers A, Corkill DD, Jennings NR. Agent technologies for sensor networks. IEEE Intelligent Systems. 2009;**24**(2):13-17

[2] Sayed AH. Adaptation, learning, and optimization over networks. Foundations and Trends® in Machine Learning. 2014;**7**(4-5):311-801

[3] Burg B. & FIPA VP. Foundation for Intelligent Physical Agents. Official FIPA presentation, Lausanne, February, 2002. Foundation for Intelligent Physical Agents, http://www.fipa.org/

[4] FIPA00002, S. FIPA Agent Management Specification. 2000. http://www.fipa.org/specs/fipa00023/index.html

[5] Poslad S. Specifying protocols for multi-agent systems interaction. ACM Transactions on Autonomous and Adaptive Systems (TAAS). 2007;**2**(4):15

[6] Bomarius F. A Multi-Agent Approach towards Modeling Urban Traffic Scenarios. Research Report RR-92-47, Deutches Forschungszentrum für Künstliche Intelligenz, September 1992.

[7] Adler JL, Satapathy G, Manikonda V, Bowles B, & Blue VJ. A multi-agent approach to cooperative traffic management and route guidance. Transportation Research Part B: Methodological, 2005;**39**(4):297-318.

[8] Yamashita T, Izumi K, Kurumatani K, & Nakashima H. Smooth traffic flow with a cooperative car navigation system. In Proc. of the fourth international joint conference on Autonomous agents and multiagent systems (pp. 478-485), ACM. Utrecht, Netherlands, 2005.

[9] Enhamza K & Seridi H. Intelligent traffic light control using an adaptive approach, In Proc. Of IT4OD, p. 246-250, Morocco, 2014.

[10] Abdoos M, Mozayani N & Bazzan AL. Traffic light control in non-stationary environments based on multi agent q-learning, In Proc. Of 14th International IEEE Conference on Intelligent Transportation Systems (ITSC), pp. 1580-1585. Washington, DC, 2011.

[11] Azevedo T, De Araújo PJ, Rossetti RJ & Rocha APC. JADE, TraSMAPI and SUMO: A tool-chain for simulating traffic light control. In Proc. Of the 13th International Joint Conference on Autonomous Agents and Multiagent Systems, Paris, 2014.

[12] Timóteo IJ, Araújo MR, Rossetti RJ & Oliveira EC. (2010, September). TraSMAPI: An API oriented towards Multi-Agent Systems real-time interaction with multiple Traffic Simulators. In Proc. Of 13th International IEEE Conference on Intelligent Transportation Systems (ITSC), (pp. 1183-1188). Funchal, Madeira Island, Portugal, 2010.

[13] Abdoos M, Mozayani N & Bazzan AL. Hierarchical control of traffic signals using Q-learning with tile coding. Applied Intelligence. 2014;**40**(2):201-213

[14] Tlig M & Bhouri N. A multi-agent system for urban traffic and buses regularity control. Procedia-Social and Behavioral Sciences. 2011;**20**:896-905

[15] Bellifemine F, Poggi A & Rimassa G. JADE–A FIPA-compliant agent framework. In Proceedings of PAAM. 1999;**99**:97-108, p 33. Available online at: http://jade.tilab.com/

[16] Christian B & Griffiths T. Algorithms to live by: The computer science of human decisions. Macmillan, USA, 2016.

[17] Barceló J. Fundamentals of traffic simulation. New York: Springer. 2010;**145**:439.

[18] Krajzewicz D, Hertkorn G, Rössel C & Wagner P. SUMO (Simulation of Urban MObility)-an open-source traffic simulation. In Proc. of the 4th middle East Symposium on Simulation and Modelling (MESM20002). Sharjah, United Arab Emirates, 2002; 183-187.

[19] Vaudrin F & Capus L. Experiment of a common sense based-approach to improve coordination of Traffic Signal Timing System with SUMO. In Proc. Of Intermodal Simulation for Intermodal Transport SUMO 2015. Berlin, 2015

[20] Bellifemine FL, Caire G & Greenwood D. Developing multi-agent systems with JADE. John Wiley & Sons, 2007:**7**.

[21] Adler JL, Satapathy G, Manikonda V, Bowles B & Blue VJ. (2005). A multi-agent approach to cooperative traffic management and route guidance. Transportation Research Part B: Methodological. **39**(4):297-318.

[22] Wegener A, Piórkowski M, Raya M, Hellbrück H, Fischer S & Hubaux JP. (2008). TraCI: an interface for coupling road traffic and network simulators. In Proc. of the 11th communications and networking simulation symposium (pp. 155-163). ACM, 2008

Section 3

Crowds and Evacuation Modelling

Chapter 4

Time Critical Mass Evacuation Simulation Combining A Multi-Agent System and High-Performance Computing

Leonel Aguilar, Maddegedara Lalith and
Muneo Hori

Additional information is available at the end of the chapter

http://dx.doi.org/10.5772/intechopen.69844

Abstract

This chapter presents an application of multi-agent systems to simulate tsunami-triggered mass evacuations of large urban areas. The main objective is to quantitatively evaluate various strategies to accelerate evacuation in case of a tsunami with a short arrival time, taking most influential factors into account. Considering the large number of lives in fatal danger, instead of widely used simple agents in 1D networks, we use a high-resolution model of environment and complex agents so that wide range of influencing factors can be taken into account. A brief description of the multi-agent system is provided using a mathematical framework as means to easily and unambiguously refer to the main components of the system. The environment of the multi-agent system, which mimics the physical world of evacuees, is modelled as a hybrid of a high-resolution grid and a graph connecting traversable spaces. This hybrid of raster and vector data structures enables modelling large domain in a scalable manner. The agents, which mimic the heterogeneous crowd of evacuees, are composed of different combinations of basic constituent functions for modelling interaction with each other and environment, decision-making, etc. The results of tuning and validating of constituent functions for pedestrian-pedestrian, car-car and car-pedestrian interactions are presented. A scalable high-performance computing (HPC) extension to address the high-computational demand of complex agents and high-resolution model of environment is briefly explained. Finally, demonstrative applications that highlight the need for including sub-meter details in the environment, different modes of evacuation and behavioural differences are presented.

Keywords: tsunami-triggered mass evacuation, multi-agent system, mixed mode evacuation, parameter tuning, high-performance computing

INTECH
open science | open minds

1. Introduction

There are several advantages of applying multi-agent systems to study mass evacuations like those triggered by mega tsunamis. Undoubtedly, the widely used simple methods like 1D-networks and queue models for simulating mass evacuation are quite useful in disaster mitigation efforts. However, they have many limitations. Considering the number of human lives in fatal danger, it is of great interest to use more sophisticated models which are close-to-reality models of environments and agents which can mimic evacuees' behaviours of significance. Unlike widely used 1D-networks or queues, multi-agent systems provide a great flexibility in the level of sophistication and allow one to gradually develop a close-to-reality model.

Details of a multi-agent system developed for simulating tsunami-triggered mass evacuation in large coastal regions are presented in this chapter. The multi-agent system is developed with the aim of including a sub-meter resolution model of the environment including the interior of buildings, dynamic changes in the environment, etc., and agents capable of perceiving this environment as evacuees do and mimic evacuees' behaviours of significance. It is essential to utilize high-performance computing (HPC) resources like computer clusters to meet the significantly high-computational demand of such multi-agent systems. A scalable HPC extension is included in the developed system so that an area of several hundreds of square kilometres with millions of agents can be simulated. The amount of computations involved should not be a great concern in developing such multi-agent systems. The rapid progress of HPC technologies will enable one to do sophisticated and large scale simulations on a workstation class computer, within few decades.

The rest of the chapter is structured as follows. Section 2 discusses a mathematical framework for the specification of multi-agent systems. Section 3 details the multi-agent system including the evacuee modelling features and the techniques for efficient modelling of environments. Parallel computing extension to efficiently utilize HPC resources is briefly presented in Section 4. Section 5 presents the validation of the model. Finally, Section 6 provides demonstrative examples showing the necessity of such models.

2. Framework

The multi-agent system is specified using a mathematical framework adapted from the field of dynamical systems, see [1] for further details. This section provides generic definitions for an agent, agent's local system, and the multi-agent system as a dynamical system. The purpose of this section is to provide a clear language to refer to the different parts and properties of the system.

Let the ith agent, a_i, be defined as a collection $a_i = \{s_i, f_i\}$, where s_i represents the agent's state and f_i its local update function. The local update function f_i encompasses all the possible actions, interactions, behaviours and thought processes an agent can exhibit. On a system with n agents, the set of all agents is given by $A = \{a_i \mid i = 1, \cdots, n\}$. The state s_i is further composed by two sub-states $s_i = \{s_i^{int}, s_i^{ext}\}$. s_i^{int} is the agent's internal state which holds the information that would not been available to other agents without explicit communication (e.g. gathered experiences, final destination). In contrast, the agent's external state s_i^{ext} contains information inferable by to other agents without explicit communication (e.g. speed, moving direction, etc.).

For every agent a local system is defined which captures the individual effects of the agent on its neighbourhood. Agent a_i's neighbourhood N_i is composed by its visible physical surrounding, N_i^{env}, and a set of agents it can interact with, N_i^{agent}; $N_i = \{N_i^{env}, N_i^{agent}\}$ and $N_i^{env} \subset E$, where E denotes the whole environment. The discrete time evolution of an agent's local system state $x_i = \{s_i, N_i\}$ due to the agent's actions is defined by $x_i^{t+\Delta t} = f_i(x_i^t)$. Actions of each individual agent make the multi-agent system to evolve from state $\{x_i^t \mid i = 1, \dots, n\}$ to $\{x_i^{t+\Delta t} \mid i = 1, \dots, n\}$.

In addition to the agents' actions, the changes in the environment due to natural causes like earthquakes, tsunami, etc. are modelled by applying environment update functions $\Lambda = \{\lambda_j \mid j = 1, \dots, m\}$ in appropriate order.

The multi-agent system is conceptualized as a parallel discrete dynamical system. In this system next state is independent of the order of execution of the agents, and only depends on the former state. Temporary copies of the agent states are used to preserve the properties of the parallel dynamical system. The time evolution of the whole system is defined by updating of the environment followed by updating of all the n number of agents, as follows.

$$\begin{aligned} E^{t+\Delta t} &= (\lambda_1 \circ \lambda_2 \cdots \circ \lambda_m)(E^t) \\ x_i^{t+\Delta t} &= f_i(x_i^t) \text{ for } i = 1, \dots, n \end{aligned} \tag{1}$$

3. The multi-agent system

As customary to most multi-agent systems, an agent system for evacuation simulation is also composed of two main components: agents and environment. The agents model the evacuees, while the environment provides the physical context in which the evacuation happens. This section provides an overview on the models of agents and environment.

3.1. Agents

Agents are composed by combining elementary functions that enable them to perceive their visible surroundings, take decisions based on their previous knowledge and current experiences, navigate in dynamically changing environment updating their memory, etc.

The logic to model evacuees' possible actions, interactions, behaviours, thought processes, etc. is embedded in the agent's local update function f_i. Local update functions, f_i, are built through the composition of basic constituent functions g^j's, $f_i = g^1 \circ g^2 \cdots \circ g^p$. These constituent functions include elementary functions that enable agents to perceive their visible surroundings, take decisions based on their previous knowledge and current experiences, navigate in dynamically changing environment updating their memory, etc. Brief descriptions of some of the implemented constituent functions are given below.

g^{eye}: scans N_i^{env} and creates a boundary of visibility in s_i^{int} according to a_i's eye sight.

$g^{find\_way\_out}$: analyzes the boundary of visibility and identifies ways out in the visible neighbourhood.

$g_{pedestrians}^{navigate}, g_{cars}^{navigate}$: defines the way pedestrians and vehicles navigate through the environment given the available information.

$g^{find\_inteact}$ finds agents to interact with, based on visibility, interaction radius, etc.

g^{coll_av} : finds a collision free velocity to move along the path chosen in $g^{navigate}$, evading collision with neighbours identified with g^{find_inter} it is based on Optimal Reciprocal Collision Avoidance (ORCA) [2].

g^{path_plan} : finds paths to a suitable destination, satisfying desired requirements like shortest, perceived to be safest, etc., taking any past experiences into account [1].

$g^{is\_path\_blocked}$: visually identifies whether a current path is blocked.

$g^{find\_a\_followee}$: finds an agent to be followed.

$g^{follow\_an\_agent}$: follows any agent identified with $g^{find\_a\_followee}$.

$g^{seek\_not\_evacuating}$: seeks for agents who have not started to evacuate.

$g^{order\_to\_evacuate}$: orders an agent, identified with $g^{seek\_not\_evacuating}$, to start evacuation immediately.

$g^{execute\_an\_action}$: executes a desired action such as move.

g^{update} : updates an agent's state.

The heterogeneity inherent of human crowds can be modelled by changing the agents' properties or by changing its logic. The components in each agent's state, s_i can be varied and assigned based on observed data. Properties like speed are drawn from observed distributions within a valid range for each age group. Agents belonging to the same age group are instantiated using the same distributions for their parameters. Different combinations of the constituent functions give rise to different behavioural models. For practical reasons, only a small set of local update functions are defined to represent the major roles and aspects of interest in the evacuation; $\{f^{\tau}\} = \{f^{resident}, f^{visitor}, f^{car}, \ldots\}$ where τrepresents the different agent types.

3.2. Specialized agent types—a^{τ}

The functionality provided by the different constituent functions can be separated into three main groups pertaining to human actions; *see, think* and *act*. *See* contains constitutive functions related to the acquisition of the information of the surroundings, *think* provides functions related to the cognition and decision-making, and finally *act* executes the decisions, actions and interactions chosen by the agent. Different behavioural models are created by specializing *think* with different constituent functions. As the focus of the evacuation simulator is on the evacuees' movement, the main way of interaction happens through the collision avoidance.

http://dx.doi.org/10.5772/intechopen.69844

To exemplify different modes of evacuation and behavioural models this chapter demonstrates the usability of the simulator using cars and pedestrians. Pedestrians are further subdivided in residents, visitors all of them provided with different information, and abilities.

Residents agents are used to model people familiar with the surroundings. They are able to use their knowledge to plan their path to the nearest evacuation area. **Figure 1** provides a sketch off the implementation of a resident agent, $f^{resident}$. Resident's *think* is composed by $g^{find\_way\_out}$, $g^{navigate}$, g^{find_inter} and g^{coll_av}. *Act* is composed of $g^{execute\_actions}$ and g^{update}. s^{int} is provided with a topological map of the environment, which is used for gathering past experiences, planning paths with desired constraints, etc.

Visitor agents are used to model people unfamiliar with their surroundings. They navigate using the information they acquire through their vision and the experiences they collect while evacuating. They perceive the details of the surroundings with g^{eye} and $g^{identify\_env}$. They seek a visible safe place like high grounds or follow other evacuees using $g^{follow\_an\_agent}$ in order to evacuate. Visitors can dynamically build their own mental maps as they explore the area and collect experiences.

Other agent types such as official agents that model figures of authority such as law enforcement, event staff, etc. are implemented. Their role is to help in the evacuation of other agents. They possess full information of the state of the environment and are assumed to be able to communicate with each other and collectively plan their actions.

Cars model a different mode of evacuation. They differ from pedestrians in the way they navigate and avoid collisions with each other and the pedestrians. While pedestrians are able to use the walkways or roads, cars movements are restricted to the road lanes. Cars are able to identify intersections. Due to the complexity of the intersections a simple queue model is used to model the effect of the intersections. Cars are able to recognize multi and single road lanes and use them accordingly. Cars are have access to the information of the environment and are able to plan their paths accordingly.

3.3. Environment—E

The environment provides the physical context in which the evacuation is happening. Formally the active environment is given by the union of all local neighbourhoods, $E^* = \bigcup_{i=1}^{n} N_i^{env}$. Although, $E^* \subset E$, for practical purposes they will be referred without distinction.

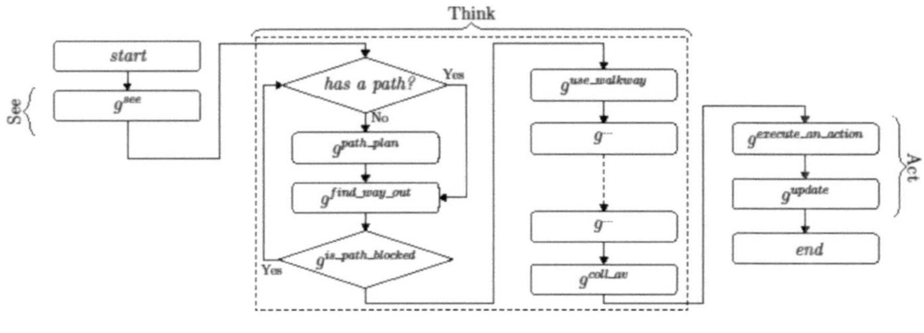

Figure 1. A simplified version of local system update function of the resident agents, $f^{resident}$.

Agents move in a continuous 2D space defined by walkable areas and roads. A hybrid model of environment consisting of raster and vector data is used to include the details of the physical environment and restrict the agents' movements, see **Figure 2**. Details of the empty spaces, obstacles, inundated areas and safe evacuation areas are provided by a grid, currently using resolutions of 1 m × 1 m cells. Agents are able to perceive these details visually and incorporate information such as blocked paths to their experiences. The topological abstraction of the traversable spaces is represented with a graph. This graph is static and represents the agent's knowledge of the undamaged domain before the start of the evacuation. The use of raster and vector data enable the efficient representation of details (grid) and efficient execution of cognitive tasks involving past experiences (graph). As an example, in large domains of several square kilometres, path planning on the graph is several orders of magnitudes faster compared to that of grid. In contrast to other large scale evacuation simulators the environment provides perceivable information and obstacles, but it does not provide an explicit constraint on the movement based on the model resolution. For example, different cell sizes, or graph connectivity can provide more or less information but do not explicitly constrain the movement of the agents in contrast to cellular automata models, graph and queuing models commonly used in other large scale evacuation simulators.

Changes in the environment, λ_j, are included by coupling the evacuation simulator with other simulators. $\lambda_{earthquake}$, includes damage models based on the results of a seismic response analysis tool. **Figure 3** provides a sketch of the integration with the seismic response analysis and the evacuation simulator.

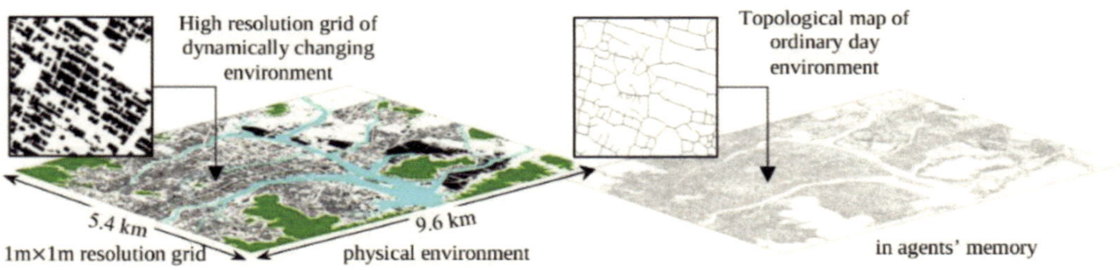

Figure 2. Hybrid model of the environment consisting of a high-resolution grid and topological graph. Grid is dynamically updated according to the changes in the environment. The graph is static and represents the path network before the disaster.

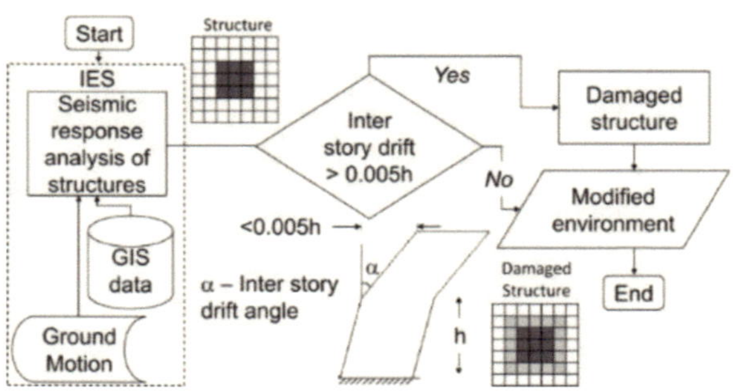

Figure 3. Integration of the seismic response analysis damage models with the evacuation simulator.

Additionally, $\lambda_{tsunami}$, provides information about the state of the inundated spaces due to tsunami. This information is provided by a tsunami inundation simulator with updates in 10 min intervals, see **Figure 4**.

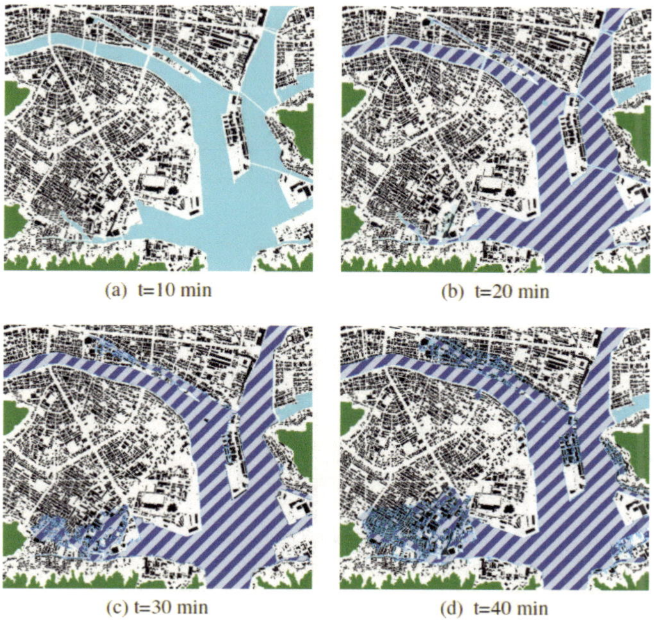

Figure 4. Snapshots of the tsunami inundation. Normal water level in cyan, inundated water level in blue (hatched).

4. Validating the model

One of the major challenges for the simulation of evacuations is providing confidence in the model. It has to be shown that the model is able to capture the essential characteristics of the evacuation (validation) and that the results are due to the emergence from those characteristics and not the result of an artefact in the simulation (verification). The validation of evacuation simulators is an area that requires further study and more and better techniques to provide the desired confidence.

This section provides an overview about the ongoing validation process. This first stage on validating the model is based on tuning the agents' interactions, specifically their collision avoidance with field observations and showing that after the tuning process the agents are capable to reproduce these observed results. This section is intended to provide a general idea of the validation process, for details on the parameters governing the interactions and the resulting values from the tuning process please refer to Ref. [3].

The pedestrian-pedestrian interaction is validated by re-enacting observations in [4] in the simulator. Monte Carlo simulations are performed varying the initial pedestrian densities and obtaining 100 samples for each in a one directional pedestrian flow. **Figure 5** shows the results of comparing the simulations results (whisker box plots with outliers) with the regression over the data [4].

A similar procedure is performed with the car agents, their characteristics are tuned with data obtained in field observations in the Lincoln tunnel [5] and the results are plotted against these observations, see **Figure 6**.

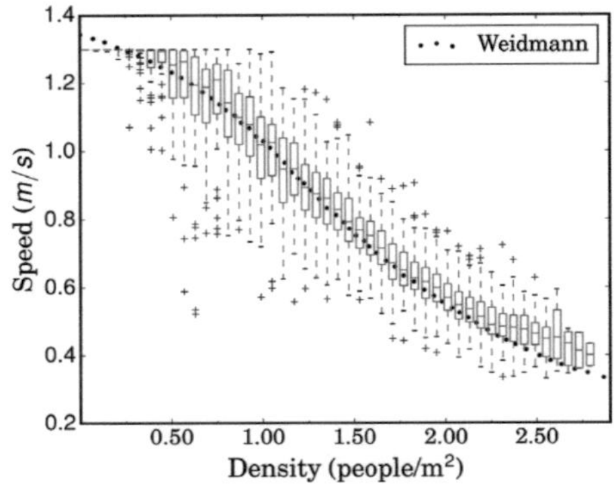

Figure 5. Comparison between simulation results and field observations for the pedestrian-pedestrian interaction.

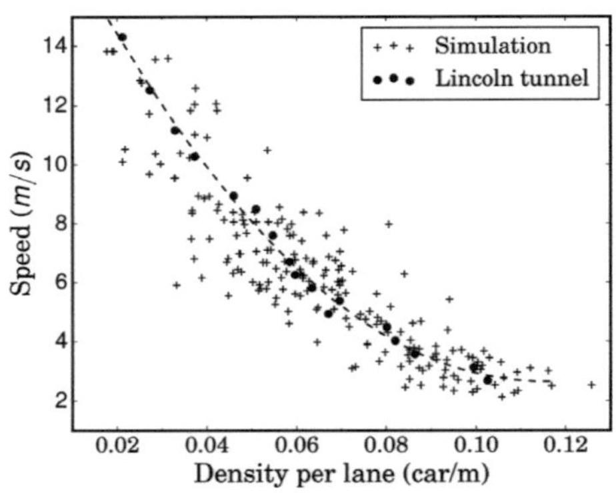

Figure 6. Comparison between simulation results and field observations for the car-car interaction.

Finally, the interactions between cars and pedestrians are validated. For these observations of cars and pedestrians interactions in Tokyo are recorded using a camera and quantified by hand frame by frame. These observations involved cars moving through crowds of pedestrians. The quantities are the cumulative amount of pedestrians in a square region in front of the car and the time it took the car to cross the study area, dividing the study area length by this time is what is referenced as the average flux speed. **Figure 7** shows the results of the tuning of parameters and the comparison of the simulation results with the field observations.

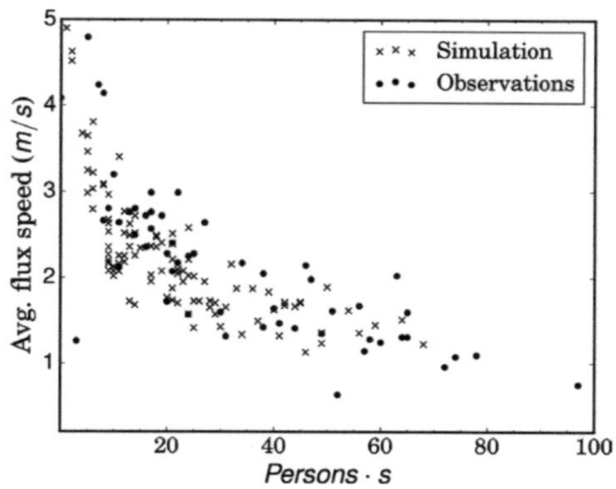

Figure 7. Comparison between simulation results and field observations for the car-pedestrian interaction.

Further parts of the evacuation simulator should be validated and verified, for example, reproducing macroscopic fundamental diagrams extracted from mobility data from cell phones.

5. Parallel computing extension

As the simulator possess the ability to model and evaluate a large number complex and heterogeneous evacuees in environments with sub-meter details the resulting high-computational load needs to be considered. The evacuation simulator takes advantage of high-performance computing (HPC) infrastructure consisting of computing nodes containing several CPU cores sharing memory within a node. These nodes are interconnected through a high-speed network.

To take advantage of the HPC infrastructure the simulation needs to be segmented in smaller pieces that can be dealt by individual computing nodes. For this purpose the environment, E, gets divided into rectangles and the information about the evacuees currently in that area is what is henceforth referred as a partition of the domain.

Hybrid parallelism using Message Passing Interface (MPI) and Open Multi-Processing (OpenMP) is used to create the parallel framework [6]. MPI messages are used to communicate the information between computing nodes and OpenMP is used to thread parallelize the execution of the agents within a partition considering each agent's execution a task. A run-time weighted 2D-tree-based domain decomposition is used for determining the partitions in the domain, see **Figure 8**. The use of a runtime weighted KD-tree for the domain decomposition allows assigning approximately a similar execution load to each partition. The partitions are provided with a ghost layer around it that keeps track of agents in neighbouring partitions, this to ensure continuity and consistency in the simulations. The communication overhead is amortized by executing the agents whose information need to be exchanged first and overlap the communication with the execution of the agents whose information does not need to be exchanged [7].

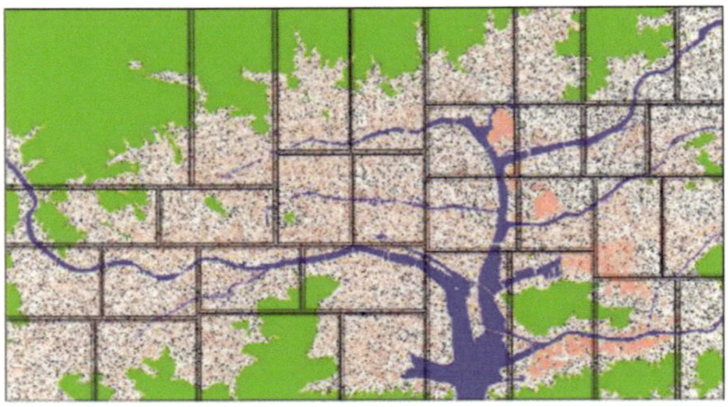

Figure 8. Domain decomposition example.

Intra and internode scalability is measured separately to evaluate how it degrades and where are the highest chances of improvement. Intra node scalability measures how the thread-parallel part (OpenMP) of the implementation degrades as the tasks of executing an agent are shared among a larger number of threads. The inter node scalability shows the performance of using flat-MPI as the number of processes (and partitions) increases. The intra-node scalability is tested using 100,000 agents in Kochi City area for 4000 time-steps. Measures for intra-node scalability are taken using a single node in The University of Tokyo's FX10 system, 16-core SPARC64 IXfx processor with 32 GB of RAM in the computing node. The inter node scalability is tested using 2 million agents in an 81 km^2 area of Tokyo for 400 time-steps using RIKEN's K computer, 8-core SPARC64 VIIIfx processor with 16 GB of RAM per computing node using flat MPI. **Figures 9** and **10** show a comparison with the ideal scalability.

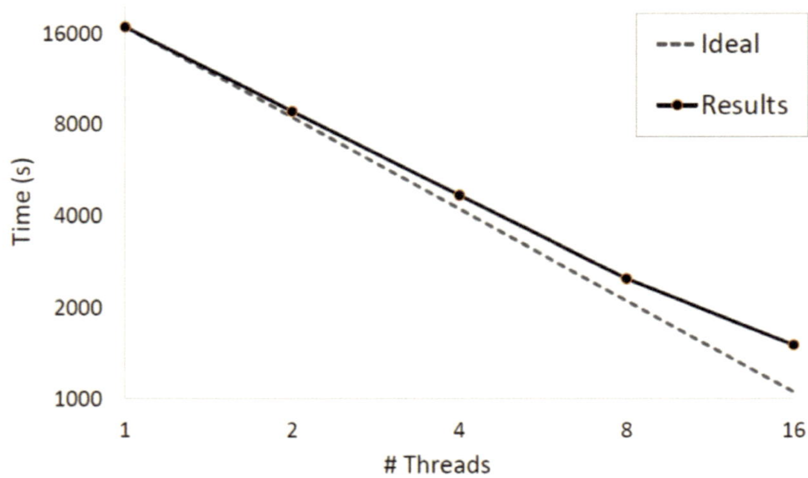

Figure 9. Intra node scalability.

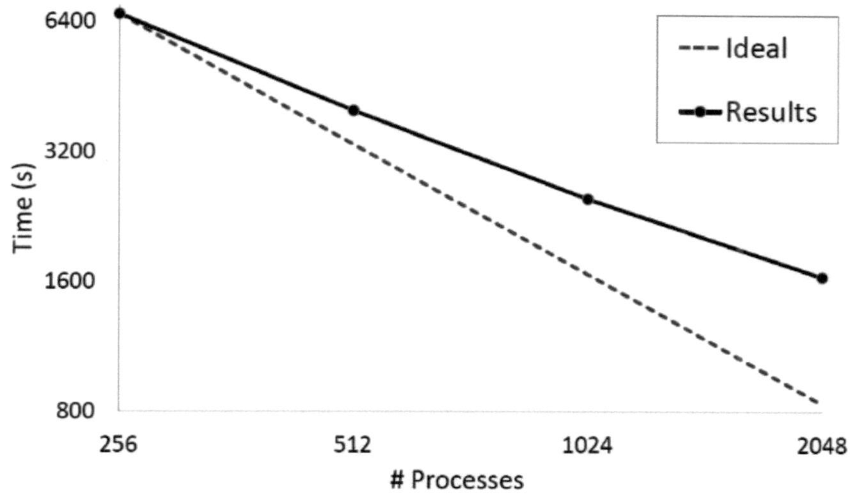

Figure 10. Inter node scalability.

6. Demonstrative examples

This section demonstrates the usage of the mass evacuation simulator it emphasizes the need of incorporating fine level details and mixed mode evacuations. For a proof of concept demonstration on the use of the evacuation simulator in an automatic evacuation management system see [8]. Some of the selected hypothetical scenarios demand a detailed model of environment, use of all available traversable area and complex agent functions, like the detection of blocked paths, navigation, etc. The ability to incorporate complex models of agents and details in the environment highlights the advantages over the simplified 1-D models. The purpose of these demonstrations is to show the capabilities of the simulator, they are not intended to provide reliable results. Providing reliable results would require a group of experts of different fields building and evaluating the behavioural models and assumptions about the evacuation.

The demonstrations are separated into two groups: pedestrian only and multi modal evacuation (pedestrian and cars). The robustness and variability of the scenarios in each category is evaluated through Monte Carlo simulations and converged results are provided for the relevant scenarios.

6.1. Pedestrian only scenarios

This section presents scenarios involving pedestrian only evacuations where changes in the environment, different evacuation behaviours and mitigation measures are tested to highlight the need of detailed modelling in mass evacuations and demonstrate the capability of the software to evaluate scenarios in a quantitative manner. First evacuation during daytime is evaluated, then evacuation during night time and finally night time evacuation during a special event are contrasted.

6.1.1. Common settings

For the pedestrian only demonstrations, a coastal city located in the southern part of Honshu island of Japan is considered. This city was chosen as it has suffered from several historical tsunamis. The domain considered is 9.6×5.4 km^2, in a 1 m × 1 m resolution grid, see **Figure 11**. An evacuation involving 57,000 persons is assumed. The evacuees are divided into two age groups, below and above 50 years, and their properties are set according to **Table 1**. Regions with an elevation above 30 m, shown in green, are considered as the safe evacuation areas. Evacuation to nearby tall buildings is not considered since only a few tall buildings are available in this coastal city. All the areas not occupied by buildings or water bodies are considered traversable.

The earthquake induced damages, $\lambda_{earthquake}$, in the region are estimated using a physics based seismic response analysis simulator [9], with the strong ground motion of 1995 Kobe earthquake. The damage state of buildings are evaluated based on a simple standard criterion used in earthquake engineering; buildings are considered to be damaged if the inter-story drift angle is larger than 0.005 [10]. The occupied area is increased by 40% of the building height

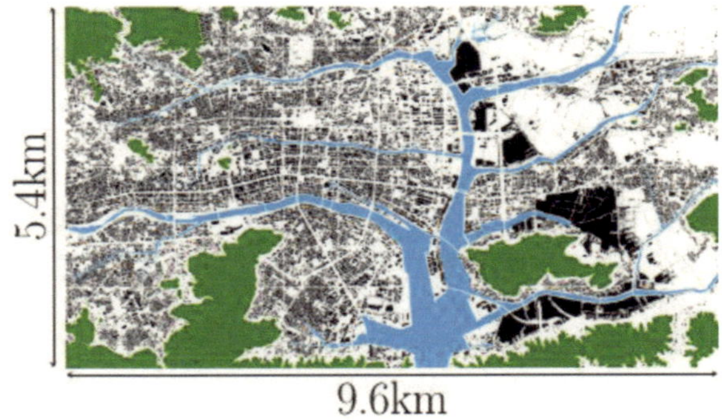

Figure 11. Environment for pedestrian only demonstrative examples.

	Younger than 50 years (55%)	Older than 50 years (45%)
Speed mean (m/s)	1.43	1.39
Speed S.D. (m/s)	0.11	0.19
Sight distance (m)	50	50
Pre-evacuation time mean (s)	1000	1000
Pre-evacuation time S.D. (s)	600	600

Table 1. Properties of the two age groups of agents for the pedestrian only scenarios.

[11], if a building is deemed damaged. The grid is updated every 5 min, according to [12], to mimic the tsunami inundation (i.e. $\lambda_{tsunami}$); the arrival time of the tsunami is 15 min.

6.1.2. Monte Carlo simulations

The results of simulations have a certain degree of uncertainty due to the presence of various random variables. In order to improve the reliability of the simulation results, taking the effects of these uncertainties into account, Monte Carlo simulations are conducted. The only random variables considered in the present simulations are the distribution of evacuees and their speeds.

To decide a sufficient number of simulations required for each Monte Carlo simulation, 1000 (=N) sets of evacuation simulations are conducted, and the convergence of standard deviation of an influential quantity with respect to the number of simulations n, $1 < n \leq N$, is analyzed. As for the settings, the 1000 simulations are composed of randomly generated agents' initial locations and speeds, while the scenario considered is evacuation to high grounds in the absence of earthquake disaster or tsunami inundation.

The standard deviation of the total number of agents evacuated after 40 min is considered as the influencing factor, in deciding the necessary number of simulations per Monte Carlo simulation, since total number of agents evacuated is one of the influential quantities. As shown in **Figure 12**, the standard deviation of the total number of people evacuated at 40 min converges (i.e. has negligibly low variation) for $n > 400$. In addition to the fore-mentioned global measure, statistical data of number of agents evacuated at each 30 s interval are compared as a local measure. **Figure 13** shows the mean number of agents evacuated at each 30 s interval, for the two cases with $n = 1000$ and $n = 400$. As is seen, both the cases have nearly identical mean values and standard deviations. Since both of above considered global and local measures have converged when $n > 400$, 400 is set to be the sufficient number of simulations for the convergence of Monte Carlo simulations. The value of sufficient n, depends on

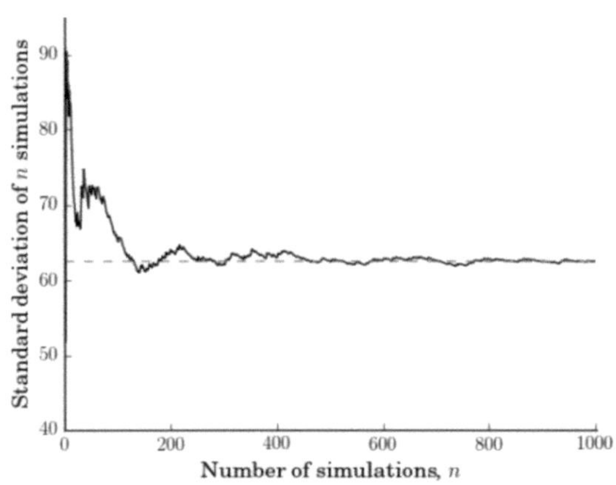

Figure 12. Standard deviation (S.D.) of cumulative number of agents evacuated by 40 min, from 2 to 1000 simulations.

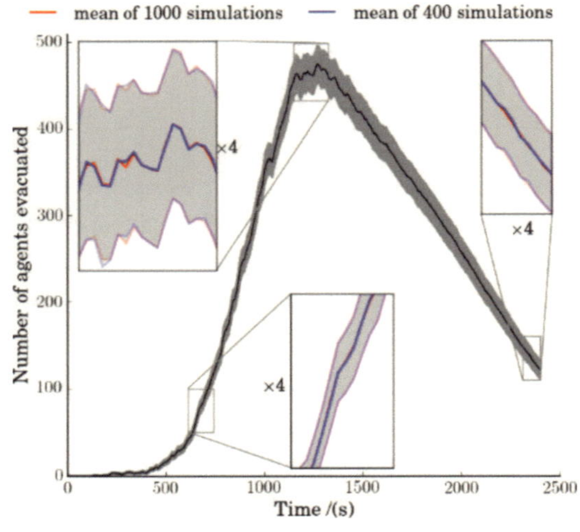

Figure 13. Mean number of agents evacuated at each 30 s intervals.

the number and the nature of the random variables considered, and the real applications may require a larger value.

6.1.3. Day time evacuation during an ordinary day

Under day time evacuation, four scenarios are considered; without any damages to the environment, with earthquake disaster; with tsunami inundation; and with both the earthquake damages and tsunami inundation. For all these cases, the 57,000 resident agents are considered, while they are positioned within 20 m proximity of buildings initially.

Figure 14 shows the time histories of cumulative number of agents evacuated for each of the four scenarios. As is seen, both the earthquake damages and tsunami inundation reduces the number of evacuees almost by the same amount. The effect of the tsunami inundation is mostly attributed to the inundation of a few critical bridges in the study area. Comparing the effect of manually blocking these bridges with the effect of the tsunami inundation shows similar results, see **Figure 15**.

However, while the effects of earthquake damages start to appear at early stages, the effect of tsunami inundation appears after 20 min; as the tsunami arrival time is 15 min.

6.1.4. Night time evacuation in an ordinary day

Due to various factors like low lighting conditions, being tired, sleepy, etc., evacuees tends to have different behaviours in night time evacuations, compared to those of day time; late to start evacuation, have slower walking speeds, may seek for safer routes, etc. The scenarios considered here aim to model mainly the effects of lower visibility and the tendency to take safer roads.

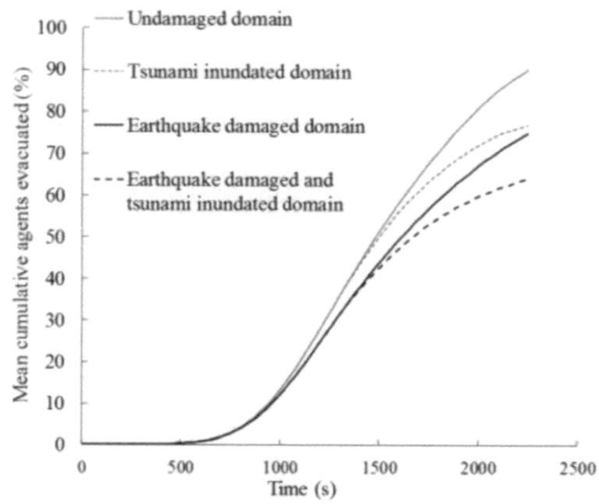

Figure 14. Time history of cumulative number of agents evacuated (mean of 400 simulations). Effect of environmental damage.

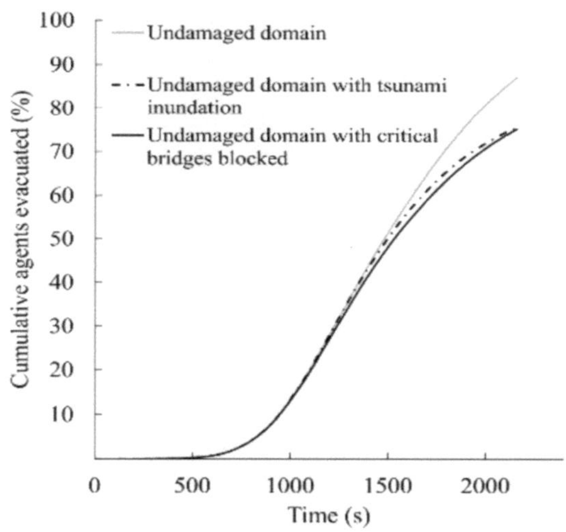

Figure 15. Time history of cumulative number of agents evacuated (mean of 400 simulations). Effect of damaged bridges.

It is assumed to be a full moon light and the earthquake has damaged the environment causing a complete power failure. Accordingly, agents' maximum sight distance is reduced to 15 m [13]. Due to the lack of information on the effect of lighting condition on the walking speed, the walking speed of the two groups of agents are set according to **Table 2** [14]. The lower visibility not only lowers the walking speed, but also makes it slow the identifying of blocked roads; require making close examinations to confirm their paths are blocked.

When evacuating right after an earthquake, like the present scenario, people tend to take paths with longer stretches of wider roads to lower the probability of encountering blocked

Max visibility radius	Younger than 50 years (%)	Older than 50 years (%)
15 m visibility (0.2 lx)	70	50
30 m visibility with 15 lx	90.6	83

Table 2. Pedestrian speeds under different lighting conditions (the value is set as a percentage of their desired speed, for example, if the desired speed is 1 m/s the modified desired speed is set to 0.5 m/s if the agent is older than 50 years old and under 0.2 lux lighting condition).

roads, depending on the intensity of ground shaking they experienced. The standard path planning algorithms like Dijkstra algorithm allow the use of strong constraints like the minimum width of a road, etc. However, the present scenario requires weaker constraint to find paths with longer stretches of wider roads as far as possible, while strictly satisfying strong constraints on total time or/and distance. As an example, an evacuee may prefer to take wider roads or avoid narrow roads as far as possible, and while ensuring to reach a safe place before the tsunami arrives. In order include such weak constraints, the standard Dijkstra algorithm is slightly modified [1] by introducing two distance measures; the actual distance, and a perceived distance. When estimating the perceived distance, the roads wider than the preferred width are reduced in length according to the level of preference.

Figure 16 compares the ordinary day time evacuation with that of night time with and without the effects of earthquake and tsunami. As is seen, there is nearly 30% reduction in number of evacuees between the day and night scenarios without earthquake and tsunami effects. The damages in the environment further reduce the number of evacuees by almost 8%, at the end of 40 min. These results highlight the ability of the developed system to take different influencing factors like lighting conditions and the preference of safer roads.

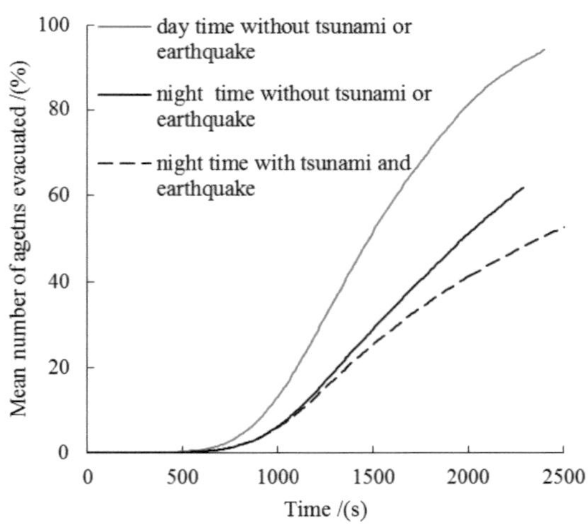

Figure 16. Time histories of total number of evacuated agents for day time and night time evacuations and in an ordinary day.

6.1.5. Night time evacuation during festival occasion

This scenario involving large number of visitors further emphasizes the need of detailed model of environment and complex agent functions, while those are necessary even for the former scenarios. The visitors are assumed to have no knowledge of the environment, and following others, with $g^{find\_a\_followee}$ and $g^{follow\_an\_agent}$, is their only way of reaching a safe place. That makes their visibility, which requires both detailed model of environment and complex agents, crucially important for the survival of visitors.

Just as in the previous night time evacuation scenario, it is assumed to be a full moon night, an earthquake has damaged the environment causing a power failure, and a tsunami is expected to arrive in 15 min. 18,000 visitors and 18,000 residents are assumed to be participating in the festival, which takes place in a 14 km^2 rectangular area shown in **Figure 17**. Agents participating the festival are distributed across the streets and open spaces, while another 39,000 residents are distributed over the whole domain. With full moon, 0.2 lx of lighting and 15 m sight distance are assumed, as in the former scenario. Another scenario with 30 m visibility is considered, in order to explore the mitigation measures of installing emergency lighting of 15 lx [14] at 30 m spacing which is equal to common street lighting. Maximum speeds of agents under these lighting conditions are set according to **Table 2**. Further, it is assumed that evacuees prefer to take safer paths, as in the previous scenario.

Figure 18 presents the results under the two lighting conditions considered. As seen, the low lighting conditions have significantly reduced the number of agents evacuated, compared that of an ordinary day. Further, it is observed that providing lighting of 15 lx significantly enhances the ability of the visitor agents to locate and follow others. An additional scenario with moon lighting without the earthquake induced damages is simulated to further explore the effect of lighting conditions. As seen in **Figure 18**, for this specific setting, the influence of lighting conditions is significantly higher than the earthquake induced damages.

6.2. Multi-modal evacuation with pedestrians and cars

In order to demonstrate the ability to perform large scale urban area evacuation simulations with sub-meter details considering the effect of car-pedestrian interactions a fictitious

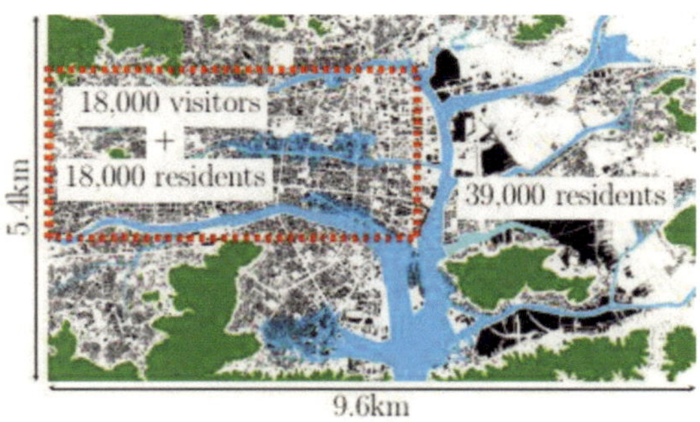

Figure 17. The area of study during the festival.

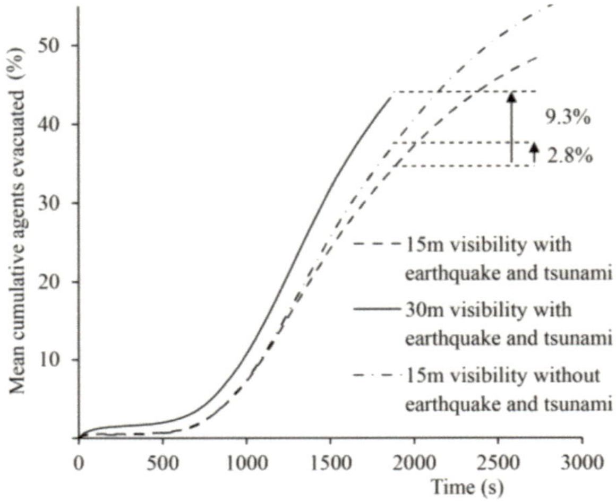

Figure 18. Simulation results under different visibility conditions.

tsunami-triggered evacuation in a coastal city of Japan is simulated. The effect of different strategies and mitigation measures are evaluated. The aim of this section is not to provide specific results to a real case scenario but to highlight the possibilities enabled by the introduction of mixed mode evacuation and interactions to the evacuation model.

6.2.1. *Setting*

The fictional setting is a 6 × 6.5 km^2 area of a coastal city in Japan, see **Figure 19**. 40,000 evacuees are considered with the properties shown in **Table 3**. The tsunami arrival time is assumed to be 40 min as observed during the 2011 Great East Japan Earthquake and Tsunami which struck that region. The pre-evacuation time, the time it takes for an evacuee to start evacuating after the first earthquake shock, is assumed to follow a normal distribution.

Figure 19. Environment for multimodal evacuation simulation.

http://dx.doi.org/10.5772/intechopen.69844

	Younger than 50 years	Older than 50 years	
Percentage	50	50	Variable
Speed mean (m/s)	1.5	1.00	9.00
Speed S.D. (m/s)	0.4	0.4	2.00
Sight distance (m)	30	30	30
Pre-evacuation time mean (s)	900	900	900
Pre-evacuation time S.D. (s)	300	300	300

Table 3. Properties of the synthetic population used for the mixed mode evacuation scenarios.

The mean and standard deviation for this pre-evacuation time for pedestrians is obtained from literature [15]. A significant fraction of the population in this area is elderly, hence, the population is divided into two groups each constituting half of the population; *pedestrians fast* representing young people, and *pedestrians slow* representing elder people. The speed of each of each group is assumed to follow a normal distribution. Each vehicle is considered to carry two evacuees, representing a pessimistic usage of vehicles. Evacuees plan their evacuation route to the nearest evacuation areas.

6.2.2. Monte Carlo simulations

The instantiation of the synthetic population involves the initialization of random variables according to a given probability density function, for example, speed, pre-evacuation time, position in the domain. This allows to consider some of the uncertainties involved in real life. By relying on the law of large numbers, with a sufficient number of results, a stable average outcome can be provided. Furthermore, with an estimate of the results distribution, the robustness of the results of different scenarios can be compared. **Figure 20** shows the convergence of the standard deviation of the results with the number of draws/simulations.

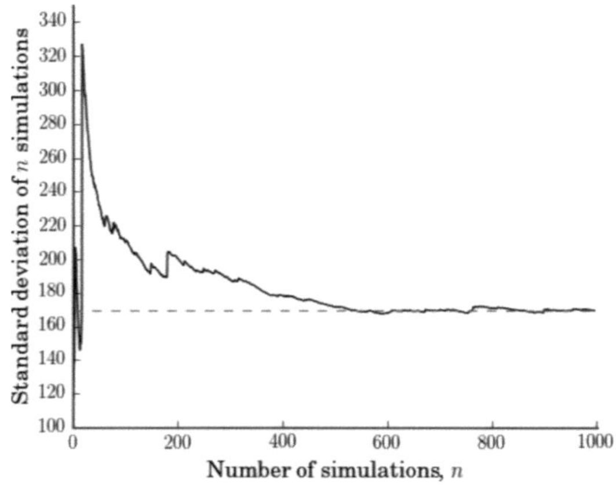

Figure 20. Convergence of the standard deviation of the results with the number of draws/simulations.

After about 600 simulations the standard deviation has already converged this contrasts with the pedestrian only simulations where convergence was achieved after 400 simulations, see **Figure 12**. **Figure 21** shows the mean and the standard deviation of the results of the cumulative number of agents evacuated with 1000 Monte Carlo simulations. The zoomed in box on the upper right corner shows a standard deviation of 0.42% in the throughput after 40 min, and in the lower right corner 0.29% after 25 min. Additionally, **Figure 22** shows the convergence of a more sensitive measure, the number of agents evacuated at each 10 s interval. The rest of the graphs present a single simulation result or the mean of 100 simulations; 600 simulations are not conducted for each scenario to reduce the computational resources used for this demonstration.

6.2.3. *Indiscriminate use of cars*

The first set of simulations explore a scenario where anyone, irrespective of their physical abilities, is allowed to use vehicles. **Figure 23**, compares the evacuation throughput with different percentages of evacuees using cars. It can be observed that as the percentage of evacuees using cars increases the total throughput after 40 min of evacuation decreases. There is an initial boost in the evacuation throughput especially during the first 25 min of evacuation.

Closer inspection shows the emergence of car queues along the roads connecting to some evacuation areas. This is considered the main reason for the throughput decrease.

6.2.4. *People in need restriction*

In order to evaluate the effect of selective usage of cars a scenario where only people in need are allowed to use cars is evaluated. People in need are defined as the evacuees having the slowest evacuation speed in the synthetic population.

The results obtained by restricting the use of cars can be seen in **Figure 24**. It can be seen that by applying this restriction an improvement in the total evacuation throughput of about 7% over the base scenario is achieved. Additionally, higher percentages up to 50% of the population can use cars without a significant impact in the total evacuation throughput. Moreover, it can be observed that the queue emergence remains as a problem.

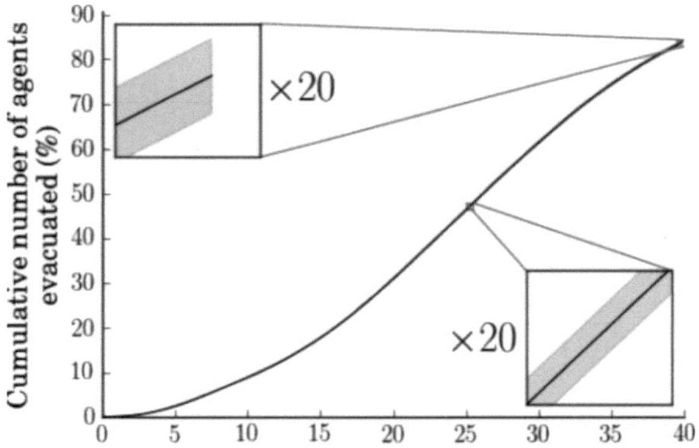

Figure 21. Time history of the evacuation, mean and the standard deviation of the cumulative number of agents evacuated with 1000 Monte Carlo simulations.

http://dx.doi.org/10.5772/intechopen.69844

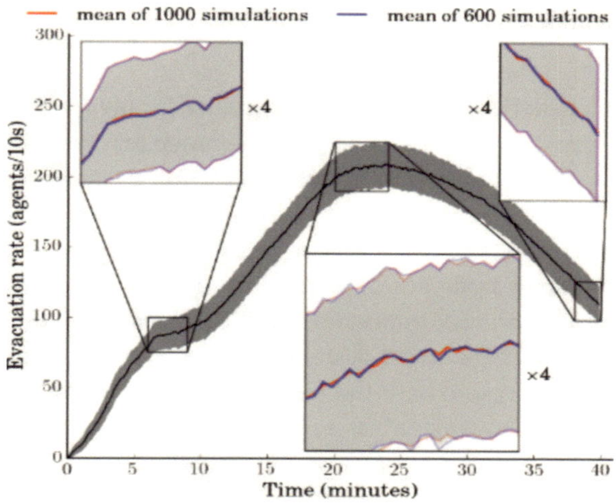

Figure 22. Convergence of the number of agents evacuated at each 10 s interval.

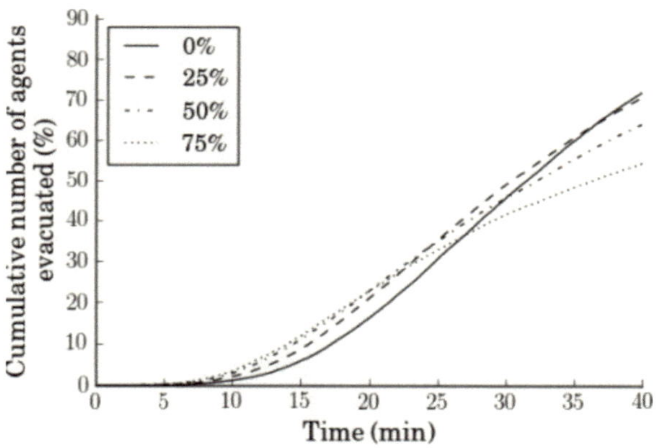

Figure 23. Time history of the evacuation varying the percentage of car usage. Anyone is allowed to use cars.

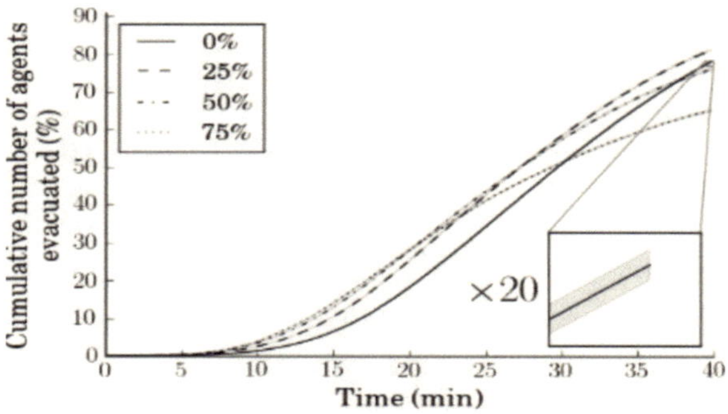

Figure 24. Time history of the evacuation varying the percentage of car usage. Only the elder people are allowed to use cars. 100 simulations mean and standard deviation.

7. Concluding remarks

This chapter provides a generic mathematical framework usable for the specification of other agent based systems providing a needed common language for comparison between models. The techniques and results of tuning the agents' interaction parameters are shown, showing the constrained validity of the model but also providing a data driven future for modelling agent's interactions. The results of scalability measures showing intra node strong scalability up to 8 threads and inter node strong scalability up to 2048 processes are shown. The techniques used for the domain decomposition and load balancing are generic enough to be easily extrapolated to other agent based systems. Finally, the demonstrative applications of the simulator show a usage case where the detailed models of environment and the detail of interactions are not only convenient but a necessity, highlighting the need of multi-agent systems considering the micro level interactions and details.

Author details

Leonel Aguilar, Maddegedara Lalith* and Muneo Hori

*Address all correspondence to: lalith@eri.u-tokyo.ac.jp

Earthquake Research Institute, The University of Tokyo, Tokyo, Japan

References

[1] Leonel A, Lalith W, Hori M, Ichimura T, Tanaka S. A scalable workbench for large urban area simulations, comprised of resources for behavioural models, interactions and dynamic environments. Lecture Notes in Computer Science. 2014;**8861**:166-181

[2] Van Den Berg, Jur, et al. "Reciprocal n-body collision avoidance." Robotics research. Springer Berlin Heidelberg, 2011. 3-19.

[3] Aguilar. Enhancements and applications of a scalable multi-agent based large urban area evacuation simulator with emphasis on the use of cars [PhD Thesis]. The University of Tokyo; 2015

[4] Weidmann U. Transporttechnik der Fussgnger. Transporttechnische Eigenschaften des Fussgngerverkehrs (Literturauswertung), Schriftenreihe des IVT Nr. 90, 2. Zurich; 1993

[5] Dhingra, S. L., and Ishtiyaq Gull. "Traffic flow theory historical research perspectives." The fundamental diagram for traffic flow theory (2008): 45.

[6] Melgar LEA, Lalith M, Ichimura T, Hori M. On the performance and scalability of an HPC enhanced multi agent system based evacuation simulator. In: International Conference on Computational Science, ICCS2017. 2017

[7] Lalith W, Leonel A, Hori M, Ichimura T, Tanaka S. HPC enhanced large urban area evacuation simulations with vision based autonomously navigating multi agents. Procedia Computer Science. 2013;**18**:1515-1524

[8] Aguilar L, Lalith M, Ichimura T, Hori M. Automatic evacuation management using a multi agent system and parallel meta-heuristic search. In: International Conference on Principles and Practice of Multi-Agent Systems. 2016

[9] Hori M, Ichimura T. Current state of integrated earthquake simulation for earthquake hazard and disaster. Journal of Seismology. 2008;**12**(2):307-321

[10] Galambos TV, Ellingwood B. Serviceability limit states: Deflection. Journal of Structural Engineering, ASCE. 1986;**112**(1):67-84

[11] Xue M, Ryuzo O. Examination of vulnerability of various residential areas in china for earthquake disaster mititgation. In: Proceedings of the 9th International Conference on Urban Earthquake Engineering/4th Asia Conference on Earthquake Engineering, Tokyo, 1931-1936.

[12] Baba, Toshitaka, et al. "Tsunami inundation modeling of the 2011 Tohoku earthquake using three-dimensional building data for Sendai, Miyagi Prefecture, Japan." Tsunami events and lessons learned. Springer Netherlands, 2014. 89-98.

[13] Nichols TF, Powers TR. Moonlight and night visibility. U.S. Army Training Center Human Research Unit, Presidio of Monterey. 1964. URL http://www.dtic.mil/dtic/tr/fulltext/u2/438001.pdf.

[14] Ouellette MJ, Rea MS. Illuminance requirements for emergency lighting. Journal of the Illuminating Engineering Society. 1989;**18**(1):37-42

[15] Dulam R. Enhancement of multi agent simulation with smart agent interaction and high performance computing [Master Thesis]. The University of Tokyo; 2012

Section 4

Processes Control in Industrial Applications

Chapter 5

Robust Adaptive Cooperative Control for Formation-Tracking Problem in a Network of Non-Affine Nonlinear Agents

Muhammad Nasiruddin bin Mahyuddin and
Ali Safaei

Additional information is available at the end of the chapter

http://dx.doi.org/10.5772/intechopen.69352

Abstract

In this chapter, a decentralized cooperative control protocol is proposed with application to any network of agents with non-affine nonlinear multi-input-multi-output (MIMO) dynamics. Here, the main purpose of cooperative control protocol is to track a time-variant reference trajectory while maintaining a desired formation. The reference trajectory is defined to a leader, which has at least one information connection with one of the agents in the network. The design procedure includes a robust adaptive law for estimating the unknown nonlinear terms of each agent's dynamics in a model-free format, that is, without the use of any regressors. Moreover, an observer is designed to have an approximation on the values of control parameters for the leader at the agents without connection to the leader. The entire design procedure is analysed successfully for the stability using Lyapunov stability theorem. Finally, the simulation results for the application of the proposed method on a network of nonholonomic wheeled mobile robots (WMR) are presented. Desirable leader-following tracking and geometric formation control performance have been successfully demonstrated through simulated group of wheeled mobile robots.

Keywords: cooperative protocol, formation control, decentralized control, robust adaptive law, distributed observer, mobile robot, non-affine nonlinear system

1. Introduction

Great attention has been paid to the problems of the multi-agent network ranging from consensus, collective behaviours of flocks and swarms, formation control of multi-robot systems, leader-following, algebraic connectivity of complex network, rendezvous, containment and so on [1–6].

The formation control problem is an interesting issue in biology, automatic control, robotics, artificial intelligence and so on, which requires each agent to move according to the prescribed trajectory. Various control strategies have been formulated to achieve the group control objectives.

The systems are usually in nonlinear form due to unpredictable environmental disturbances, unmodelled dynamics or other uncertainties. A class of nonlinear first-order multi-agent systems with external disturbances consensus problem was discussed in Ref. [7], whereas other works that involve second-order and higher order nonlinear multi-agent systems are reported in Refs. [8] and [9], respectively. Wang et al. [10] reported the design of distributed state/output feedback cooperative control approaches for uncertain multi-agents in undirected communication graphs. This is later extended to a condition of directed graphs containing a spanning tree [11]. To remedy the problem of a non-affine system for a general class, several reported works such as Ref. [12] employ a direct adaptive approach using an artificial neural network (ANN) to approximate an ideal controller. By employing a system transformation, a non-affine system can be transformed into an affine system as demonstrated in Ref. [11]. However, the transformation technique to convert a multi-agent non-affine system to a multi-agent affine system is still new and open to further studies which are to be discussed in this chapter.

Hou et al. [13] illustrate the method of dealing with non-affine multi-agent system by incorporating dynamic surface control or DSC but it is limited to a single-input-single-output (SISO) type of system, that is, with one control input. A similar approach is reported in Ref. [14] where the distributed dynamic surface design approach is used to design local consensus controllers using the transformation to convert the system to an affine strict-feedback multi-agent system. The work is also limited to a single control input per agent.

In this chapter, several novel contributions can be highlighted, that is, the introduction of transformation techniques from a non-affine multi-agent system to an affine multi-agent system for a network of generic nonlinear multi-input-multi-output (MIMO) systems, that is, a single agent may have more than one control input and more than one output. The second contribution to be highlighted in the chapter is the estimation of nonlinear terms in the dynamics without requiring the linear-in-parameter condition (LIP), that is, the dependence on any model regressor is elevated. The lumped nonlinear function existing in the model agent can be estimated online despite time-varying characteristics. This implies that the estimation is model free. By virtue of a sigma-modified adaptive law with projection algorithm that drives the estimation using the cooperative consensus error, the unknown nonlinear function can be reconstructed. The proposed cooperative control scheme requires a robust adaptive observer which can reconstruct the control signal from all agents to be used in the consensus formation control. Owing to the robustification term in the observer, the control signals can be estimated in finite time. The proposed robust adaptive formation control is to be exemplified in a form of simulation of multi nonholonomic mobile robots with differential drive configurations. They are commissioned to follow the leader trajectory while at the same time required to maintain predefined geometric formation guaranteeing safe inter-agent separation.

The chapter is organized into preliminaries, problem definition, design procedure of the proposed robust adaptive formation control algorithm, simulated results and lastly the conclusion of the chapter.

http://dx.doi.org/10.5772/intechopen.69352

2. Preliminaries

2.1. Mean value theorem

Suppose that the function $\mathcal{F}$ is continuous on the closed interval $[a, b]$ and differentiable on the open interval (a, b) (i.e. $\mathcal{F}$ is Lipschitz). Then, there is a point $\mathcal{X}_0$ in the open interval (a, b) at which [15]

$$\dot{\mathcal{F}}(\mathcal{X}_0) = \frac{\mathcal{F}(b) - \mathcal{F}(a)}{b - a} \tag{1}$$

In physical terms, the mean value theorem says that the average velocity of a moving object during an interval of time is equal to the instantaneous velocity at some moment in the interval [15].

2.2. Kronecker product

The Kronecker product of matrices $\mathcal{A} \in \mathbb{R}^{m\times n}$ and $\mathcal{B} \in \mathbb{R}^{p\times q}$ is defined as [16]

$$\mathcal{A} \otimes \mathcal{B} = \begin{bmatrix} a_{11}\mathcal{B} & \dots & a_{1n}\mathcal{B} \\ \vdots & \ddots & \vdots \\ a_{m1}\mathcal{B} & \dots & a_{mn}\mathcal{B} \end{bmatrix} \tag{2}$$

which satisfies the following properties [16]

$$\begin{aligned} (\mathcal{A} \otimes \mathcal{B})(\mathcal{C} \otimes \mathcal{D}) &= (\mathcal{A}\mathcal{C}) \otimes (\mathcal{B}\mathcal{D}) \\ (\mathcal{A} \otimes \mathcal{B})^T &= \mathcal{A}^T \otimes \mathcal{B}^T \\ \mathcal{A} \otimes (\mathcal{B} + \mathcal{C}) &= \mathcal{A} \otimes \mathcal{B} + \mathcal{A} \otimes \mathcal{C} \end{aligned} \tag{3}$$

2.3. Schur complement lemma

For any constant symmetric matrix $S = \begin{bmatrix} S_{11} & S_{12} \\ S_{12}^T & S_{22} \end{bmatrix}$, the following statements are equivalent [17]

$$\begin{aligned} &- \ S > 0 \\ &- \ S_{11} > 0\ .\ S_{22} - S_{12}^T S_{11}^{-1} S_{12} > 0 \\ &- \ S_{22} > 0\ .\ S_{11} - S_{12} S_{22}^{-1} S_{12}^T > 0 \end{aligned} \tag{4}$$

2.4. Graph theory preliminaries

Consider a network consisting of N agents. Let $\mathcal{G}(\mathcal{V}, \mathcal{E}, A)$ be a graph with the set of N *nodes* $\mathcal{V} = \{v_1, v_2, \dots, v_N\}$, a set of *edges* $\mathcal{E} = \{e_{ij}\} \in \mathbb{R}^{N\times N}$ and associated *adjacency matrix* $A = (a_{ij}) \in \mathbb{R}^{N\times N}$. An edge e_{ij} in $\mathcal{G}$ is a link between a pair of nodes (v_j, v_i), representing the flow of information from v_j (as parent) to v_i (as child). The e_{ij} is in existence if and only if $a_{ij} > 0$. The graph is *undirected*, that is, the e_{ij} and e_{ij} in $\mathcal{G}$ are considered to be the same. We name v_i and v_j

as neighbors if $e_{ij} \in \mathcal{E}$. A path is defined as a sequence of connected edges in a graph. A graph is *connected* if there is a path between every pair of the nodes. The degree matrix $D_L = diag\{d_1, d_2, \dots, d_N\} \in \mathbb{R}^{N\times N}$, where each d_i is the input degree to each node, which is equal to the number of all edges through it (i.e. $d_i = \sum_{j=1:N} a_{ij}$). Hence, we can define *Laplacian Matrix* (L) as below [16, 18, 19]

$$L = D_L - A \tag{5}$$

Furthermore, we can define an adjacency matrix for the leader as follows

$$B = diag\{b_1, b_2, \dots, b_N\} \in \mathbb{R}^{N\times N} \tag{6}$$

where each b_i indicates the existence of a communication link between the leader and each agent [16, 18, 19]. Besides, we would have,

$$H = L + B \tag{7}$$

3. Problem definition

Consider a network of N agents with general non-affine nonlinear dynamics for each of them. The problem is to design a set of decentralized control protocols for all agents to enhance a *desired formation* in the state space and also track a *reference trajectory* on state variables. Here, a virtual node is considered as the *leader*, which knows the desired trajectory and has at least one communication link with the agents in the network. It means that some agents are unaware about the leader states and also their control inputs. The whole problem in a general format can be considered as a platform for any possible state space in diverse applications.

For a MIMO system, one can define the following general nonlinear formulation

$$\begin{aligned} \dot{x}_{i1} &= h_1(x_i) + R_1(x_i) + f_1(x_i, u_i) \\ \dot{x}_{i2} &= h_2(x_i) + R_2(x_i) + f_2(x_i, u_i) \\ &\vdots \\ \dot{x}_{in} &= h_n(x_i) + R_t(x_i) + f_n(x_i, u_i) \end{aligned} \tag{8}$$

where n is the number of states for the system, t is the total number of nonlinear terms in the system (which $t \le n$), $x_i \in \mathbb{R}^n$ is the states vector, $u_i \in \mathbb{R}^m$ is the input (or control parameters) vector, m is the number of control parameters, h_j for $j = [1, n]$ is any linear combination on x_i, R_j for $j = [1, n]$ is any Lipschitz continuous nonlinear function on x_i and f_j for $j = [1, n]$ is any Lipschitz continuous nonlinear function on both x_i and u_i. The last term defines the non-affine property of the system which represents the completely coupled inter-relation between states and control parameters. Each agent dynamic can be represented in matrix form as follows

http://dx.doi.org/10.5772/intechopen.69352

$$\begin{aligned}
\dot{X}_i &= CX_i + R_i + F_i \\
X_i &= [x_{i1}, x_{i2}, \dots, x_{in}]^T \; C \; : constant\ matrix \\
R_i &= [R_1(x_i), R_2(x_i), \dots, R_t(x_i)]^T, \; t \le n \\
F_i &= [F_1(x_i, u_i), F_2(x_i, u_i), \dots, F_n(x_i, u_i)]^T
\end{aligned} \tag{9}$$

where $C \in \mathbb{R}^{n \times n}$ is a constant matrix including the multipliers for each state. The elements of C define the dependence of each state's derivative to the other states.

For a network of N of similar agents (or systems), dynamics for each agent i can be represented by Eq. (9). Also, the dynamic of the leader node can be proposed by this format. The difference is that the control parameters for the leader are defined with respect to a time-varying reference trajectory, that is

$$\begin{aligned}
\dot{x}_{01} &= h_1(x_0) + h'_1(u_0) \\
\dot{x}_{02} &= h_2(x_0) + h'_2(u_0) \\
&\vdots \\
\dot{x}_{0n} &= h_n(x_0) + h'_n(u_0)
\end{aligned} \tag{10}$$

where h'_j for $j = [1, n]$ is any linear combination on the leader control parameters (i.e. reference trajectory u_0). Actually, the reference trajectory is a set of inputs which provide certain dynamics in state space for the leader agent. The leader dynamics can be represented in the matrix form as the following:

$$\dot{X}_0 = CX_0 + Du_0 \tag{11}$$

$$\begin{aligned}
&X_0 = [x_{01}, x_{02}, \dots, x_{0n}]^T, \; u_0 = [u_{01}, u_{02}, \dots, u_{0m}]^T \\
&C \;\&\; D \; : constant\ matrices
\end{aligned}$$

where $D \in \mathbb{R}^{n \times m}$ is a constant matrix including the multipliers for each control parameters.

Moreover, the desired formation among the agents in a network can be presented by a set of constant values $\mathcal{F} \in (\mathbb{R}^N \times \mathbb{R}^n)$, which determines the relative distance between agents in the state space.

The problem is to enhance $\mathcal{F}$ among the network agents and track the reference trajectory defined by (x_0, u_0) at the leader node with inter-agent communication topology defined by the communication graph.

4. Design procedure for robust adaptive cooperative control protocol

This section is dedicated to presenting the design process for cooperative control protocol, an observer to estimate the control parameters of the leader at each agent and a robust adaptive law to estimate the nonlinear terms at each agent. The design process is initiated by dealing with the non-affinity property of the agents.

4.1. Dealing with non-affinity property

Using the mean-value theorem presented in Section 1, for the nonlinear functions f_j, which has a coupled terms of x_i and u_i, we have [19]

$$\frac{\partial f_j(x_i, u_i)}{\partial u}\Big|_{u=u^*} = \mu = \frac{f_j(x_i, u_i) - f_j(x_i, \overline{u_i})}{u_i - \overline{u}_i}, \ \overline{u}_i < u^* < u \tag{12}$$

and without any loss of generality we can consider $\mu = 1$ and $\overline{u}_i$ is any constant value.

$$\begin{aligned} f_j(x_i, u_i) &= u_i + q_j(x_i) \\ q_j(x_i) &= f_j(x_i, \overline{u}_i) - \mu \overline{u}_i \end{aligned} \tag{13}$$

where $q_j(x_i)$ is an unknown nonlinear function depending only on x_i. As can be seen, the non-affine nonlinear function $f_j(x_i, u_i)$ is converted to an affine form. Now, the dynamics of each agent can be modified as

$$\begin{aligned} \dot{x}_{i1} &= h_1(x_i) + R_1(x_i) + h'_1(u_i) + q_1(x_i) \\ \dot{x}_{i2} &= h_2(x_i) + R_2(x_i) + h'_2(u_i) + q_2(x_i) \\ &\vdots \\ \dot{x}_{in} &= h_n(x_i) + R_t(x_i) + h'_N(u_i) + q_t(x_i) \end{aligned} \tag{14}$$

Considering

$$g_j(x_i) = R_j(x_i) + q_j(x_i), \ j \in [1, t], \ t \le n \tag{15}$$

where $g_j(x_i)$ is an unknown nonlinear function depending on x_i, the matrix format for each agent dynamics can be presented as

$$\begin{aligned} \dot{X}_i &= CX_i + Du_i + D_1 G_i \\ D \;\&\; D_1 &: \textit{constant matrices} \\ G_i &= [g_1(x_i), g_2(x_i), \ldots, g_t(x_i)]^T \end{aligned} \tag{16}$$

where $D \in \mathbb{R}^{n \times m}$ is a constant matrix including the multipliers for each control parameter. Actually, the elements of D define the dependence of each state's derivative to each control parameters. Moreover, $D_1 \in \mathbb{R}^{n \times t}$ is a diagonal matrix defining the existence of nonlinear functions in the equation for derivative of each state. Elements of D_1 can only be one or zero. It should be noted that since $t \le n$, we may have some states' derivatives which do not include any nonlinear terms.

In the following subsections, the elements of G_i, which define the unknown nonlinear functions on each state's derivative, would be estimated (adapted) online using consensus error of the network.

4.2. Cooperative protocol for formation and tracking problem

For a network of N agents with the dynamics described by Eq. (16), we can have a lumped formulation for the dynamics of all agents using the Kronecker product,

$$\begin{aligned} &\dot{X} = (I_N \otimes C)X + (I_N \otimes D)U + (I_N \otimes D_1)G \\ &X = X_{Nn\times 1} = [X_1, X_2, \dots, X_N]^T, \ U = U_{Nm\times 1} = [u_1, u_2, \dots, u_N]^T \\ &G = G_{Nt\times 1} = [G_1, G_2, \dots, G_N]^T, \ I_N = diag\{1, 1, \dots, 1\} \in \mathbb{R}^{N\times N} \end{aligned} \tag{17}$$

For this network, we can define the combined formation and tracking errors in a single formulation in relation to the neighbouring information available to each agent i via the communication graph [16]

$$e_i = \sum_{j=1}^{N} a_{ij}\Big((X_i - X_j) - (\Delta_i - \Delta_j)\Big) + b_i\Big((X_i - X_0) - (\Delta_i - \Delta_0)\Big) \tag{18}$$

where $\Delta \in \mathbb{R}^{n\times 1}$ is the vector of desired values for states of agents and also the leader. We can consider e_i as the consensus error for agent i. Hence

$$e_i = \sum_{j=1}^{N} a_{ij}\Big((X_i - \Delta_i) - (X_j - \Delta_j)\Big) + b_i\Big((X_i - \Delta_i) - (X_0 - \Delta_0)\Big) \tag{19}$$

By changing the variables, we have

$$\begin{aligned} &e_i = \sum_{j=1}^{N} a_{ij}(Z_i - Z_j) + b_i(Z_i - Z_0) \\ &Z_i = X_i - \Delta_i \\ &Z_j = X_j - \Delta_j \\ &Z_0 = X_0 - \Delta_0 \end{aligned} \tag{20}$$

Trying to lump the consensus errors of all agents in an N-array format, we have

$$\begin{aligned} &E = (H \otimes I_n)Z - (B \otimes Z_0)\underline{1} \\ &Z = Z_{Nn\times 1} = [Z_1, Z_2, \dots, Z_N]^T \\ &I_n = diag\{1, 1, \dots, 1\} \in \mathbb{R}^{n\times n}, \underline{1} = [1, 1, \dots, 1]^T \in \mathbb{R}^{N\times 1} \end{aligned} \tag{21}$$

Besides, considering Eq. (17), we can have an N-array form for dynamics of agents in the changed variables space

$$\dot{Z} = (I_N \otimes C)Z + (I_N \otimes D)U + (I_N \otimes D_1)G \tag{22}$$

If the consensus errors of all agents converge to zero, then both formation and tracking objectives are reached, that is

$$\lim_{t\to\infty} E = \underline{0} \tag{23}$$

Here, the cooperative protocol U is designed using the Lyapunov stability theorem to ensure Eq. (23) is reached. Consider the following Lyapunov function

$$V = \frac{1}{2}E^T E \tag{24}$$

Then,

$$\begin{aligned} \dot{V} &= E^T\Big((H\otimes I_n)\dot{Z} - (B\otimes \dot{Z}_0)\underline{1}\Big) \\ \dot{V} &= E^T\Big((H\otimes I_n)(I_N\otimes C)Z + (H\otimes I_n)(I_N\otimes D)U + (H\otimes I_n)(I_N\otimes D_1)G - (B\otimes \dot{Z}_0)\underline{1}\Big) \end{aligned} \tag{25}$$

Considering Eq. (3), we have

$$\begin{aligned} (H\otimes I_n)(I_N\otimes D) &= (H\otimes D) \\ (H\otimes I_n)(I_N\otimes D_1) &= (H\otimes D_1) \end{aligned} \tag{26}$$

Besides, using Eqs. (3) and (21), we have

$$(H\otimes I_n)(I_N\otimes C)Z = (I_N\otimes C)E + (B\otimes CZ_0)\underline{1} \tag{27}$$

Then, Eq. (25) leads to,

$$\dot{V} = E^T\Big((I_N\otimes C)E + (B\otimes CZ_0)\underline{1} + (H\otimes D)U + (H\otimes D_1)G - (B\otimes \dot{Z}_0)\underline{1}\Big) \tag{28}$$

Forcing $\dot{V} < 0$ and referring to Eq. (11), we have

$$\begin{aligned} &(I_N\otimes C)E + (B\otimes Du_0)\underline{1} + (H\otimes D)U + (H\otimes D_1)G = -PE \\ &P = P^T > 0\,,\ P\in\mathbb{R}^{Nn\times Nn} \end{aligned} \tag{29}$$

Hence,

$$(H\otimes D)U = -\Big(P + (I_N\otimes C)\Big)E - (B\otimes Du_0)\underline{1} - (H\otimes D_1)G \tag{30}$$

Based on Lyapunov stability theorem, using $U\in\mathbb{R}^{Nm\times 1}$ in Eq. (30) as the cooperative control protocol will ensure that $\dot{V} < 0$ and that E reaches zero asymptotically. Hence, the objectives in formation problem and tracking problem have been accomplished. Expressing the control signal at agent level for agent i

$$\sum_{j=1}^{N} H_{ij} D u_j = -(P_i + C)e_i - b_i D u_0 - \sum_{j=1}^{N} H_{ij} D_1 G_j \tag{31}$$

$$P_i = P(k^*, r^*)\ ,\ k^*, r^* = \left[\left((i-1)\times n + 1\right) : (i \times n)\right]\ ,\ H_{ij} = H(i,j)$$

and then

$$H_{ii} D u_i = -(P_i + C)e_i - b_i D u_0 - \sum_{j=1}^{N} H_{ij} D_1 G_j \ - \sum_{j=1 \neq i}^{N} H_{ij} D u_j \tag{32}$$

Finally, the control parameter for agent i can be presented as the following

$$u_i = \frac{1}{H_{ii}} (D^T D)^{-1} D^T \Big(-(P_i + C)e_i - b_i D u_0 - \sum_{j=1}^{N} H_{ij} D_1 G_j \ - \sum_{j=1 \neq i}^{N} H_{ij} D u_j \Big) \tag{33}$$

Here, a pseudo-inverse method is employed on D.

There are two required conditions on achieving this goal, which are explained in the following assumptions.

Assumption 1. The communication graph should be undirected and connected. It means sufficient information can be available on agents.

Assumption 2. The dynamics of each agent should be completely controllable, that is D matrix should be full rank. It leads us to a state transformation in some applications.

Looking at the proposed cooperative control protocol in Eq. (33), there are two terms, which are not totally available to all agents:

i. u_j (fourth term in the prentices in Eq. (33)), which is the control parameter for the neighbouring agent at the current moment.

ii. G_j (third term in the prentices in Eq. (33)), which includes the unknown nonlinear terms for dynamics of neighbouring agents.

By reaching consensus on the states of agents, we can conclude that the control parameters of each agent has converged to the values of leader control parameters [20]

$$\lim_{t\to\infty}(u_j - u_0) = \underline{0}\ ,\ j \in [1, N] \tag{34}$$

Hence, the control parameters for the neighbouring agent (u_j) are approximated by the control parameter of the leader, which in turn will be observed locally at each agent. It means that each agent has its own estimation on u_0 and sends it to the neighbouring agents as its control parameter. The observed data will be transmitted to the neighbouring agents via communication graph to compute the control protocols.

The unknown nonlinear terms (G_j) also will be estimated using the consensus error of each agent. Similarly, the adapted data are shared with neighbouring agents through the communication graph.

4.3. Observer design for leader control parameters

Here, the objective is to have consensus on the value of u_0 among the all agents in the network. For this objective, we can define the following consensus error for each agent

$$\Delta_{c_i} = \sum_{j=1}^{N} a_{ij}(\hat{T}_i - \hat{T}_j) + b_i(\hat{T}_i - u_0) \tag{35}$$

where $\hat{T}_i \in \mathbb{R}^{m\times 1}$ is the observed vector at agent i for the leader control parameter, and again the a_{ij} and b_i are the elements of adjacency matrix for the communication graph in the network. Eq. (35) can be represented in a lumped format as the following

$$\begin{aligned} \Delta_c &= (H \otimes I_m)\hat{T} - (B \otimes u_0)\underline{1} \\ \Delta_c &= \Delta_{cNm\times 1} = [\Delta_{c1}, \Delta_{c2}, \ldots, \Delta_{cN}]^T \\ \hat{T} &= \hat{T}_{Nm\times 1} = [\hat{T}_1, \hat{T}_2, \ldots, \hat{T}_N]^T \end{aligned} \tag{36}$$

If the equation

$$\lim_{t\to\infty} \Delta c = \underline{0} \tag{37}$$

is satisfied, we can say that the observation objective is achieved. Considering the following Lyapunov function, we have

$$V_1 = \frac{1}{2}\Delta_c^T \Delta_c \tag{38}$$

Then,

$$\dot{V_1} = \Delta_c^T\left((H \otimes I_m)\dot{\hat{T}} - (B \otimes \dot{u}_0)\underline{1}\right) \tag{39}$$

Since the summation of all elements in each row of the Laplacian matrix is zero, we can say that

$$(L \otimes \dot{u}_0)\underline{1} = 0 \tag{40}$$

and recalling Eq. (7), Eq. (39) can be written as following,

$$\dot{V_1} = \Delta_c^T(H \otimes I_m)\dot{\hat{T}} - \Delta_c^T(H \otimes \dot{u}_0)\underline{1} \tag{41}$$

Considering $\dot{\hat{T}} = -\Delta_c + \hat{T}'$, we have

$$\dot{V}_1 = -\Delta_c^T(H\otimes I_m)\Delta_c + \Delta_c^T(H\otimes I_m)\hat{T}' - \Delta_c^T(H\otimes \dot{u}_0)\underline{1} \tag{42}$$

where since $(H\otimes I_m)$ is the positive definite recalling the Schur Complement Lemma, the first term is surely negative. To achieve $\dot{V}_1 < 0$, we should show that

$$\dot{V}_{11} = \Delta_c^T(H\otimes I_m)\hat{T}' - \Delta_c^T(H\otimes \dot{u}_0)\underline{1} \le 0. \tag{43}$$

Recalling Eq. (3), we have

$$(H\otimes \dot{u_0}) = (H\otimes I_m)(I_N\otimes \dot{u}_0) \tag{44}$$

Hence, the Eq. (43) is,

$$\dot{V}_{11} = \Delta_c^T(H\otimes I_m)\hat{T}' - \Delta_c^T(H\otimes I_m)(I_N\otimes \dot{u}_0)\underline{1}\dot{V}_{11} \le \Delta_c^T(H\otimes I_m)\hat{T}' + ||\Delta_c^T(H\otimes I_m)||\ (I_N\otimes \dot{U}_{0M})\underline{1} \tag{45}$$

where $\dot{U}_{0M}$ is the upper band or maximum absolute value for $\dot{u}_0$. This value should be available beforehand. Now, we should only show that

$$\Delta_c^T(H\otimes I_m)\hat{T}' + ||\Delta_c^T(H\otimes I_m)||\ (I_N\otimes \dot{U}_{0M})\underline{1} = 0 \tag{46}$$

Hence,

$$\begin{aligned} \Delta_c^T(H\otimes I_m)\hat{T}' &= -||\Delta_c^T(H\otimes I_m)||\ (I_N\otimes \dot{U}_{0M})\underline{1} \\ \Delta_c^T(H\otimes I_m)\hat{T}' &= -\Delta_c^T(H\otimes I_m)\ sign\left(\Delta_c^T(H\otimes I_m)\right)(I_N\otimes \dot{U}_{0M})\underline{1} \end{aligned} \tag{47}$$

where $sign\left(\Delta_c^T(H\otimes I_m)\right) \in \mathbb{R}^{Nm\times Nm}$ is a diagonal matrix whose diagonal elements are the signs of each element in $\Delta_c^T(H\otimes I_m)\in\mathbb{R}^{1\times Nm}$. Finally, since we have

$$\left(\Delta_c\Delta_c^T(H\otimes I_m)\right)^{-1}\Delta_c\Delta_c^T(H\otimes I_m) = I_N\otimes I_m \tag{48}$$

the second term in $\dot{\hat{T}} = -\Delta_c + \hat{T}'$, is

$$\hat{T}' = -\ sign\left(\Delta_c^T(H\otimes I_m)\right)(I_N\otimes \dot{U}_{0M})\underline{1} \tag{49}$$

and recalling Eq. (36), the rate for the observed parameter is

$$\dot{\hat{T}} = -(H\otimes I_m)\hat{T} + (B\otimes u_0)\underline{1}\ -\ sign\left(\Delta_c^T(H\otimes I_m)\right)(I_N\otimes \dot{U}_{0M})\underline{1}. \tag{50}$$

By using $\dot{\hat{T}}$ from Eq. (50), we can have $\dot{V}_1 \leq 0$, which in turn shows that the consensus error on observation (i.e. Δ_c) is stable in accordance to the Lyapunov stability theorem. It is obvious that the observed values for u_0 (i.e. $\hat{T}$) at each agent are computed iteratively using the rate value proposed in Eq. (50).

The lumped format for rate of observer parameter in Eq. (50) can be presented for each agent as the following

$$\begin{aligned} \dot{\hat{T}}_i &= -\Delta_{ci} - \left(\sum_{r=1}^{m} sign(y_{ir}) \times \dot{u}_{0Mr}\right) \\ y_i &= \sum_{j=1}^{N} H_{ij}\Delta_{cj} = [yi_1, y_{i2}, \ldots, y_{im}], \quad \dot{U}_{0M} = [\dot{u}_{0M1}, \dot{u}_{0M2}, \ldots, \dot{u}_{0Mm}] \end{aligned} \tag{51}$$

where Δ_{ci} is defined as in Eq. (35).

4.4. Adaptive law design for unknown nonlinear terms in each agent dynamics

In this subsection, the objective is to estimate the values of unknown nonlinear terms in each agent dynamics (i.e. G in Eq. (30)). Since, there is not any data available on exact values of G, the estimation error for adaptation process is not available. Hence, the adaptation should be handled using the output error which in this problem is the consensus error (i.e. E in Eq. (21)).

Considering the consensus error in Eq. (21) and the agent dynamics according to Eq. (22), the derivative for consensus error is

$$\dot{E} = (I_N \otimes C)E + (B \otimes Du_0)\underline{1} + (H \otimes D)U + (H \otimes D_1)G \tag{52}$$

where G here is the exact value for nonlinear terms. If we put the designed cooperative control protocol (from Eq. (30))

$$(H \otimes D)U = \; -\left(P + (I_N \otimes C)\right)E - (B \otimes Du_0)\underline{1} - (H \otimes D_1)\hat{G} \tag{53}$$

with $\hat{G}$ is the adapted value for the unknown nonlinear terms, into Eq. (52), we have

$$\dot{E} = -PE + (H \otimes D_1)\tilde{G}, \; \tilde{G} = G - \hat{G} \tag{54}$$

Using the following positive definite Lyapunov function

$$V_2 = \frac{1}{2}E^T E + \frac{1}{2}\tilde{G}^T \Gamma^{-1}\tilde{G} \tag{55}$$

where $\Gamma \in \mathbb{R}^{Nn \times Nn}$ is a positive definite matrix, we have

http://dx.doi.org/10.5772/intechopen.69352

$$\begin{aligned} \dot{V_2} &= E^T \dot{E} + \tilde{G}^T \Gamma^{-1} \dot{\tilde{G}} \\ \dot{V_2} &= -E^T P E + E^T (H \otimes D_1) \tilde{G} + \tilde{G}^T \Gamma^{-1} \dot{\tilde{G}} \end{aligned} \tag{56}$$

where the first term in the last equation is the negative definite. To show $\dot{V_2} < 0$, we have

$$E^T (H \otimes D_1) \tilde{G} + \tilde{G}^T \Gamma^{-1} \dot{\tilde{G}} = 0 \tag{57}$$

Then,

$$\tilde{G}^T \Gamma^{-1} \dot{\tilde{G}} = -E^T (H \otimes D_1) \tilde{G} \tag{58}$$

which in turn leads to this adaptive law

$$\begin{aligned} &\dot{\hat{G}} = -\dot{\tilde{G}} = +\Gamma (H^T \otimes D_1^T) E \\ &\Gamma = diag\{\gamma_1, \gamma_2, \ldots, \gamma_N\}, \; \gamma_i = diag\{\gamma_{i1}, \gamma_{i2}, \ldots, \gamma_{it}\}, \; t \leq n \end{aligned} \tag{59}$$

Considering the Lyapunov stability theorem for the function in Eq. (55), if $\hat{G}$ is updated using the rate value proposed in Eq. (59) iteratively, $\tilde{G}$ converges to zeros asymptotically. It means that the adapted parameter $\hat{G}$ will converge to the actual value of the nonlinear terms in agent dynamics. One of the important issues of the proposed adaptive law in Eq. (59) is that it is not required to include any set of nonlinear basis functions as regressors in the adaptive law. It is only based on the consensus error of the network, which may have sufficient information to tune the adaptive parameter.

Since the adapted signals are always vulnerable for being distracted and diverged by unknown terms, two robusting methods are provided to make the designed adaptive law robust against the divergence [21].

i. Parameter projection method

$$\dot{\hat{G}} = \begin{cases} \Gamma (H^T \otimes D_1^T) E, & if\ \hat{G}^T \hat{G} < \underline{M_0^T M_0} \\ \left(I - \dfrac{\Gamma G G^T}{G^T \Gamma G} \right) \Gamma (H^T \otimes D_1^T) E, & otherwise \end{cases} \tag{60}$$

$$\underline{M_0} = [\underline{M_{0_1}}, \underline{M_{0_2}}, \ldots, \underline{M_{0_N}}]^{\mathrm{T}}, \; \underline{M_{0_i}} = [M_{0_1}, M_{0_2}, \ldots, M_{0_t}]^{\mathrm{T}}, \; t \leq n$$

where M_{0_i} is chosen so that $M_{0_i} \geq |g_i|$. The value for M_0 should be defined beforehand. The algorithm is named as parameter projection in the literature [21].

ii. σ-modification or leakage method;

$$\dot{\hat{G}} = +\Gamma \left((H^T \otimes D_1^T) E - \rho \hat{G} \right), \; \rho > 0 \in \mathbb{R} \tag{61}$$

Hence, the complete robust adaptive control for estimating the nonlinear terms in each agent's dynamics is presented as the following

$$\dot{\hat{G}} = \begin{cases} \Gamma(H^T \otimes D_1^T)E - \rho\Gamma\hat{G} \,, \; if \; \hat{G}^T\hat{G} < \underline{M_0^T M_0} \\ \left(I - \dfrac{\Gamma G G^T}{G^T \Gamma G}\right)\left(\Gamma(H^T \otimes D_1^T)E - \rho\Gamma\hat{G}\right), \quad otherwise \end{cases} \tag{62}$$

$$\underline{M_0} = [\underline{M_{0_1}}, \underline{M_{0_2}}, \ldots, \underline{M_{0_N}}] \,, \; \underline{M_{0_i}} = [M_{0_1}, M_{0_2}, \ldots, M_{0_t}] \,, \; t \le n$$

The lumped format for the rate of adaptive parameter in Eq. (60) can be presented for agent i as the following

$$\dot{\hat{G}}_i = \begin{cases} \gamma_i \left(\sum_{j=1}^{N} Q_{ij} e_j - \rho \hat{G}_i \right), \; if \; \hat{G}_i^T \hat{G}_i < \underline{M_0^T M_0} \\ \left(I_n - \dfrac{\gamma_i G_i G_i^T}{G_i^T \gamma_i G_i} \right) \gamma_i \left(\sum_{j=1}^{N} Q_{ij} e_j - \rho \hat{G}_i \right), \; otherwise \end{cases} \tag{63}$$

$$Q = (H^T \otimes D_1^T) \,, \; M \in \mathbb{R}^{Nt \times Nn}$$

$$Q_{ij} = Q(k^*, r^*) \,, \; k^* = [\left((i-1) \times t + 1\right) : (i \times t)] \,, \; r^* = [\left((j-1) \times n + 1\right) : (j \times n)]$$

5. Application: wheeled mobile robot

In this section, application of the proposed cooperative control protocol on a team including three nonholonomic wheeled mobile robots (WMRs) is presented. The robots are moving on a smooth planar surface with a constraint on the speed (**Figure 1**). They can only move in the direction of their attitudes and speed in the perpendicular direction is zero. This is a nonholonomic constraint. Few number of researches can be found in literatures, which deal with the cooperative control of the multi-agent of WMRs taking account of each agent's WMR dynamics [22, 23].

5.1. Problem definition

Here, the kinematics and dynamics for motion of ith WMR are considered as the following

$$\begin{gathered} \dot{x}_i = v_i \cos\theta_i \,, \; \dot{y}_i = v_i \sin\theta_i \,, \; \dot{\theta}_i = \omega_i \\ \dot{v}_i = \frac{1}{m} F_i \,, \; \dot{\omega}_i = \frac{1}{J} T_i \end{gathered} \tag{64}$$

where x_i and y_i represent the position of a single WMR in the inertial coordinate system, θ_i is the orientation of the WMR, v_i is the translational speed in the WMR's pose direction and ω_i is the angular speed of WMR about the Z axis. Also, m and J are the mass and moment of inertia for WMR. Moreover, F_i and T_i are the force and torque generated by the electric motors disclosed in each wheel of WMR. The last parameters are the control parameters for motion of each WMR. By transforming the kinematics of WMR to a local coordinate system fixed to the WMR, [24]

http://dx.doi.org/10.5772/intechopen.69352

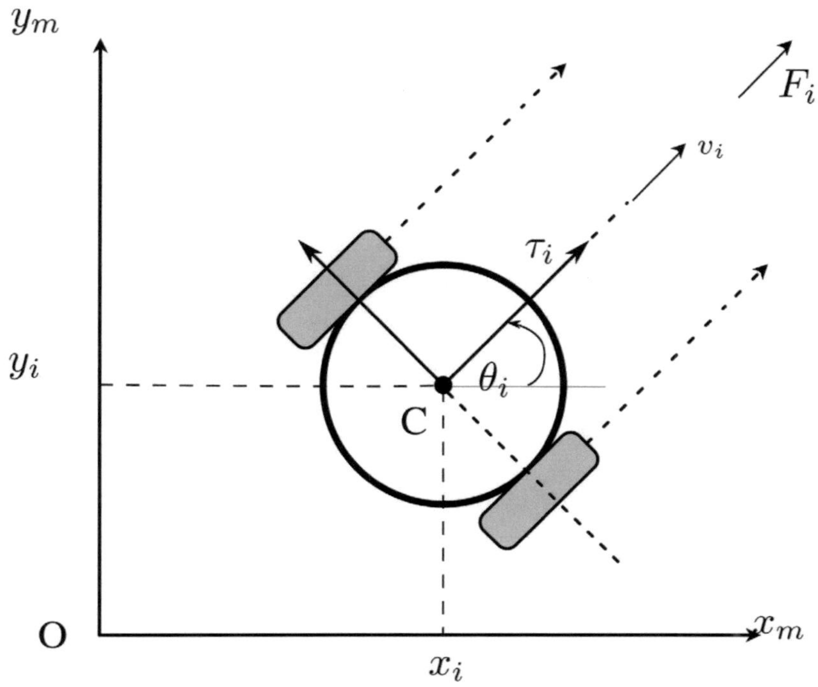

Figure 1. A diagram for kinematics of a nonholonomic planar wheeled robot.

$$\begin{bmatrix} x_{i1} \\ x_{i2} \\ x_{i3} \end{bmatrix} = \begin{bmatrix} \cos\theta_i & \sin\theta_i & 0 \\ -\sin\theta_i & \cos\theta_i & 0 \\ 0 & 0 & 1 \end{bmatrix} \begin{bmatrix} x_i \\ y_i \\ \theta_i \end{bmatrix} \tag{65}$$

Then by considering $x_{i4} = v_i$ and $x_{i5} = \omega_i$, we have

$$\begin{aligned} \dot{x}_{i1} &= x_{i4} + x_{i5}x_{i2}\ ,\ \dot{x}_{i2} = -x_{i5}x_{i1} \\ \dot{x}_{i3} &= x_{i5}\ ,\ \dot{x}_{i4} = u_{i1}\ ,\ \dot{x}_{i5} = u_{i2} \end{aligned} \tag{66}$$

where $u_{i1} = \frac{1}{m}F_i$ and $u_{i2} = \frac{1}{J}T_i$. The state-space system can be represented in matrix form similar to Eq. (16), as the following

$$\begin{aligned} &\dot{X}_i = CX_i + Du_i + D_1G_i \\ &X_i = [x_{i1}, x_{i2}, x_{i3}, x_{i4}, x_{i5}]^T,\ u_i = [u_{i1}, u_{i2}]^T,\ G_i = [x_{i5}x_{i2}, -x_{i5}x_{i1}]^T \\ &C = \begin{bmatrix} 0 & 0 & 0 & 1 & 0 \\ 0 & 0 & 0 & 0 & 0 \\ 0 & 0 & 0 & 0 & 1 \\ 0 & 0 & 0 & 0 & 0 \\ 0 & 0 & 0 & 0 & 0 \end{bmatrix},\ D = \begin{bmatrix} 0 & 0 \\ 0 & 0 \\ 0 & 0 \\ 1 & 0 \\ 0 & 1 \end{bmatrix},\ D_1 = \begin{bmatrix} 1 & 0 \\ 0 & 1 \\ 0 & 0 \\ 0 & 0 \\ 0 & 0 \end{bmatrix} \end{aligned} \tag{67}$$

As can be seen, D is not full rank. According to assumption 2, we need a change of variables to have D in the full-rank form. Recalling the idea of the back-stepping method [25] we have

$$\delta_{i1} = v_i - s_{i1} \ , \ \delta_{i2} = \omega_i - s_{i2} \tag{68}$$

Applying the back-stepping method

$$s_{i3} = u_{i1} - \dot{s}_{i1} \ , \ s_{i4} = u_{i2} - \dot{s}_{i2} \tag{69}$$

we have

$$\begin{aligned} \dot{x}_{i1} &= \delta_{i1} + \delta_{i2} x_{i2} + s_{i1} + x_{i2} s_{i2} \\ \dot{x}_{i2} &= -\delta_{i2} x_{i1} - x_{i1} s_{i2} \\ \dot{x}_{i3} &= \delta_{i2} + s_{i2} \ , \ \dot{\delta}_{i1} = s_{i3} \ , \ \dot{\delta}_{i2} = s_{i4} \end{aligned} \tag{70}$$

Then, the state-space representation of a single WMR can be represented in following format

$$\begin{aligned} \dot{\overline{X}}_i &= \overline{C}\,\overline{X}_i + \overline{D}\,\overline{u}_i + \overline{D_1}\,\overline{G}_i \\ \overline{X}_i &= [x_{i1}, x_{i2}, x_{i3}, \delta_{i1}, \delta_{i2}]^T \ , \ \overline{u}_i = [s_{i1}, s_{i2}, s_{i3}, s_{i4}]^T \\ \overline{G}_i &= [\Big(\delta_{i2} x_{i2} + q_{i1}(x_{i2})\Big) , \Big(- \delta_{i2} x_{i1} + q_{i2}(x_{i1})\Big)]^T \\ \overline{C} = C \ , \ \overline{D} &= \begin{bmatrix} 1 & 1 & 0 & 0 \\ 0 & 1 & 0 & 0 \\ 0 & 1 & 0 & 0 \\ 0 & 0 & 1 & 0 \\ 0 & 0 & 0 & 1 \end{bmatrix} , \ \overline{D_1} = D_1 \end{aligned} \tag{71}$$

which has a full rank $\overline{D}$ matrix. Hence, assumption 2 is satisfied and the proposed cooperative controller can be implemented. Hence, we have five state variables, four control parameters and two nonlinear terms for each WMR. At each agent within the network, the nonlinear terms will be adapted using Eq. (63) and the control parameters of the leader will be observed using Eq. (51).

Here, the desired formation is a rectangle with four agents and four equal edges. The length of each edge is equal and is r. The virtual leader is positioned at the centroid of the geometry (**Figure 2**). Moreover, the communication graph for this network is shown in **Figure 2**. The leader information is only available to agent 1. Hence, the adjacency matrices are defined as the following

$$A = \begin{bmatrix} 0 & 1 & 0 & 0 \\ 1 & 0 & 1 & 0 \\ 0 & 1 & 0 & 1 \\ 0 & 0 & 1 & 0 \end{bmatrix} , \ D_L = \begin{bmatrix} 1 & 0 & 0 & 0 \\ 0 & 2 & 0 & 0 \\ 0 & 0 & 2 & 0 \\ 0 & 0 & 0 & 1 \end{bmatrix} , \ B = \begin{bmatrix} 1 & 0 & 0 & 0 \\ 0 & 0 & 0 & 0 \\ 0 & 0 & 0 & 0 \\ 0 & 0 & 0 & 0 \end{bmatrix} \tag{72}$$

There is a well-known reference trajectory for this problem in the literature [20], which is presented as the following,

$$x_0 = \frac{v_r}{\omega_r}\sin\theta_0\ ,\ y_0 = -\frac{v_r}{\omega_r}\cos\theta_0\ ,\ \theta_0 = \omega_r t \tag{73}$$

where v_r and ω_r can be any known time-varying functions. Usually, these functions are considered as constant values. In Eq. (73), t is time.

5.2. Simulation results

The simulation for the problem defined in Section 5.1 is performed by MATLAB/Simulink. The constant values for running the simulation are presented in **Table 1**.

Moreover, the values of P_i as the gain values for cooperative control protocol at each agent (see Eq. (33)) are as follows

$$\begin{matrix} P_1 = diag\{10, 10, 100, 10, 10\},\ P_2 = diag\{10, 10, 12, 10, 10\} \\ P_3 = diag\{10, 10, 30, 10, 10\},\ P_4 = diag\{10, 10, 55, 10, 10\} \end{matrix} \tag{74}$$

The values in P_i are determined in a way to ensure that the whole matrix P is positive definite and the sufficient transient performance of the whole network is achieved.

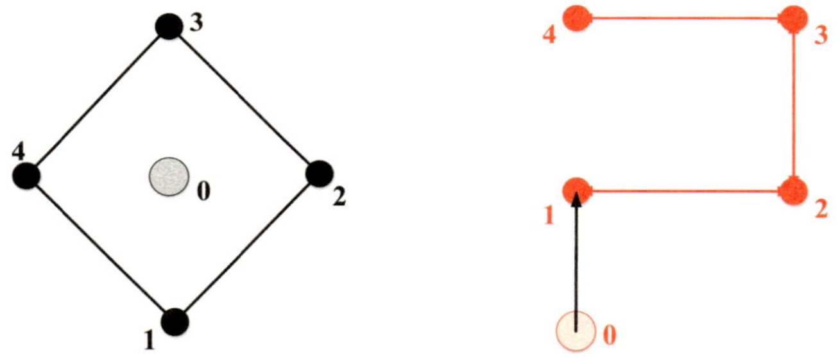

Figure 2. (Left) A diagram for the desired positions of four agents in a network; (right) the communication graph for a network of four agents and a leader.

Parameter	Value
Mass of each agent (M)	1 kg
Inertia of each agent (J)	1 kg/m^2
Relative position of agents in the network (r)	4 m
Reference velocity (v_r)	5 m/s^2
Reference angular velocity (ω_r)	0.25 rad/s
The adaptation rates (γ_1, γ_2)	0.01 & 0.1
The leakage factor (ρ)	100
The maximum value for rate of u_0 ($\dot{U}_{0M}$)	*ones* (4,1)
The maximum value for adapted signal ($\underline{M_0}$)	10 × *ones* (2, 1)

Table 1. The constant parameters for simulation of a network of WMRs.

The simulation results for this problem are presented in the following figures. The position of all agents in the X-Y plane is shown in **Figure 3**. The consensus on both reference trajectory and the desired formation can be seen. Actually, the desired formation is achieved gradually. In addition, the position of the centroid of all agents is compared with the reference trajectory in **Figure 4**. Moreover, the signals for translational and angular speeds of agent 4 are presented in **Figure 5**. Finally, the observed data for control parameters of the leader and also the adapted nonlinear terms at agent 4 are shown in **Figures 6** and **7**. Appropriate performance of proposed algorithms can be inferred by these figures.

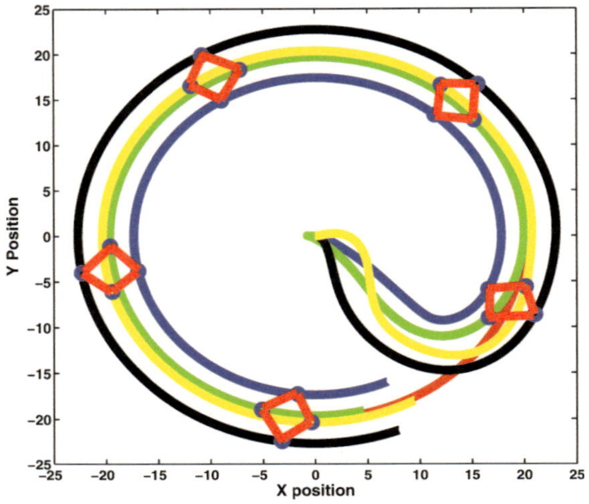

Figure 3. The reference trajectory (red) and position of agents in the desired formation (agent #1: blue, agent #2: green, agent #3: black and agent #4: yellow).

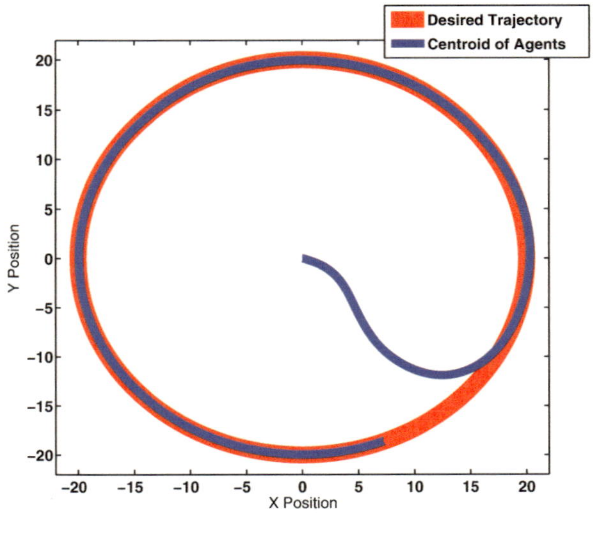

Figure 4. The reference trajectory and position of the centroid of the agents in the desired formation.

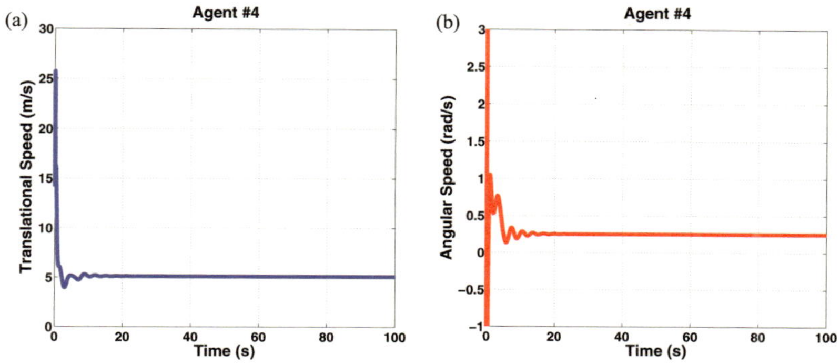

Figure 5. Translational and angular speed of agent #4.

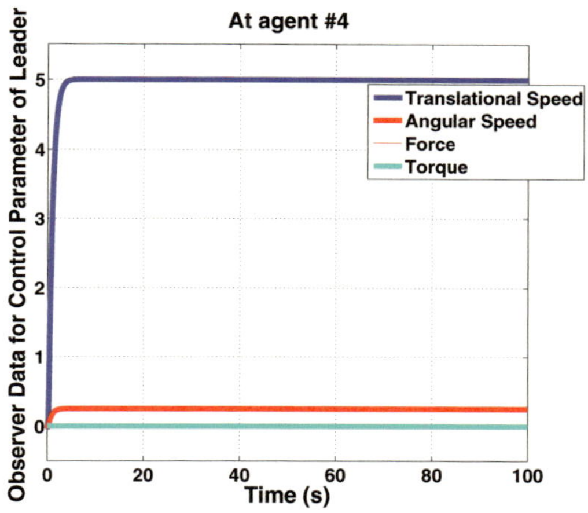

Figure 6. Observed data for control parameters of the leader at agent #4.

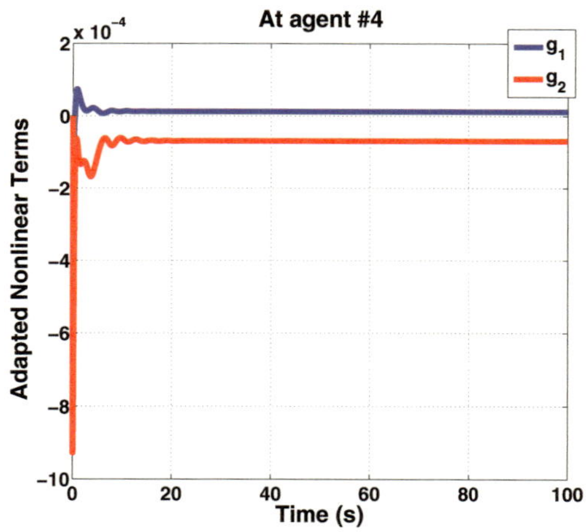

Figure 7. Adapted nonlinear terms at agent #4.

6. Conclusion

This chapter is dedicated to the design procedure of a cooperative control protocol for any network consisting of agents with non-affine nonlinear dynamics and multi-input multi-output structure. The main goal is to satisfy a tracking problem for the whole network while maintaining a predefined formation topology in the state space of the agents' dynamics. The proposed design procedure is including an adaptive law incorporated with a robustification method to estimate the unknown nonlinear terms in the agents' dynamics. In addition, an observer is designed using the consensus-type error for estimating the leader's control parameters at each agent. Since there are no complete information links between the leader and all agents, the observed control parameters of the leader are required at each agent to construct the cooperative control protocol. The entire design procedure is analysed successfully for the stability using Lyapunov stability theorem. The presented simulation results for a team of wheeled mobile robots show the appropriate performance of the proposed method.

Acknowledgements

This chapter is supported by the Fundamental Research Grant Scheme (FRGS) under Grant No. (FRGS-203/PELECT/6071290), awarded by Ministry of Education Malaysia. Besides, this chapter is under a USM-TWAS Postgraduate Fellowship.

Author details

Muhammad Nasiruddin bin Mahyuddin* and Ali Safaei

*Address all correspondence to: nasiruddin@usm.my

School of Electrical and Electronics Engineering, Universiti Sains Malaysia, Pulau Pinang, Malaysia

References

[1] Mahyuddin MN, Herrmann G, Lewis FL. Finite-time adaptive distributed control for double-integrator leader-agent synchronization. In: 2012 IEEE International Symposium on Intelligent Control (ISIC); Dubrovnik, Croatia

[2] Mahyuddin MN, Herrmann G, Lewis FL. Distributed adaptive leader-following control for multi-agent multi-degree manipulators with finite-time guarantees. In: 52nd IEEE Conference on Decision and Control; Florence, Italy

[3] Wang Q, Wang Y, Zhang H. The formation control of multi-agent systems on a circle. IEEE/CAA Journal of Automatica Sinica. 2016;(99): pp. 1–7

[4] Fathian K, Rachinskii DI, Spong MW, Gans NR. Globally asymptotically stable distributed control for distance and bearing based multi-agent formations. In: 2016 American Control Conference (ACC); Boston, MA. 2016. pp. 4642–4648

[5] Han T, Zheng R, Lin Z, Fu M. A barycentric coordinate based approach to formation control of multi-agent systems under directed and switching topologies. In: 2015 54th IEEE Conference on Decision and Control (CDC); Osaka. 2015. pp. 6263–6268

[6] Yang Y, Dong Y, Jie D, Deming Y. Distributed control of uncertain nonlinear multi-agent systems in non-affine pure-feedback form using DSC technique. In: 2015 34th Chinese Control Conference (CCC); Hangzhou. 2015. pp. 7380–7385

[7] Das A, Lewis FL. Cooperative adaptive control for synchronization of second-order systems with unknown nonlinearities. International Journal of Robust and Nonlinear Control. 2011;**21**(13):1509–1524

[8] Zhang HW, Lewis FL. Adaptive cooperative tracking control of higher-order nonlinear systems with unknown dynamics. Automatica. 2012;**48**(7):1432–1439

[9] Peng ZH, Wang D, Sun G, Wang H. Distributed cooperative stabilisation of continuous time uncertain nonlinear multi-agent systems. International Journal of Systems Science. 2014;**45**(10):2031–2041

[10] Wang W, Wang D, Peng ZH. Cooperative fuzzy adaptive output feedback control for synchronisation of nonlinear multi-agent systems under directed graphs. International Journal of Systems Science. 2014:1–14. DOI: 10.1080/00207721.2014.886135 [ahead-of-print]

[11] Zhao Y, Chen G. Distributed adaptive tracking control of non-affine nonlinear multi-agent systems. In: 2016 Chinese Control and Decision Conference (CCDC); Yinchuan, China; 28-30 May 2016; pp. 1518–1523

[12] Meng WC, Yang QM, Jagannathan S, Sun YX. Adaptive neural control of high-order uncertain nonaffine systems: A transformation to affine systems approach. Automatica. 2014;**50**:1473–1480

[13] Hou ZG, Cheng L, Tan M. Decentralized robust adaptive control for the multi-agent system consensus problem using neural networks. IEEE Transactions on Systems, Man, and Cybernetics, Part B: Cybernetics. 2009;**39**(3):636–647

[14] Hovakimyan N, Calise AJ, Kim N. Adaptive output feedback control of a class of multi-input multi-output systems using neural networks. International Journal of Control. 2004;**77**(15):1318–1329

[15] Marsden J, Weinstein A. Calculus Unlimited. Menlo Park, CA: Benjamin/Cummings Publishing Company Inc.; 1981

[16] Li Z, Duan Z. Cooperative Control of Multi-Agent Systems. Boca Raton, FL: CRC Press, Taylor & Francis Group; 2015

[17] Boyd S, El Ghaoui L, Feron E, Balakrishnan V. Linear Matrix Inequalities in System and Control Theory. Philadelphia, PA: SIAM; 1994

[18] Lewis FL, Zhang H, Hengster-Movric K, Das A. Cooperative Control of Multi-Agent Systems. London: Springer-Verlag; 2014

[19] Wu L, Qin X, Zhang D. Cooperative adaptive fuzzy control for a class of uncertain nonlinear multi-agent systems with time delays. Journal of Control and Decision. 2016;**4**(3): 131–152

[20] Dong W. Tracking control of multiple-wheeled mobile robots with limited information of a desired trajectory. IEEE Transactions on Robotics. 2012;**28**(1): 262–268

[21] Ioannou P, Fidan B. Adaptive Control Tutorial. Philadelphia: SIAM; 2006

[22] Peng Z, Yang S, Wen G, Rahmani A. Distributed consensus-based robust adaptive formation control for nonholonomic mobile robots with partial known dynamics. Mathematical Problems in Engineering. 2014;**2014**:Article ID 670497

[23] Koh KC, Cho HS. A smooth path tracking algorithm for wheeled mobile robots with dynamics constraints. Journal of Intelligent and Robotic Systems. 1999;**24**:367–385

[24] Fierro R, Lewis FL. Control of a nonholonomic mobile robot: Backstepping kinematics into dynamics. In: Proceedings of the IEEE 34th Conference on Decision & Control; New Orleans, LA., USA; 13-15 December 1995; pp. 3805-3810

[25] Khalil HK. Nonlinear Systems. 3rd ed. Prentice Hall, Inc.; New Jersey, USA; 2002

Management of a Single-User Multi-Robot Teleoperated System for Maintenance in Offshore Plants

Seungyeol Lee and Jeon-Il Moon

Additional information is available at the end of the chapter

http://dx.doi.org/10.5772/intechopen.69351

Abstract

This chapter proposes a new approach to management method of a single-user multi-robot teleoperated system for maintenance in offshore plants. The management method is designed to perform a 1:*N* mode (here, "1" refers to the number of operators and "*N*" denotes the number of slave robots), in which a single operator teleoperates a number of slave robots directly to conduct a maintenance task, or in an autonomous cooperation mode between slave robots in order to overcome the limitations of the aforementioned 1:1 teleoperation mode. The aforementioned management method is responsible for the role sharing and integration of slave robots to divide the operation mode of the slave robots into various types according to the operator's intervention level and the characteristics of the target maintenance task beforehand and to perform the target maintenance task using the robot operation mode selected by the operator.

Keywords: multi-robot, teleoperated system, management, maintenance, offshore plants

1. Introduction

A typical teleoperated robotic system consists of a master device that collects motion commands from a remote user for a slave robot, and a slave robot that follows those commands. The 1:1 teleoperation method is most frequently used in typical teleoperated robotic systems, and involves a master device that collects target task commands from an operator to the slave robot that carries out those commands [1, 2]. For example, Heikkila et al. proposed functional design of a manufacturing robot cell [3]. Yamada et al. introduced construction telerobot system with virtual reality [4]. Zhao et al. developed a construction telerobotic system that has wide applications in restoration work in stricken areas [5]. Kwon et al. developed a microsurgical telerobot system [6]. Geerinck et al. introduced the operability of an advanced demonstration platform incorporating reflexive teleoperated control concepts developed on a mobile robot system [7]. The 1:1 teleoperation mode that can be expected in offshore plants, includes operations conducted by a robot manipulator, such as manipulating door knobs (open, close) and pressing buttons and other types of switches; operations of mobile platform movement, including evading obstacles; and inspection operations, such as inspecting inner pipes, gauges, and oil or water leakage by cameras and other instruments. But 1:1 teleoperation method is unsuitable due to limits of the robotic workspace or power of only one slave robot. When this method is applied to maintenance (e.g., handling large valves) in offshore plants, one slave robot is insufficient for performing the maintenance processes because of the length and weight of the mechanical parts in offshore plants. When two of these systems are used for the maintenance in offshore plants, communication between the operators and cooperation between the robots through the two master devices are not smooth, and this reduces the work efficiency. Furthermore, if user operations are repeated regularly, an operator may lose concentration due to the repetition of simple motion commands [8].

A "shared telerobotics" has recently been proposed in which a general operating command is issued and the robot autonomously performs the specific task [9–20]. Operating on a valve that is located between multiple obstacles and must not come in contact with a nuclear facility, enables an operator to simply provide a direction to the robot and move the robot and its end effector to a desired location to perform the operation through an obstacle avoidance algorithm, without having to meticulously control the robot to avoid the obstacles. In this chapter, a single-operator multi-robot (SOMR, 1:*N*) teleoperation system that can conduct specific operations with cooperation between multi-robots to overcome the limitations of the 1:1 teleoperation systems is briefly explained. The system presented in this chapter can perform teleoperation with respect to remotely placed robots through a single operator, and is designed to perform particular operations through autonomous cooperation between robots with minimal input from an operator. In particular, software for efficient robot management, such as role sharing and changing between robots in the SOMR teleoperation system, is explained in detail.

2. Framework of single-operator multi-robot system

Figure 1 shows the framework diagram of a system that allows single operator to remotely control multiple units of robots (N; positive integers). As shown in **Figure 1**, operators transmit action commands to a master device; the commands are converted into action control signals for the robot system through the device and processed through a communication system, which includes the remote-control device, to be delivered to the corresponding module (such as a robot arm, mobile platform, or camera) of the slave robot. In addition, data on the contact force that occurs through interactions between robots and the surrounding environment while in operation, data on the actual robot motions, and data on the current action status are measured by various sensors on the slave robots. The measured data are then delivered to the master device through a communication system to ultimately provide necessary data (such as contact force, robot motion status, and action status) to operators through the controllers and drivers inside the device.

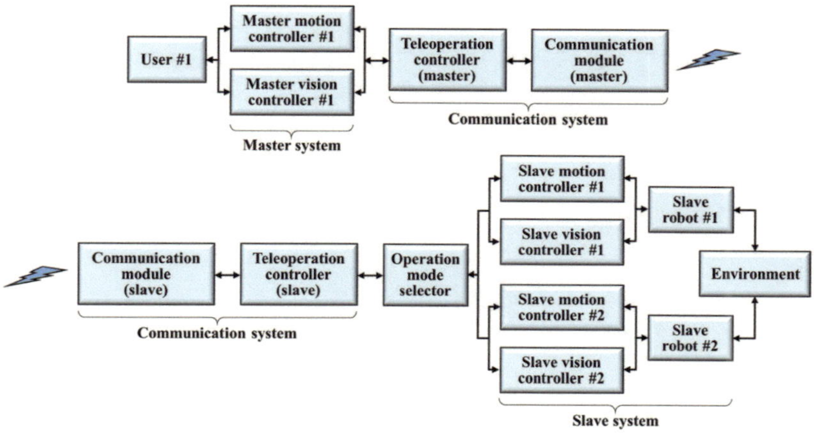

Figure 1. Framework diagram of a single-operator multi-robot system.

In addition, an operation mode selector is included in the slave circuits. This device supports predefined parameters for each of the following four cases: when separating action commands (such as robot motion and measurement Degree Of Freedom) delivered from the operators by the master device, when separating action commands delivered from the master devices by the slave system, when separating data on robot motion and action status measured from the environment by the slave system, and when separating data on the current motion of robots and action status delivered from the slave systems by the master device. Therefore, an operating scenario is determined by the operators controlling each parameter, and action commands are distributed by the operators to control the robots' cooperation. When the action commands are delivered to the slave system, they are distributed by a slave robot to ensure they are delivered to the necessary slave robots. Likewise, the measurement and observation DOF of the slave robots are distributed by the slave system, and when the data are delivered back to the master system, they are distributed by the master system to ensure they are delivered to the appropriate operators.

Figure 2 shows the structure of a typical master system (including master arms), which includes the master motion controllers inside the master system (**Figure 1**) and the signal input-output relationship. As shown in the **Figure 2**, when operators move the handle of the master arm, the rotational displacement of the joint is converted into pulse values through an encoder inside the arm and is converted again into angle values through a decoder. The converted angle values are then subjected to forward kinematics analysis to be converted into desired location coordinates of the rectangular coordinate system to which the slave robot is to be directed, and are subsequently processed through a communication module (remote-controlled) to be delivered to the slave robot. In general, the data on the contact force that occurs when slave robots come in contact with the surrounding environment are measured by force/torque sensors installed inside the robots, and the data pass through the communication module to be delivered to the master controller. The delivered data then undergo an internal conversion process to obtain the desired torque value for the master arm joint and are modified to the current values for each motor required to generate the same torque again. Therefore, the data on contact force measured by the initial slave robot through the driving mechanism

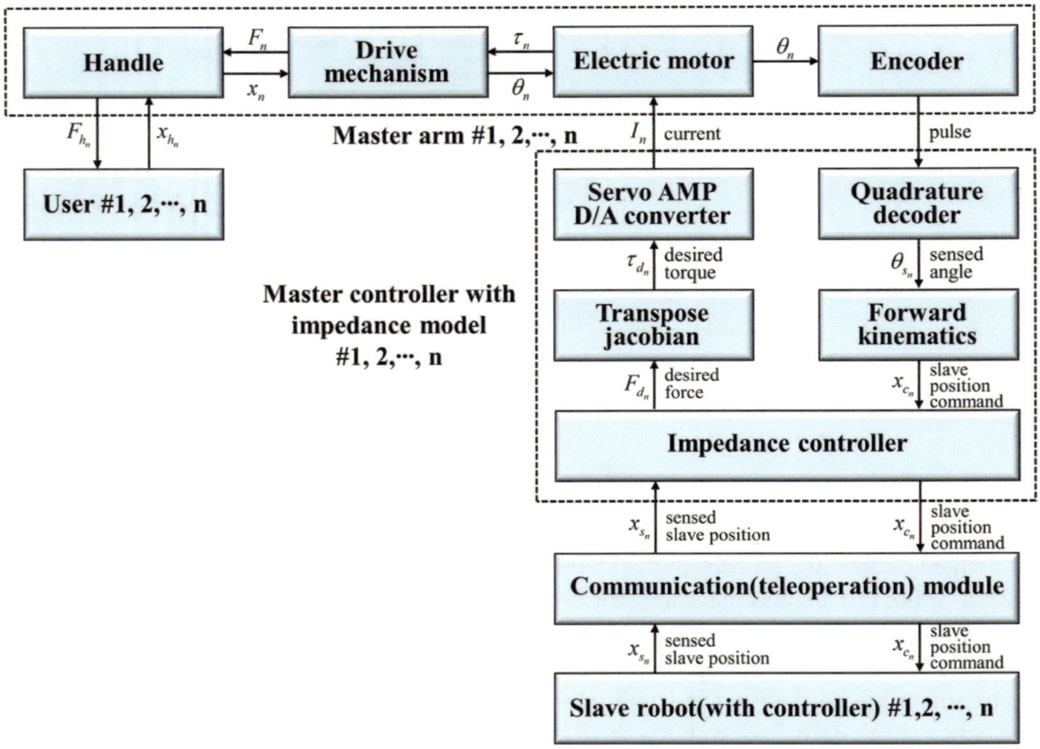

Figure 2. Structure diagram of a master device.

that includes the motor inside the master arm are ultimately converted into the data for the force/torque of the master arm and are delivered to the operators.

Figure 2 also represents the structure diagram of a master device that can provide operators with the data on contact force without force/torque sensors inside the slave robots. This means that the master device differs in the following two aspects: there are deviations between the operators' action commands inside the master controller and the current motion data of the robots and the device estimates the data of the desired contact force from a virtual environment model in Eq. (1), which is determined by impedance parameters. The virtual environment model is determined from the impedance parameters (*K*, *D*) and can be adjusted according to the operators' requests. As for a PHANToM™ haptic device, a haptic equipment that has been launched commercially, its impedance parameters are fixed to recommended values upon factory release, and operators are unable to adjust the values. However, they are able to adjust the degree of force/torque they sense to a certain proportion by parameter "ε" in Eq. (1).

$$\varepsilon \underline{\tilde{F}}_{\mathrm{d}} = K \Delta \underline{x}_{\mathrm{ds}} - D \Delta \underline{\dot{x}}_{\mathrm{ds}} \quad (1)$$

where $\underline{\tilde{F}}_{\mathrm{d}}$: is the desired contact force estimated from the impedance (virtual environment) model; *K*, *D*: are hardness and damping parameters, respectively. ε: is the contact force adjusting parameters that are fed back to operators.

http://dx.doi.org/10.5772/intechopen.69351

$$\Delta \underline{x}_{\rm ds} = \underline{x}_{\rm d} - \underline{x}_{\rm s},\ \Delta \dot{\underline{x}}_{\rm ds} = \dot{\underline{x}}_{\rm d} - \dot{\underline{x}}_{\rm s} \tag{2}$$

To realize the SOMR (1:*N*) system, the signal input-output relationship for remote-controlled robots is shown in **Figure 3**. When the initial operator issues "commands for robot's motion ($R_{\rm u}$)/ robot's action ($P_{\rm u}$)," the commands are processed through a communication system and delivered to slave (robot) systems. Then, as the robots follow the motion/action commands above, the "data on robot's motion ($R_{\rm e}$)/robot's action ($P_{\rm e}$) (current motion status of robots, surrounding environment, and action status)," which are measured through various internal sensors, are processed through the communication system again to be delivered to the master system. These data on the motion/action ultimately provide operators with various necessary data through the internal controller of the master system. This means that the motion/action commands issued from the initial operator and delivered to the robots are executed in the form of robots actually initiating the commands or observing the surrounding environment and situation. The robots then deliver the result of their motion/action to operators to inform them about the execution status of the commands and the current action status. As such, there must be a clear input-output relationship between the motion/action commands for robots that are input by the operators and the motion/action data that are output from the robots, and it must be accompanied by the 1:1 mapping between the input data and output data. Unlike on the SOMR (1:1 teleoperation) system, an operation mode selector is included in the slave system section in the 1:*N* teleoperated system. Parameters are included within the operation mode selector for determining the 1:*N* teleoperation mode. These parameters, as shown in **Figure 3**, consist of a parameter (β) that separates the action commands delivered from the master (operator) by the slave and a parameter (γ) that separates the data on the robot's current motion/action status measured from the operation environment by the slave. Therefore, the 1:*N* teleoperation mode is determined because an operator selects this parameter, and cooperative control between robots becomes possible because action commands are distributed by the slave robot. The data measured or observed from the environment are distributed by the slave, providing the necessary data to the slaves.

To explain in detail, in the 1:*N* teleoperation mode, a single operator first establishes a distribution plan for tasks (classified into two cases: distributed as the robot motion task, and measurement task of the surrounding environment and situation by robots; the proportion of cooperation is adjusted while performing the robot motion task and measurement task simultaneously) to be performed by a specific number (*N*) of slave robots (assumption *N* = 2) and determines the

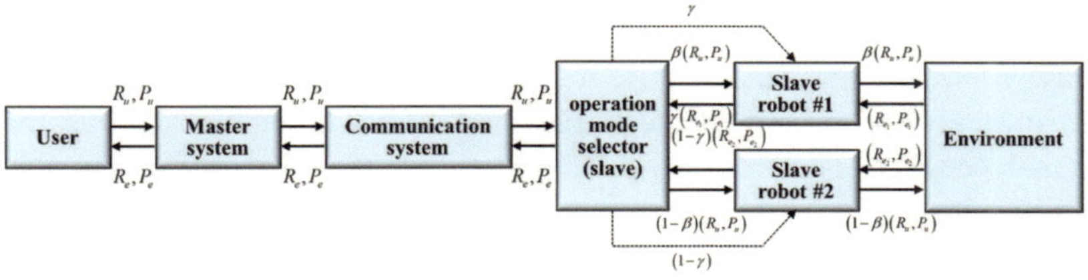

Figure 3. Structure diagram of a master device in a SOMR system.

parameter β within the operation mode selector on the basis of the task distribution plan. Then, the action command delivered to the master device from the operator is processed through a communication system and delivered to each respective slave robots as $\beta(R_{u_1}, P_{u_1}), (1-\beta)(R_{u_2}, P_{u_2})$, as shown in Eq. (3).

$$(R_u, P_u) = \beta(R_{u_1}, P_{u_1}) + (1-\beta)(R_{u_2}, P_{u_2}) \tag{3}$$

where (R_{u_1}, R_{u_2}): is the robot action commands input into slave robots 1 and 2; (P_{u_1}, P_{u_2}): is the ancillary action commands input into slave robots 1 and 2.

$$R_u = R_{u_1} + R_{u_2}, \; P_u = P_{u_1} + P_{u_2} \tag{4}$$

In addition, there is a parameter γ within the operation mode selector that functions to separate the data on the robot's current motion/action status measured from the environment by the slave. To explain in detail, when the data on the robot's motion (R_e) and ancillary action (P_e) are measured from the sensors inside the slave robots, the data are distributed and measured according to $\gamma(R_{e_1}, P_{e_1}), (1-\gamma)(R_{e_2}, P_{e_2})$ by slave robots 1 and 2 by the parameter γ Eq. (4). Because the data measured by each slave must be delivered to a single operator through communication system and a single master system, they require reintegration to (R_e, P_e) within the operation mode selector, as shown in Eq. (4).

$$(R_e, P_e) = \gamma(R_{e_1}, P_{e_1}) + (1-\gamma)(R_{e_2}, P_{e_2}) \tag{5}$$

(R_{e_1}, R_{e_2}): is the data on robot's motion provided to slave robots 1 and 2; (P_{e_1}, P_{e_2}): is the data on ancillary action provided to slave robots 1 and 2.

$$R_e = R_{e_1} + R_{e_2}, \; P_e = P_{e_1} + P_{e_2} \tag{6}$$

3. Integrated robot management software

The SOMR system allows an operator to remotely control multi-robots and aims to perform tasks that cannot be done with a single robot (e.g., large volume required or heavy objects handle works) through the cooperation of multiple robots. In the above system, each robot has a single robotic manipulator mounted in an upper part of a single mobile platform, as well as various sensors, including a camera. The development goal of the SOMR teleoperation system is to improve work efficiency by performing particular tasks with multiple robots where a single robot would be either inefficient at or incapable of functioning optimally.

Figure 4 shows the schematic diagram of the SOMR system with integrated robot management (IRM) software. An operator determines the number of robots required for executing the specific maintenance tasks, the cooperation mode of the robots, and the authority needed for carrying out the work between human operators and robots first via the GUI in the master device connected to the IRM software. An operator then selects from four modes the behavior most suited to the task required: general teleoperation with 1:1 systems, cooperation between an operator and robots, and cooperation between robots with (or without) an operator's operational command in the GUI. Once the cooperation mode determined for each process is delivered to the remote IRM device as various control signal types, the IRM

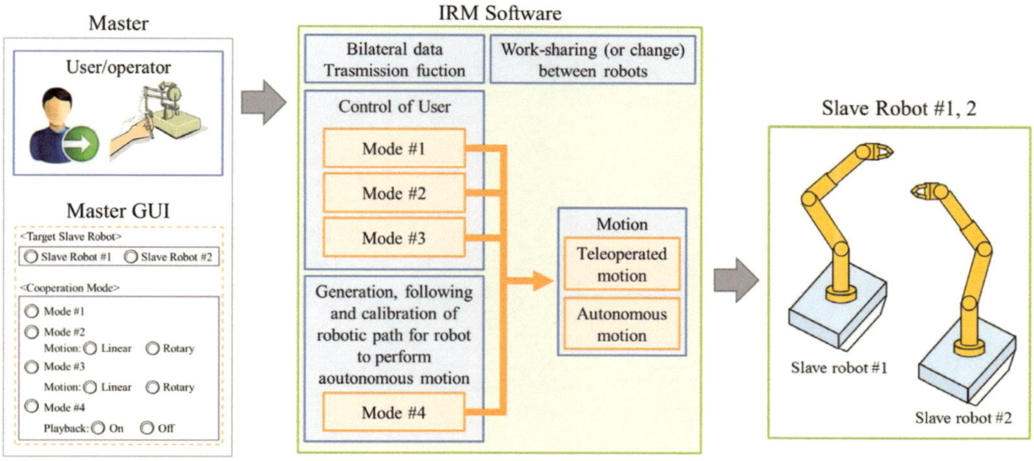

Figure 4. SOMR system with IRM (integrated robot management) software.

software performs functions, such as the switching of input/output signals between operator and robots and the generation (or calibration) of each robotic path in order to conduct cooperative motion between robots according to the cooperation mode chosen.

The IRM software is utilized in the IRM device inside the SOMR system described in **Figure 4**. This software is an integrated management software that includes role sharing (or change) between robots and the generation (calibration) of each robotic path to allow cooperation between two or more robots for tasks that are difficult for a single teleoperated robot. Initially, the IRM software classifies works in advance into four categories, primarily, by the degree of operator intervention required during the operation of the robots, based on the characteristics of the initial work (difficulty or risk level). Later on, it classifies each of the above work groups into four detailed work groups, secondarily, according to the physical motion characteristics. Thus, the various tasks that can be performed are classified into 16 types of work. Also proposed is the mode in the SOMR system that is applicable to each work group, so that the proposed SOMR system can secure universal generality and efficiency at the same time.

The proposed IRM software is mainly responsible for the bilateral data transmission function between an operator and robots, the management function of transmitted data, and the operation function of cooperation between robots for specified tasks. In more detail, the proposed IRM software includes, firstly, a function of work-sharing (or change) between robots to ensure cooperation between an operator and robots, and cooperation between robots with (or without) operator's operational commands; secondly, a function of control of operator intervention according to the nature of the tasks (difficulty or risk level) during cooperation between an operator and robots; and thirdly, a function of generation, following, and calibration of robotic paths for robots to perform autonomous motion (operator's intervention is 0%).

As shown in **Figure 5**, whether robots perform teleoperated motion or autonomous motion is determined among the remote robots according the mode (#1–#4) selected through the GUI in the master device by an operator. The mode can also be divided into straightforward or circular motion according to the physical motion characteristics of the robot that performs the

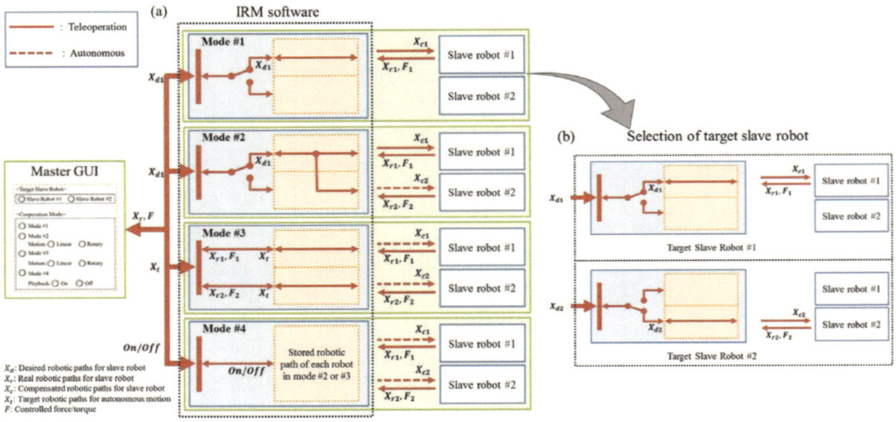

Figure 5. Structure of (a) IRM software (modes #1–#4) and (b) selection of target slave robot.

particular task. Thus, commands relating to the robotic path created via the master device by an operator are transferred to a specific robot, which performs the teleoperated motion (mode #1), while robotic paths for autonomous motion for other robots are created to assist the motion of that specific robot (mode #2). In addition, an operator can also create operational commands (from the viewpoint of motions for target objects) via the master device. These operational commands are transformed into robotic paths for autonomous motion for each robot via the IRM software (mode #3). Finally, in those instances where a task is repeatedly performed, the robotic path of each robot that corresponds to a single iteration can be stored and repeated as necessary (mode #4).

4. Verification of integrated robot management software

Figure 6 shows the simple experimental setup of SOMR system for valve handling (one of maintenance tasks) in offshore plants. The SOMR system is intended to work in places where people cannot easily access due to safety concerns and/or geographical restrictions, such as remote offshore plants, disaster relief sites, or nuclear power plants. Such simulated environments simulate the various types of maintenance work common across a variety of fields in offshore plants. In particular, the experiment aims to validate feasibility of operation of the SOMR system for the rotation of large valves, which cannot be accomplished with a single robot. The valve handling experiment was accomplished by cooperation motions between two robots through the SOMR system using the modes #2 and #3 (including linear, rotational and combination modes) of the IRM software. To evaluate the efficiency of the SOMR system and IRM software, the total time required to accomplish the valve handling task was compared with that required by two sets of the existing 1:1 teleoperated system under the same conditions, as presented in **Table 1**. As indicated in **Table 1**, the total valve handling time was reduced by about 80% of the proposed 1:N (N = 2) teleoperated robotic system compared to the existing 1:1 system.

http://dx.doi.org/10.5772/intechopen.69351

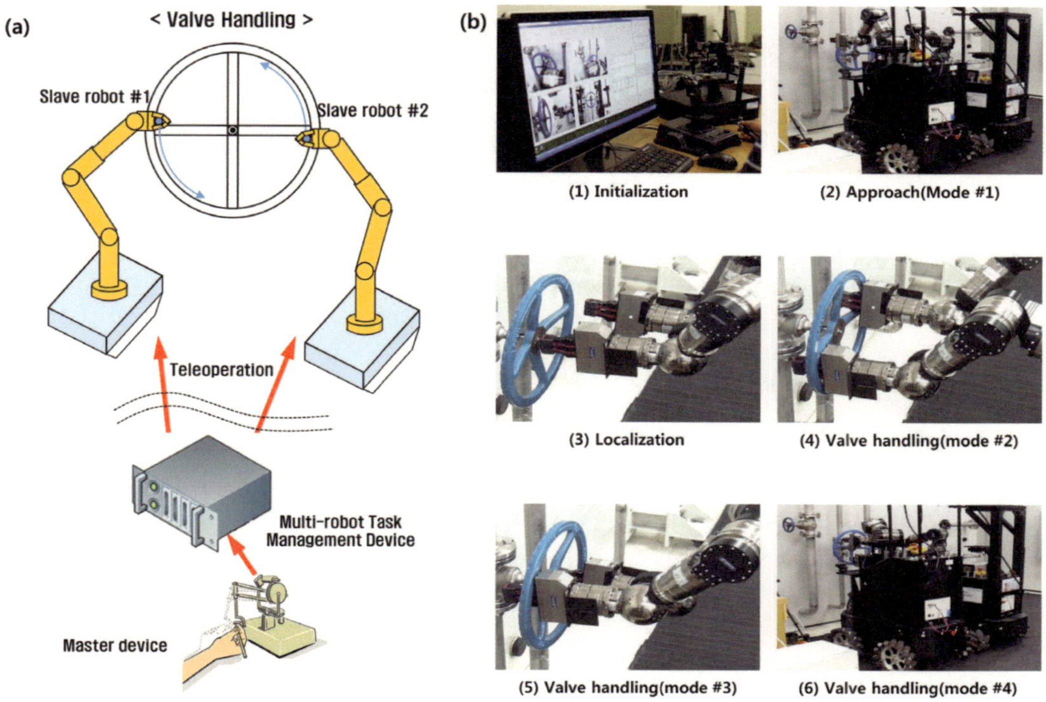

Figure 6. Experiment of a SOMR system. (a) Experimental setup and (b) experiment process.

	1:1 (s)	1:2 (s)	Decrement ratio (%)
1st	72.9	56.6	16.3
2nd	83.4	68.5	14.9
3rd	80.9	69.0	11.9
4th	99.5	70.9	28.6
5th	101.3	79.1	22.2

Table 1. Comparison of working time between 1:1 teleoperated robot system and 1:N (N = 2) teleoperated robot system.

5. Conclusion

This chapter is presented as a research in the area of multiagent systems. Research in the area of multiagent and multi-robot systems is concerned with the effective coordination of autonomous agents to perform tasks so as to achieve high quality overall system performance. Multiagent coordination challenges include the lack of single point of control, local views of each agent that provide only incomplete information, private goals and solution procedures of the agents, communication asynchrony, dynamic environments, and uncertainty. In the case of robotic remote maintenance, such as the proposed 1:*N* teleoperated robotic system in this chapter, the research focuses on robot software architectures for multi-robot coordination, task planning for automated maintenance, detecting when multiagent motions are likely to fail, and replanning to reformulate cooperation mode to enable humans and robots to seamlessly switch control from one to another. The proposed IRM software was developed for improved maintenance work efficiency (including valve handling) in an offshore plant, but further study will be conducted to expand the application of the system to fields involving high dimensional tasks. Studies will be conducted to verify the practical application of the IRM software to a variety of industries.

Acknowledgements

This work was supported by the Industrial Strategic technology development program, 10040132, Development of a Tele-Service Engine and Tele-Robot Systems with Multi-Lateral Feedback, funded by the Ministry of Knowledge Economy (MKE, Korea) and DGIST R&D Program of the Ministry of Science, ICT ,and Future Planning of Korea (17-ST-01, 17-IT-03).

Author details

Seungyeol Lee* and Jeon-Il Moon

*Address all correspondence to: syl@dgist.ac.kr

Collaboration Robotics Convergence Research Center, DGIST, South Korea

References

[1] Sheridan TB. Teleoperation, telerobotics and telepresence: A progress report. Journal of Control Engineering Practice. 1955;**3**(2):205–214

[2] Hokayem PF, Spong MW. Bilateral teleoperation: An historical survey. Automatica. 2006;**42**(12):2035–2057

[3] Heikkila T, Jarviluoma M, Juntunen T. Holonic control for manufacturing systems: Functional design of a manufacturing robot cell. Integrated Computer-Aided Engineering. 1997;**4**(3):202–218

[4] Yamada H, Tao N, Dingxuan Z. Construction tele-robot system with virtual reality. In: Proceedings of the Robotics, Automation and Mechatronics; September 2008; China. USA: IEEE; 2008. pp. 21–24

[5] Zhao D, Yamada H, Huang H, Gong W, Xia Y. 6 DOF presentation of realistic motion in operating a construction tele-robot system. In Proceedings of the JFPS International Symposium on Fluid Power. 2002;**2002**:507–512

[6] Kwon DS, Woo KY, Song SK, Kim WS, Cho HS. Microsurgical tele-robot system. In: Proceedings of International Conference on Intelligent Robots and Systems; 17–17 October 1998; Victoria BC. USA: IEEE; 1998. 945–950

[7] Geerinck T, Colon E, Berrabah SA, Cauwerts K, Sahli H. Tele-robot with shared autonomy: Distributed navigation development frame work. Integrated Computer-Aided Engineering. 2006;**12**(4):329–345

[8] Backes PG, Mark WS. Bilateral teleoperation: An historical survey. Automatica. 2006; **42**(12):2035–2057

[9] Backes PG, Tso KS. UMI: An interactive supervisory and shared control system for telerobotics. IEEE International Conference on Robotics and Automation; 13–18 May 1990; Cincinnati, OH. USA: IEEE; 1990. pp. 1096–1101

[10] Douglas A, Xu H. Real-time shared control system for space telerobotics. Intelligent Robots and Systems '93, IROS '93. In: Proceedings of the 1993 IEEE/RSJ International Conference on; 26–30 July 1993; Yokohama, Japan. USA: IEEE; 1993. pp. 2117–2122

[11] Hayati S, Venkataraman ST. Design and implementation of a robot control system with traded and shared control capability. In: Proceedings, 1989 International Conference on Robotics and Automation; 14–19 May 1989; Scottsdale, USA. USA: IEEE; 1989. pp. 1310–1315

[12] Crandall JW, Goodrich MA. Characterizing efficiency of human robot interaction: a case study of shared-control teleoperation. IEEE/RSJ International Conference on Intelligent Robots and Systems. 2002;**3**:1290–1295

[13] Ali KS, Arkin RC. Multiagent tele autonomous behavioral control. Machine Intelligence and Robotic Control. 2000;**1**(2):3–10

[14] Boer ER, Nakayama O, Futami T, Nakamura T. Development of a steering entropy method for evaluating driver workload. International Congress and Exposition. 1999;**1**:1–10

[15] Conway L, Volz RA, Walker MW. Teleautonomous systems: Projecting and coordinating intelligent action at a distance. IEEE Transactions on Robotics and Autonomation. 1990; **6**(2):146–158

[16] Crandall JW, Goodrich MA. Experiments in adjustable autonomy. IEEE Systems, Man, and Cybernetics. 2001;**3**:1624–1629

[17] Fong T, Thorpe C, Baur C. A safeguarded teleoperation controller. IEEE International Conference on Advanced Robotics (ICAR). ISBN 963-7154-05-1, Budapest, Hungary, August, 2001

[18] Krotkov E, Simmons R, Cozman F, Koenig S. Safeguarded teleoperation for lunar rovers: from human factors to field trials. Proc. IEEE Workshop on Planetary Rover Technology and Systems, Minneapolis, MN, April, 1996:1–20

[19] Sheridan TB. Telerobotics, Autonomation, and Human Supervisory Control. Cambridge: The MIT Press; 1992:180–181

[20] Stein MR. Behavior-based control for time-delayed teleoperation [PhD Dissertation]. University of Pennsylvania; 1994

Section 5

Data Mining and Image Processing

Chapter 7

Multiagent System for Image Mining

Nicksson Ckayo Arrais de Freitas and
Marcelino Pereira dos Santos Silva

Additional information is available at the end of the chapter

http://dx.doi.org/10.5772/intechopen.69353

Abstract

The overdone growth, wide availability, and demands for remote sensing databases combined with human limits to analyze such huge datasets lead to a need to investigate tools, techniques, methodologies, and theories capable of assisting humans at extracting knowledge. Image mining arises as a solution to extract implicit knowledge intelligently and semiautomatically or other patterns not explicitly stored in the huge image databases. However, spatial databases are among the ones with the fastest growth due to the volume of spatial information produced many times a day, demanding the investigation of other means for knowledge extraction. Multiagent systems are composed of multiple computing elements known as agents that interact to pursuit their goals. Agents have been used to explore information in the distributed, open, large, and heterogeneous platforms. Agent mining is a potential technology that studies ways of interaction and integration between data mining and agents. This area brought advances to the technologies involved such as theories, methodologies, and solutions to solve relevant issues more precisely, accurately and faster. AgentGeo is evidence of this, a multiagent system of satellite image mining that, promotes advances in the state of the art of agent mining, since it relevant functions to extract knowledge from spatial databases.

Keywords: remote sensing, database, image mining, multiagent system, agent, agent mining, data mining, AgentGeo

1. Introduction

Technological advances have provided new ways to collect spatial data: satellites, radars, unmanned air vehicle, balloons, and many others. These instruments caused an enormous accumulation of images data on remote sensing databases for many reasons. These databases are the ones with the fastest growth due to the volume of spatial information produced all day long.

The systematic and intelligent analyses of the remote sensing images provide a unique opportunity for understanding how, when, and where changes take place in our world. Precious information exploited from spatial repositories has been promoting benefits on many areas, such as agricultural [1, 2] (forecast of harvests and soil erosion), hydric [3] (use of water resources and verification of the water quality), urban [4] (urban planning and demographic inferences), forest [5–7] (monitoring deforestation and biomass control), limnology [8] (characterization of aquatic vegetation and identification of water types), meteorology [9] (weather and climate studies), air traffic [10] (information for safety in the air), and national security [11] (military strategic planning of operations and missions).

However, the manual analysis of huge databases is an extremely inconvenient task for human experts. Despite professionals such as physicists, meteorologists, and ecologists trained to analyze spatial data, the semi-automatic and intelligent interpretation of these data can be a useful tool to leverage the monitoring of the earth surface.

Data mining (DM) arises as solution to detect precious patterns semiautomatically and intelligently in huge databases. DM is defined as the nontrivial process of identifying valid, novel, potentially useful, and ultimately understandable patterns in data [12, 13]. Image mining (IM) is also a challenging field which extends traditional data mining from structured data to unstructured data such as image data [14]. IM deals with the extraction of implicit knowledge, image data relationships, or other patterns not explicitly stored in the huge image databases such as remote sensing and medical database.

Despite the success in different applications, the research community of DM has dealt with some issues mining methodology, user interaction, efficiency and scalability, diversity of database models, and data mining and society [15]. The efficiency and scalability issue is particularly significant as the amount of data currently available are increasing rapidly day by day. Therefore, it is necessary to investigate new technological resources that improve some of these issues.

A multiagent system (MAS) is composed of multiple computing elements, known as agents that interact to pursuit their goals. Agents have software architecture for decision-making systems that are embedded in an environment. Consequently, this technology has been widely adopted in numerous applications to solve significant issues.

Agent mining is a new area under development that deals with interaction and integration of between data mining and intelligent agents, and aims to join resources to solve relevant problems that cannot be tackled by a single technology with the same quality and performance. This technology provides important resources, and promises to solve particular issues of both technologies involved.

In this chapter, we present an introduction about image mining, multiagent systems, and agent mining, as well as an overview of these areas. Besides that, a tool known as AgentGeo will be presented [16–18]. It is a multiagent system for satellite image mining that uses the agent resources to mine image data in remote sensing databases. AgentGeo improves the analysis and application of satellite image mining when compared to other systems. The agents leverage the process of image mining due to properties such as autonomy, interaction, reaction, and initiative. This system has been developed in Java and its functionalities are the creation, edition

http://dx.doi.org/10.5772/intechopen.69353

and selection of agents, selection and creation of the environment, and the use of agents to mine the satellite images. These agents can support many tasks of the image mining process, as well as improve the performance of the steps of preprocessing, transformation and feature extraction, and classification and evaluation.

The chapter is structured as follows: Section 2 discusses image mining, Section 3 describes multiagent systems, Section 4 presents the agent mining, Section 5 focuses on AgentGeo, and finally, Section 6 presents conclusion and mentions future research work.

2. Image mining

Data from computing systems are produced constantly, thereby causing the unbridled growth in the institutions, industries, and corporations databases. This explosive development is caused by several factors, including: internet versatility, reduction in the price of data storage devices, improvement of data collection tools, popularity of embedded systems, increasing of online work, among others. In addition, data are being made available in various formats such as video, text, image, and spreadsheet.

The data variety and volume are so immense that relevant information becomes hidden within databases. Unfortunately, it is difficult or even impossible for a human being to detect patterns handling huge and diversified databases. Several specialists such as economists, statisticians, forecasters, and communication engineers worked with the idea that patterns from data can be reached automatically, identified, validated, and used for various purposes [19]. Therefore, the need to assist the specialist in the extraction of knowledge from huge databases originated the knowledge discovery databases (KDD).

KDD is defined as the nontrivial process of identifying valid, novel, potentially useful, and ultimately understandable patterns in data [12]. This process is composed by the following steps selection, preprocessing, transformation, data mining, and interpretation/evaluation [12, 13]. Data mining (DM) is a particular step in KDD process, where specific algorithms for extracting patterns are applied [12, 13]. However, the term data mining has become popular in the database field, used by statisticians and data analyst like synonymous for KDD.

Data mining technology is application oriented and incorporates a variety of techniques, tools, and algorithms capable of extracting relevant information from a wide and diversified collection of databases. Image mining (IM) is a potential technology for data mining, and also a challenging field which extends traditional data mining from structured data to unstructured data such as satellite images, medical images, and digital pictures. Structured data patterns are different from unstructured data patterns. Extracted patterns from image databases are not easily interpreted and understood. Consequently, IM is considered more than just an extension of data mining. It is an interdisciplinary endeavor that incorporates knowledge of important areas such as machine learning, image processing, computer vision, data mining, database, and artificial intelligence [20, 21].

In fact, IM is different from computer vision and image processing. The focus of these areas is extracting specific features from a single image, whereas the IM makes efforts for extraction patterns stored in the huge image databases. This implies in all aspects of databases such as the indexing scheme, the storage of images, and the image retrieval [20, 21].

The image mining process is shown in **Figure 1**. Everything starts from an image database where data are being stored. There are often inconsistent data that need to pass through a preprocessing step in order to improve the level of database quality. Image processing techniques are applied on this step, which are mathematical operations to change the pixel values of images, such as filtering, histogram equalization, image subtraction, image restoration, and others [22]. In the transformation and feature extraction, the images undergo some transformations until identified the relevant objects present in these data. Then features from these objects are extracted, such as edge shape, texture, and length. Obtained such features, the mining step can be carried out using data mining techniques to discover significant patterns automatically or semiautomatically. These patterns need to be evaluated and interpreted by a specialist to obtain the knowledge, which can be applied to applications and can be useful on decision-making processes or on problem understanding.

Image mining process is analogous to data mining process. However, there are important differences between relational databases and image databases [20]. Some differences are as follows:

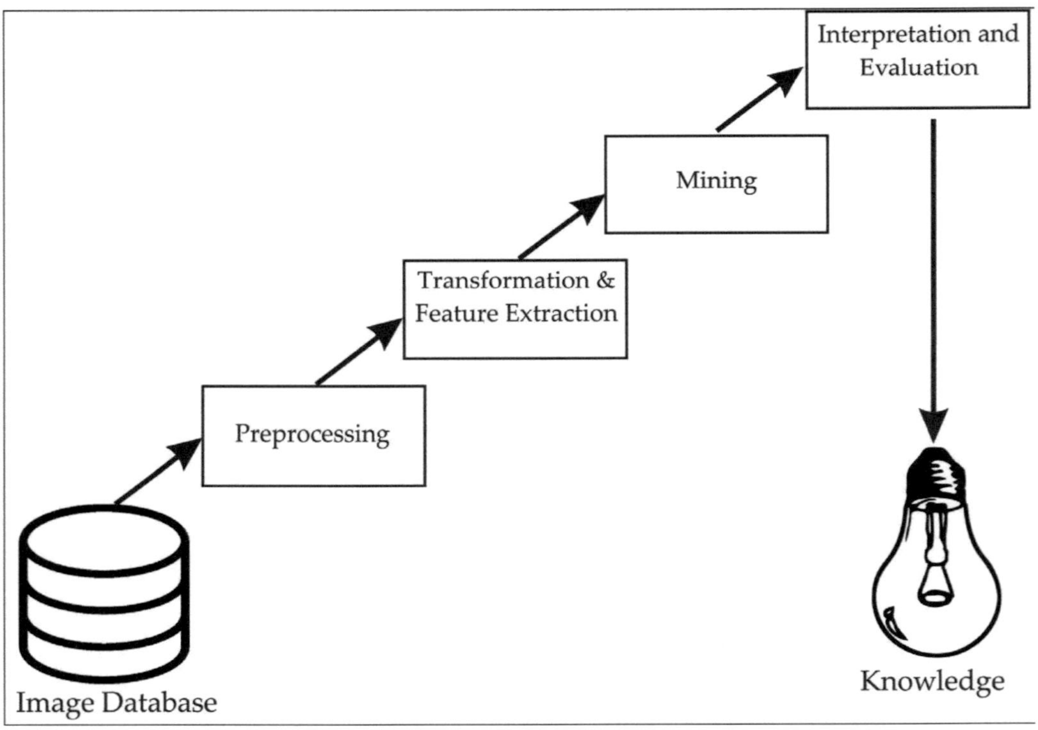

Figure 1. Image mining process [20].

- *Domain dependency*. Real-world activities belong to a given domain, and consequently have specific features and elements. In relational databases, the data values are semantically meaningful. However, at image databases, the identification of elements, their classes, and relationships are linked to the context itself, and a same image can have different information inherent to different domains.
- *Spatial information* (independent versus dependent position). In image databases, a simple image is composed by several elements (pixels). Each pixel is related to its neighbors, often forming a homogeneous region. Due to this, the image miners try to overcome this problem by extracting position-independent features from images before mining useful patterns.
- *Unique versus multiple interpretation*. In relational databases, the data values are easily understood. For example, field person is Paul; we already understood that the field stores a person's name. However, in image databases, an image data may reproduce ambiguous interpretations for the same visual pattern. For example, a simple intensity data can be seen like red, orange, or yellow.

Image mining is a promising and vast field, incorporating mature techniques. Despite the field is under development, there are techniques frequently used for object recognition, image indexing and retrieval, image classification and clustering, association rule mining, and neural network [23–26]. Besides that, image mining has become increasingly important die to its application in many areas such as health, meteorology, aerospace, agriculture, industry, air traffic, spatial research, among others.

2.1. GeoDMA: geographic data mining analyst

Satellite image mining, also known as remote sensing image mining, is an image mining process. Remote sensing image mining deals specifically with the challenge of capturing patterns, processes, and agents present in the geographic space, in order to extract specific knowledge for problem understanding or decision making related to a set of relevant topics, including land change, climate variations, and biodiversity studies. Events like deforestation patterns, weather change correlations, and species dynamics are examples of precious knowledge contained in remote sensing image repositories [27].

The spatial and multiband characteristics of the satellite images differ from the general category of image data. Therefore, remote sensing image mining demands specific image mining tools. GeoDMA is a toolbox for remote sensing image mining that arose based on methodology proposed by Silva et al. [28]. The software incorporates resources for segmentation, feature selection, feature extraction, classification, and multitemporal methods for change detection and analysis of remote sensing data [29].

GeoDMA works as a plugin of the software TerraView GIS [30], which provides the interface for the interpreter to visualize the geographic information stored in databases, to control the database, and also to display the objects' properties [31]. The image mining process in the GeoDMA is shown in **Figure 2**. This process is composed by five steps which described below:

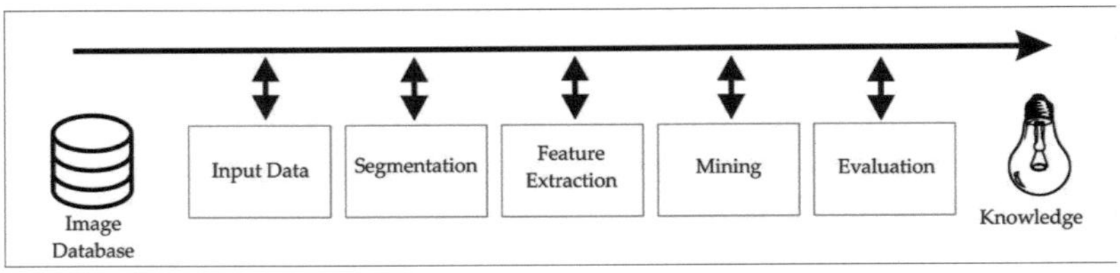

Figure 2. Image mining process at GeoDMA.

2.1.1. Input data

This step is responsible for image selection. GeoDMA can only manipulate one image at a time. Therefore, it is necessary to define an image as input for segmentation process.

2.1.2. Segmentation

Segmentation is a process where an image pass through various transformations to detect its regions or objects. The level of detail to a segmentation process depends on the application purpose. This means that a segmentation process should stop when all important objects or regions of the application have been detected [29]. Therefore, segmentation is one of the most challenging tasks into digital image processing. The GeoDMA provides four segmentation algorithms as follows:

- Region growing approach based on Ref. [32]
- Segmentation approach based on Ref. [33]
- Chessboard segmentation
- Algorithm based on Ref. [34].

2.1.3. Feature extraction

This process aims to extraction attributes as well as spectral and spatial features of objects from the images. Spectral features relate all pixel values inside a region, therefore include metrics for maximum and minimum pixel values, or mean values such as amplitude, dissimilarity, and pixels mean. Spatial features measure the shapes of the regions, including height, width, or rotation [31].

2.1.4. Mining

Mining is the process where the algorithms to find a set of models (or functions) are defined, which describe and distinguish classes or concepts. The GeoDMA provides two ways for mining [31]:

- Supervised classification using decision trees based on Ref. [35] and
- Unsupervised classification using self-organizing maps (SOM) [31].

Supervised classification can be divided in two process training and classification. Training is a process supervised by specialists, where data class to known objects is identified, and models to classification of objects are designed. Classification is a process where the build models are used to detect objects that are still unknown. Unsupervised classification is a process that searches for interpretable patterns in data and describe them forming regions known as cluster. The search is based on spectral features such as variance, mean, and light intensity.

2.1.5. Evaluation

The output of GeoDMA is a thematic map. At image mining process, specialists should analyze whether the results are satisfying to application. In the decision tree classification model, the specialist should check whether the regions classified by the built models are valid. In the classifier SOM, generally the result produces more clusters than the desired patterns. In this case, the specialist is responsible for label the patterns according to the application. However, if the results are not satisfactory in both process, previous tasks may be executed again [31].

3. Multiagent system

An agent is anything that can be viewed as perceiving its environment through sensors and acting upon that environment through actuators [36]. Perception refers to input information received by agents at a certain moment. In general, the choice of its action at any instant may depend on the entire sequence of observed perceptions. These perceptions can occur through the physical world, via graphical interface, a collection of agents, the internet, or perhaps all combined [37]. The environment, which typically is both computational and physical, might be open or closed, and might or might not contain other agents.

Agents have properties such as autonomy, social ability, reactivity, and proactiveness [37]. Autonomy is the ability to analyze the environment and take their own decisions without the intervention of humans or other agents, controlling their acts and internal state. Social ability is the agent's ability to communicate with other agents or even with human beings using some kind of communication language. Reactivity is the agent's ability to respond in a timely manner, given a history of perception. Proactiveness (or initiative) refers to the agent's capacity of taking initiative in order to achieve their goals. These properties make agents of a technology capable of the following: cooperate in solving problems; share expertise; work in parallel on common problems; develop and implemented modularly; be fault tolerant through redundancy; represent multiple viewpoints and the knowledge of multiple experts; and mainly be reusable.

We can consider four basic kinds of agents: simple reflex agents, model-based reflex agents, goal-based agents, and utility-based agents [36].

- *Simple reflex agents*. Agents that select their actions based on current perception, ignoring the rest of the perceptual history.

- *Model-based reflex agents*. They are a simple reflex agent, but with some differences. These agents maintain some sort of internal state that depends on the perception history and thereby reflects at least some of the unobserved aspects of the current state.
- *Goal-based agents*. These agents know some sort of information about their goals. Based on this information and with internal state, these agents analyze and take their actions.
- *Utility-based agents*. These agents know some sort of information about their goals and have internal state. Besides that, there is a utility function that measures goal performance. This way, these agents choose actions to maximize its utility function.

Agents can learn new concepts and techniques, they can adapt to the needs of different users, they can anticipate the needs of the user, besides others abilities. During the last years, agents have become a powerful technology, which have been adopted in several applications as a solution to solve complex issues that cannot be solved by humans. In the area of remote sensing, for example, a complex task is to analyze remote sensing images, a human being is able to analyze a single remote sensing image, but analyze a significant amount of this data is unlikely because of limited human ability to reason and interpret huge information volumes.

However, when a simple agent cannot solve the problem, a MAS can be implemented. These systems have been studied since 1980s, but were only recognized in the mid of the 1990s. At that time, scientific and industrial interests raised due to the need of exploiting information and modern computing platforms, as well as distributed, open, large and heterogeneous ones [38]. A MAS is formed by two or more agents that interact between them to solve some specific problem. In general, the agents act on behalf of users with different goals. However, agents also may have the same goals, this is determined by the purpose of the system. The interaction in the system occurs through exchanging messages, and it is determined by the ability to coordinate, cooperate, and negotiate between agents [38].

Coordination is a property which aims performing some activity in a shared environment. The degree of coordination is determined by the extent to which they avoid extraneous activity by reducing resource contention, avoiding livelock and deadlock, and maintaining applicable safety conditions [39]. In general, we consider a relevant degree of coordination, when agent activities activities agents are well balanced inside of the environment as well as the operations are being distributed and involved among agents without any failure. There are some reasons why multiple agents need to be coordinated [40], which are as follows:

- Their goals may be conflicting.
- Their goals may be interdependent.
- Agents may have different capabilities and different knowledge.
- Their goals can quickly achieve if different agents work together in a coordinated way.

Cooperation is coordination among nonantagonistic agents, while negotiation is coordination among competitive or simply self-interested agents [39]. At the MAS, agents can cooperate with each other to general goals of the system, or they can compete for their individual goals. Both features must be determined according to the general purpose of the agents into the application.

In the MAS, a key issue is how the agents will communicate. In particular, the communication among processes has long been an important research problem in computer science. In fact, concurrent processes need to be synchronized if there is a possibility that they can interfere with one another in a destructive way [41].

For example, being P1 and P2 two processes, which have access to some shared variable V, when P1 begins to update the value of V, P2 may act at the same moment, but without interfere in the P1 acts. Such communication among processes is like communication among agents. Among other reasons, agents communicate in order to coordinate actions more effectively, to distribute more accurate models of the environment, and to learn subtask solutions from one another [42]. This communication can be implemented through a determined programming language (for example, Java) or can be used an agent communication language like knowledge query and manipulation language (KQML) [41]. There are two types of communication in the multiagent systems [42]:

- *Direct communication*: agents are able to communicate with each other using direct message exchange mechanisms between them. These mechanisms may be constrained in terms of throughput, latency, locality, and agent class.
- *Indirect communication*: consists of indirect transfer of information between agents. For example, when an agent wants to send a message to other agent, it relies on the mediating agent who is responsible for the exchange of information within the environment.

Multiagent systems are increasingly being implemented in several applications such as industry, distributed applications, applications for the internet, games, air traffic control, and teaching environment (e.g., distance education sites). MAS have become more and more important in many aspects of computer science such as distributed artificial intelligence, distributed computing systems, robotics, and artificial life. Some reasons to implement a MAS are

- When the system is complex and the human being cannot or is unable to predict the behavior of that system.
- When it is expensive to keep a team of specialists working.
- When the activity involved put humans at risk.
- When the decision-making process requires performance, agents can solve the problem quickly using parallel processing.
- When it is necessary to ensure information privacy.

4. Multiagent system for image mining

Given the overview of multiagent systems and image mining, we have seen that the areas of agents and data mining emerged separately. Both independent research streams have been created and originally evolving with separate aims and objectives. The area of agents, for example, aims to study the autonomous and independent behavior of agents, and data mining, more comprehensively, dealt with the KDD process. Despite emerged separately, several similar aspects of these areas appear such as user-system interaction, human roles and involvement, constraints, dynamic modeling, life-cycle and process management, domain factor, and organizational and social factors [43].

Agents is a powerful technology, generally used to solve complex problems in distributed environments where agents can cooperate, coordinate, and communicate their activities in order to reduce the complexity of the problem. Agent research focuses on theoretical, methodological, technical, experimental, and practical issues and the means to handle system complexities [44]. Agent technologies have been contributing to many diverse domains such as software engineering, user interfaces, e-commerce, information retrieval, robotics, computer games, education and training, ubiquitous computing, and social simulation.

Data mining is an application-oriented technology that employs techniques, tools, and algorithms capable of extracting relevant information (or patterns) semi-automatically and intelligently from a massive and diversified collection of datasets. Data mining has been used in web mining services, text mining, medical data mining, meteorological data mining, governmental services, fraud detections, securities, and bioinformatics.

Agents and data mining deal with their specific problems and limitations. Both areas face critical challenges that the other technology might contribute. Agents can leverage the KDD process on data selection, extraction, preprocessing, and integration, and they are an excellent choice for peer-to-peer, parallel, and distributed computing. Agents can bridge the gap between humans and software systems by acting as interfaces that can sense and affect human-mining needs or multisource mining [44]. In the same way, the knowledge acquired through data mining processes provides more stable, predictable, and controllable models for dispatching and planning, and can be used for learning on multiagent systems.

Therefore, agents are elements that can leverage the data mining process, and data mining can contribute significantly to agent's area. A few years ago, researchers have studied means of joining forces between agent and data mining technologies. These studies have given rise to a new research field which became known as agent mining [44–49] or agent-mining interaction and integration [43, 50–52]. Agent mining is the most popular term.

Agent mining refers to the methodologies, principles, techniques, and applications for the integration and interaction of agents and data mining, as well as the community that focuses on the study of the complementarity between these two technologies, for better addressing issues that cannot be tackled by a single technology with the same quality and performance [44, 49].

Agent-mining area is under development; therefore, some issues demands research on theoretical, technological, and methodological aspects. This area follows two fronts of research, which are

- Agent-driven distributed data mining (otherwise known as multiagent-driven data mining, and multiagent data mining): studies ways to use agents to enhance data mining processes and systems. Agents can be used in data mining for different purposes such as agent-based data mining system, agent-based data warehouse, agents for information retrieval, mobile agents for distributed data mining, among others [49].

- Data mining driven agents: investigates issues related to the proper and formal representation of extracted knowledge models from data mining applications such as collaborative learning in multiagents, data mining driven agent learning, reasoning, adaptation and evolution, data mining-driven multiagent communication, planning and dispatching, data mining agent intelligence enhancement [52].

According to Seydim [53], in several steps for knowledge discovery, an agent can be used to automate the individual tasks, including data preprocessing, data mining as well as search for patterns of interest using learning and intelligence in classification, clustering, summarization, and generalization. For example, in the data mining step, an agent can perform automatic sensitivity analysis to determine which parameters should be used in learning. This would reduce the dependency of having domain experts available to examine the problem every time something changes in the environment. The great advantage of using agents in automation of data mining is indicated as their possible support for online transaction data mining [53].

This way, agents can also support and enhance the image mining process in some steps:

- Preprocessing: When an image is added in a database or when it is defined the image database, an agent can perceive these events and automatically examine the data. If the agents perceive anomalies on these images, it can automatically use digital image processing techniques to deal with them. Agent acts can be taken based on rules built by a specialist. This reduces the dependence of having domain experts available for analyzing several images.

- Transformation and feature extraction: agents can be subordinated to transformation and feature extraction task. They can be trained to work together in a much faster way on data transformation, on detecting objects and on the segmentation process.

- Mining: agents can discover significant patterns automatically or semi-automatically in image databases. For example, on classification process, agents can be trained by specialists and can perform intelligently the classification process. Besides that, agents can specialize in one standard and the process may be carried out by several agents simultaneously. This certainly increases the performance and accuracy of the classification process.

- Interpretation and evaluation: knows itself that the evaluation of knowledge is realized usually performed by specialists. In general, specialists have experience in data analysis of a particular domain. In fact, agents can learn with specialists about a particular domain, that is, they can perform this task to support or even substitute the specialists.

Agent mining is a new area with huge opportunities that brings several advantages to multiagent systems, data mining, and machine learning, as well as new derived theories, tools and applications that are beyond any individual technology. The following section presents AgentGeo, a multiagent system of satellite image mining. The tool employs agent to leverage the image mining process, and uses the knowledge of image mining process to agent learning.

5. AgentGeo

AgentGeo emerged based on the ideas proposed by [16, 17], which used agents to mine remote sensing images. This tool is being developed in Java language, and its initial version works along with GeoDMA and TerraView. This system brings advances in the state-of-the-art of multiagent systems and image mining, presenting relevant resources and precious functionalities. For example, this system implements functions such as creation, edition and selection of agents, selection and creation of the environment and use of agents for image mining. Moreover, it is capable of performing the classification process with multiple images at a time, differently from GeoDMA that is limited to only one image during the entire image mining process.

5.1. System architecture

The system architecture is shown in **Figure 3**.

The image mining process begins in TerraView, which provides the structure to insert and view the images. In fact, the database are created, and several images are inserted. GeoDMA is responsible for processing the data, therefore it receives a single image at a time, and segment and extract the characteristics of each one. These processed images are stored in the image database. AgentGeo connects to the same image database, and receives as input the processed data. So, the environment for the agents can be created, that is, the user defines the image process through GeoDMA. After that, the mining agents responsible for automatically mining these images are defined; that is an automatic process performed by agents and has as output the mined images. These images are stored in the image database, and can be visualized through TerraView. However, AgentGeo provides statistical data about the mining performed by agents, such the number of segments classified by agents. Each process presented may be performed several times.

5.2. Agent's structure

There are two agent types implemented at AgentGeo: the simple agents and a monitor agent. These agents have different properties, features, goals, functions, and behaviors. The simple agents are simple reflex ones, that is, they select their actions based on current perception, ignoring the rest of the perceptual history. Agent's perception occurs in the moment that a user defines the environment and selects the agents on the AgentGeo. Agents have a degree of autonomy, when they are pursuing their particular goals on mining process. The user is not able to forecast the agent actions, because they autonomously decide which goals to pursue.

Besides that, simple agents compete for their goals at the environment just looking to their own well-being, and when their goals conflict with other agents, a monitor agent is responsible for coordinating environmental disputes. For example, two simple agents "A" and "B" are in conflict because of resource at the environment. Soon, the monitor agent perceives the conflict, and takes initiative to finish it. Despite the monitor agent also be a simple reflex agent, we can notice that the behavior of the monitor agent is different from the simple agent. The monitor agent is cooperative and it has the ability to communicate with other agents.

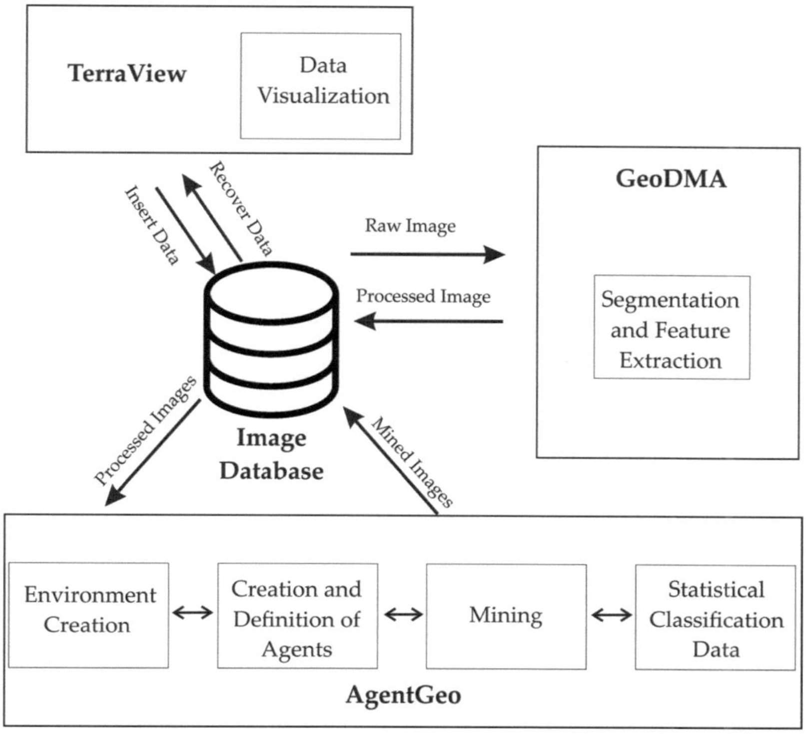

Figure 3. Image mining system architecture.

The communication at the environment occurs indirectly as shown in **Figure 4**. Simple agents only store information about their goals, whereas the monitor agent has the overview of the environment and knows the other agents. Thus, this communication architecture partially solves the communication, coordination, and negotiation problems and considerably reduces the complexity of the MAS.

The agents are implemented through a thread structure and they can perceive and act simultaneously in a certain environment. The simple agents are built by the user, and their internal structure consists of: a description (agent's name), a knowledge base (information about their goals obtained in the training step), and a metadata (extra information about the agent for the usability). This development has four steps as illustrated in **Figure 5**.

Any agent needs a knowledge base to reason about their acts. That base is built through the training phase carried out in GeoDMA and after that comes the segmentation and extraction of features. The agent's knowledge base is formed by a decision tree structure. Firstly, it is defined the image database, and the images are preprocessed on the segmentation and features extraction step. At training step, segment samples that are known to users referring to a specific class are selected by them, according to the agent goals referring to a specific class according to the agent goals. After that, the users can generate a decision tree using GeoDMA, which provides a resource to build it adapted for spatial data mining using the supervised algorithm C4.5 [35].

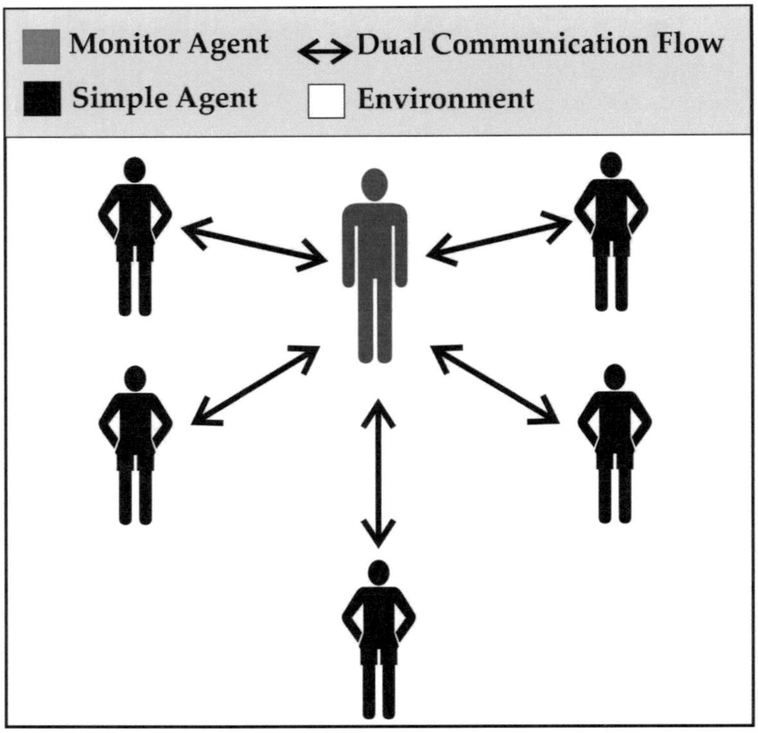

Figure 4. Communication architecture at AgentGeo.

With the decision tree model generated by GeoDMA, the mining step happens automatically. That process is performed by means of thresholds referring to the spatial and spectral attributes of the segments present in the image. All the steps are performed several times in order to have a consistent model. If the user identifies that the results of the model are not satisfactory, he can return to previous steps and perform them again. Otherwise, the model will serve as the knowledge base for the agent, which integration step occurs when the user creates the agent within AgentGeo, that is, the user informs name, metadata, and the knowledge base to the agent.

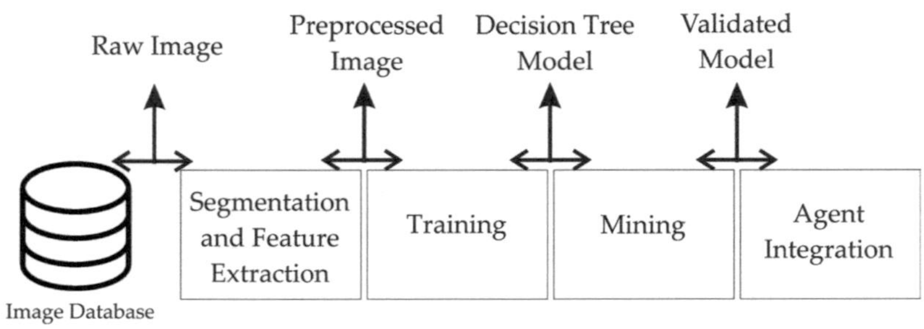

Figure 5. Steps for agent construction at AgentGeo.

All agents of AgentGeo are stored on"agentes.dat" file and can be used whenever necessary. For instance, consider the development of an agent that aims to detect water bodies. The image database is defined, and the images are preprocessed one at a time using GeoDMA. The users select several samples of water bodies and several samples of what is not water bodies. A decision tree model is gendered, and the mining process occurs at GeoDMA. After the user analyzed and evaluated positively the models, he can create the agent in AgentGeo.

5.3. Case study

In this section, we will briefly describe two case studies presented in Ref. [17]. The purpose is remote sensing images mining to detect exposed fields, vegetation fields, and water body patterns in Rio Grande Do Norte state, and water bodies patterns in 15 cities of the Ceara state, Brazil. Therefore, three agents were created to detect these patterns, using the methodology for agents construction presented in 5.2 Section.

The image database is formed by LANDSAT-8 satellite images, which are available at <https://earthexplorer.usgs.gov/>. At first, image database is build using TerraView and satellite images are inserted. Second, the study region was delimited as well as the area of Rio Grande do Norte state and cities of the Ceara state using digital image processing techniques embedded in TerraView. Third, the images were segmented using the region growing algorithm implemented in GeoDMA, and the spatial and spectral features were extracted from the image database. Fourth, the AgentGeo is loaded, the environment is defined, and the mining agents, implemented in the tool, are selected. At last, the mining results are evaluated by visual inspection using Google Maps images.

This study shows that the methodology of AgentGeo is effective, reaching 92.66% of accuracy on first study and 95.04% on second study. It is important to make it clear that the results of the mining process would be the same if you used only GeoDMA for the mining process. However, the process would occur with one image at a time, which is different from AgentGeo approach, that is capable of mining multiple images, improving the performance of mining process, and keeping the results precision.

6. Conclusion

In this work, we proposed an approach on image mining, multiagent system, agent mining, and presented AgentGeo. In the image mining section, similarities and differences between image mining, data mining, and image mining process were presented. GeoDMA is a toolbox for remote sensing image mining. At the multiagent system section, concepts, proprieties, features, behaviors, structure, and applications about agents and multiagent system were described. Multiagent system for image mining section presented an overview about the new area known as agent mining; we presented and suggested improvements in the integration and interaction of agents and data mining, and of multiagent and image mining. Finally, AgentGeo was introduced, a multiagent system for image mining which uses agent mining to exploit remote sensing databases. This promising tool brings advances in the state-of-the-art in multiagent systems and image mining, due to relevant resources that leverage the image mining process.

As future work, we hope to integrate more resources into AgentGeo to provide operational advantages, optimization, and innovation. We concluded that agents can be used in several steps in image mining process, that is, we can use them and build modules at AgentGeo for the steps of preprocessing, transformation and feature extraction, and interpretation and evaluation. We can also expand the studies by creating other agents with different goals. For example, agents to road mining, to cloud mining, to deforestation mining, or to mine any spatial object.

Author details

Nicksson Ckayo Arrais de Freitas[1,2]* and Marcelino Pereira dos Santos Silva[1]

*Address all correspondence to: nickssonarrais@gmail.com

1 Rio Grande do Norte State University (UERN), Mossoró, RN, Brazil

2 Federal Rural University of the Semi-arid Region (UFERSA), Mossoró, RN, Brazil

References

[1] Aguiar DA, Rudorff BFT, Silva WF, Adami M, Mello MP. Remote sensing images in support of environmental protocol: Monitoring the sugarcane harvest in Sao Paulo State, Brazil. Remote Sensing. 2011;**3**(12):2682-2703. DOI: 10.3390/rs3122682

[2] Alba JMF, Schroder VF, Nóbrega MRR. Land cover change detection in Southern Brazil through orbital imagery classification methods. In: Escalante B, editor. Remote Sensing—Applications. 1st ed. InTech; 2012. pp. 99-116. DOI: 10.5772/36940. Available from: https://www.intechopen.com/books/remote-sensing-applications/strategies-of-change-detection-in-southern-brazil-by-orbital-imagery-classification-methods

[3] Ding Z, Qi N, Dong F, Jinhui L, Wei Y, Shenggui Y. Application of multispectral remote sensing technology in surface water body extraction. In: International Conference Audio, Language and Image Processing (ICALIP); 2016. pp. 141-144. DOI: 10.1109/ICALIP.2016.7846565

[4] Matthieu KWK, Maeyer M, Wolff E. The mapping of the urban growth of Kinshasa (DRC) through high resolution remote sensing between 1995 and 2005. In: Escalante B, editor. Remote Sensing—Applications. 1st ed. InTech; 2012. pp. 463-478. DOI: 10.5772/38435. Available from: https://www.intechopen.com/books/remote-sensing-applications/the-mapping-of-the-urban-growth-of-kinshasa

[5] Sousa WRN, Couto MS, Castro AF, Silva MPS. Evaluation of desertification processes in Ouricuri-PE through trend estimates of times series. IEEE Latin America Transactions. 2013;**11**(1):602-606. DOI: 10.1109/TLA.2013.6502869

[6] Pizaña JMG, Hernández JMN, Romero NC. Remote sensing-based biomass estimation. Marghany M, editor. Environmental Applications of Remote Sensing. InTech; 2016. pp. 1-40. DOI: 10.5772/61813. Available from: https://www.intechopen.com/books/environmental-applications-of-remote-sensing/remote-sensing-based-biomass-estimation

[7] Maciel AM, Silva MPS, Escada MIS. Mining frequent substructures from deforestation objects. In: IEEE International. Geoscience and Remote Sensing Symposium (IGARSS). 2012. pp. 6745-6748. DOI: 10.1109/IGARSS.2012.6352557

[8] Cho HJ, Mishra D, Wood J. Remote sensing of submerged aquatic vegetation. In: Escalante B, editor. Remote Sensing—Applications. 1st ed. InTech; 2012. pp. 297-308. DOI: 10.5772/35156. Available from: https://www.intechopen.com/books/remote-sensing-applications/remote-sensing-of-submerged-aquatic-vegetation

[9] Ashraf A, Rustam M, Khan SI, Adnan M, Naz R. Remote sensing of the glacial environment influenced by climate change. In: Marghany M, editors. Environmental Applications of Remote Sensing. 1st ed. InTech; 2016. pp. 99-129. DOI: 10.5772/62134. Available from: https://www.intechopen.com/books/environmental-applications-of-remote-sensing/remote-sensing-of-the-glacial-environment-influenced-by-climate-change

[10] Zhang L, Zhang Y. Airport detection and aircraft recognition based on two-layer saliency model in high spatial resolution remote-sensing images. IEEE Journal of Selected Topics in Applied Earth Observations and Remote Sensing. 2016;**10**(4):1511-1524. DOI: 10.1109/JSTARS.2016.2620900

[11] Ardouin JP, Lévesque J, Roy V, Chestein YV, Faust A. Demonstration of hyperspectral image exploitation for military applications. In: Escalante B., editor. Remote Sensing—Applications. 1st ed. InTech; 2012. pp. 493-517. DOI: 10.5772/37681. Available from: https://www.intechopen.com/books/remote-sensing-applications/demonstration-of-hyperspectral-image-exploitation-for-military-applications

[12] Fayyad U, Piatetsky-Shapiro G, Smyth P. From data mining to knowledge discovery in databases. AI Magazine. 1996;**17**(3):37-52

[13] Fayyad U. Data mining and knowledge discovery in databases: Implications for scientific databases. In: Ninth International Conference on Scientific and Statistical Database Management; August 11-13. 1997; Olympia, Washington, USA. IEEE; 1997. pp. 2-11. DOI: 10.1109/SSDM.1997.621141

[14] Cao X, Wang S. Research about image mining technique. In: Communications and Information Processing, Aveiro, Portugal. Berlin Heidelberg: Springer-Verlag; 2012. pp. 127-134. DOI: 10.1007/978-3-642-31965-5_15

[15] Han J, Pei J, Kamber M. Data Mining: Concepts and Techniques. 3rd ed. Waltham, MA, USA: Elsevier; 2011. p. 703

[16] Moura CDG, De Freitas NCA, Silva MPS. Agentes de Mineração de Imagens. In: Proceeding of the XV Brazilian Symposium on GeoInformatics (GEOINFO), SP-Brazil; 2014. pp. 1-6

[17] De Freitas NCA, Filho PPR, Moura CDG, Silva MPS. AgentGeo: Multi-agent system of satellite images mining. IEEE Latin America Transactions. 2016;**14**(3):1343-1351. DOI: 10.1109/TLA.2016.7459619

[18] De Freitas NCA, Moura CDG, Silva MPS. Sistema multiagente para mineração de imagens de satélite. In: XVII Brazilian Symposium on Remote Sensing, PB-Brazil; 2015. pp. 7351-7358

[19] Witten IH, Frank E, Hall MA, Pal CJ. Data Mining: Practical Machine Learning Tools and Techniques. 4th ed. Cambridge, MA, United States: Todd Green; 2017. p. 621

[20] Hsu W, Lee ML, Zhang J. Image mining: Trends and developments. Journal of Intelligent Information Systems. 2002;**19**(1):7-23. DOI: 10.1023/A:1015508302797

[21] Zhang J, Wynne H, Lee ML. Image mining: Issues, frameworks and techniques. In: Proceedings of the Second International Conference on Multimedia Data Mining. Springer-Verlag; 2001. pp. 13-20

[22] Gonzales RC, Woods RE. Digital Image Processing. 3rd ed. Upper Saddle River, NJ, USA Pearson Education, Prentice Hall; 2008. p. 976

[23] Dey N, Karâa WBA, Chakraborty S, Banerjee S, Salem MMA, Azar AT. Image mining framework and techniques: A review. International Journal of Image Mining. 2015;**1**(1):45-64. DOI: http://dx.doi.org/10.1504/IJIM.2015.070028

[24] Kaur P, Kaur K. Review of different existing image mining techniques. International Journal of Advanced Research in Computer Science and Software Engineering. 2014;**4**(6):518-524

[25] Shukla VS, Vala J. A Survey on image mining, its techniques and application. International Journal of Computer Applications. 2016;**133**(9):12-15. DOI: 10.5120/ijca2016907978

[26] Tripathi A, Jangir H. A study on image mining methods and techniques. International Journal of Innovative Research in Computer and Communication Engineering. 2016;**4**(4):7047-7053. DOI: 10.15680/IJIRCCE.2016.0404136

[27] Silva MPS, Câmara G, Escada MIS. Image mining: Detecting deforestation patterns through satellites. In: Rahman H, editor. Data Mining Application for Empowering Knowledge Societies. UK/USA: IGI Global; 2009. pp. 54-75. DOI: 10.4018/978-1-59904-657-0.ch004

[28] Silva MPS, Câmara G, Souza RCM, Valeriano DM, Escada MIS. Mining patterns of change in remote sensing image databases. In: Fifth IEEE International Conference on Data Mining; November 2005; Houston, Texas, USA. Houston, Texas, USA: IEEE; 2005. p. 8. DOI: 10.1109/ICDM.2005.98

[29] Korting TS, Fonseca LMG, Câmara G. GeoDMA—Geographic data mining analyst. Computers & Geosciences. 2013;**57**:133-145. DOI: 10.1016/j.cageo.2013.02.007

[30] INPE. São José dos Campos, SP: INPE [Internet]. 2010 [Updated: TerraView 4.1.0]. Available from: www.dpi.inpe.br/terraview [Accessed: March 1, 2017]

[31] Korting TS. GEODMA: A toolbox integrating data mining with object-based and multi-temporal analysis of satellite remotely sensed imagery [thesis]. Sao Jose dos Campos, SP: INPE, Brazil; 2012. p. 97. Available from: http://urlib.net/8JMKD3MGP7W/3CCH86S

[32] Bins LSA, Fonseca LMG, Erthal GJ, Ii FM. Satellite imagery segmentation: A region growing approach. In: Brazilian Symposium on Remote Sensing; April 14-19, 1996; Brazil. Salvador: INPE; 1996. pp. 677-680

[33] Baatz M, Schape A. Multiresolution Segmentation–an Optimization Approach for High Quality Multi-Scale Image Segmentation. AGIT-Symposium Salzburg; 2000. pp. 12-23

[34] Korting TS, Fonseca LMG, Câmara G. A geographical approach to self-organizing maps algorithm applied to image segmentation. In: Advanced Concepts for Intelligent Vision Systems. Ghent, Belgium: Springer Berlin Heidelberg; 2011. pp. 162-170. DOI: 10.1007/978-3-642-23687-7_15

[35] Quinlan JR. Improved use of continuous attributes in C4.5. Journal of Artificial Intelligence Research. 1996;**4**(1):77-90. DOI: 10.1613/jair.279

[36] Russel ST, Norvig P. Artificial Intelligence: A Modern. 3rd ed. United States of America: Pearson Education; 2010. p. 1132

[37] Wooldridge M, Jennings N. Intelligent agents: Theory and practice. The Knowledge Engineering Review. 1995;**10**(2):115-152. DOI: 10.1017/S0269888900008122

[38] Wooldridge M. An Introduction to MultiAgent Systems. 2nd ed. United Kingdom: John Wiley & Sons Ltd; 2009. p. 462

[39] Weiss G. Multiagent Systems: A Modern Approach to Distributed Modern Approach to Artificial Intelligence. Cambridge, Massachusetts and London, England: The MIT Press; 2000. p. 620

[40] Bellifemine F, Caire G, Greenwood, D. Developing Multi-Agent Systems with JADE. 1st ed. United Kingdom: John Wiley & Sons Ltd; 2007. p. 285

[41] Wooldridge M. An introduction to Multiagent Systems. 1st ed. United Kingdom: John Wiley & Sons; 2002. p. 348

[42] Panait P, Luke S. Cooperative Multi-Agent Learning: The State of the Art. In: Autonomous Agents and Multi-Agent Systems. Springer Science; 2005;**11**(3):387-434. DOI: 10.1007/s10458-005-2631-2

[43] Silva CVS, Ralha CG. Detecção de Cartéis em Licitações Públicas com Agentes de Mineração de Dados. Revista Eletrônica de Sistema de Informações. 2011;**10**(1):1-19. DOI: 10:5329/RESI.2011.1001

[44] Cao L, Gorodetsky V, Mitkas PA. Agent mining: The synergy of agents and data mining. IEEE Computer Society; 2009;**24**(3):64-72. DOI: 10.1109/MIS.2009.45

[45] Cao L, Gorodetsky V, Mitkas PA. Agents and data mining. IEEE Computer Society. 2009;**24**(3):16-17. DOI: 10.1109/MIS.2009.54

[46] Cao L, Luo D, Zhang C. Ubiquitous intelligence in agent mining. In: Cao L, Gorodetsky V, Liu J, Weiss G, Philip SY, editors. Agents and Data Mining Interaction. Berlin Heidelberg: Springer; 2009;**24**(3):23-35. DOI: 10.1007/978-3-642-03603-3_3

[47] Cao L. Introduction to agent mining interaction and integration. In: Cao L, editor. Data Mining and Multi-Agent Integration. USA: Springer; 2009. pp. 3-36. DOI: 10.1007/978-1-4419-0522-2_1

[48] Cao L, Zhang C, Yu PS, Zhao Y. Agent-driven data mining. In: Cao L, Zhang C, Yu PS, Zhao Y, editors. Domain Driven Data Mining. USA: Springer; 2010. pp. 145-169. DOI: 10.1007/978-1-4419-5737-5_7

[49] Cao L, Weiss G, Yu PS. A brief introduction to agent mining. Autonomous Agents and Multi-Agent Systems. 2012;**25**(3):419-424. DOI: 10.1007/s10458-011-9191-4

[50] Ralha CG, Silva CVS. A multi-agent data mining system for cartel detection in Brazilian. Expert Systems with Applications. 2012;**39**(14):11642-11656

[51] Ralha CG. Towards the integration of multiagent applications and data mining. In: Cao L, editor. Data Mining and Multi-Agent Integration. USA: Springer; 2009. pp. 37-46. DOI: 10.1007/978-1-4419-0522-2_2

[52] Cao L, Luo C, Zhang C. Agent-mining interaction: An emerging area. In: Gorodetsky V, Zhang C, Skormin VA, Cao L, editors. Autonomous Intelligent Systems: Multi-Agents and Data Mining. St. Petersburg, Russia, June 3-5: Berlin Heidelberg: Springer; 2007. pp. 60-73. DOI: 10.1007/978-3-540-72839-9_5

[53] Seydim AY. Intelligent agents: A data mining perspective. TechReport. 1999. p. 19

Section 6

Emergence, Cognition and Context Awareness

Chapter 8

A Toolbox to Analyze Emergence in Multiagent Simulations

Danilo Saft and Volker Nissen

Additional information is available at the end of the chapter

http://dx.doi.org/10.5772/intechopen.69749

Abstract

The field of complexity science often employs multiagent simulations to investigate complex and emergent behavior. Authors in complexity science have suggested that the discussion of complex systems could benefit from a more systematic approach and a more compact mathematical way to describe the behavior of such systems in addition to the common observations and interpretations taking place today. Regarding quantitative measures to capture emergent phenomena, several approaches have been published, but have not yet been put to wide systematic use in the research community. One reason for this could be the manual effort required to investigate multiagent systems in a quantitatively accurate form. Toward this end, there has so far been a lack of appropriate and easy-to-use IT-based tools. To eliminate this deficiency, we present a software library, which enables researchers to integrate emergence measurements into experiments with multiagent modeling tools such as Repast and NetLogo. The major benefit for researchers is that this toolbox enables them to make comparable, quantitatively well-grounded statements about the emergent behavior of the model at hand. The toolbox therefore provides researchers with a standardized artifact that can be employed in a systematic methodological approach to the analysis of multiagent systems.

Keywords: multiagent system, emergence measures, complexity mathematics, toolbox, agent-based simulation, evaluation

1. Brief introduction, problem statement, and research goals

The field of complexity science is interdisciplinary and extends broadly into areas of science such as physics, biology, sociology, economics, and others [4]. Agent-based systems can be considered as computational laboratories [5–7] that provide research insights analogously to conventional laboratories. The research community usually concentrates investigations on the study of the system behavior and on the relation of input and output variables within multiagent simulations. Authors in complexity science have suggested that the discussion of complex systems could benefit from a more systematic approach and a more compact mathematical way to describe the behavior of such systems in addition to the common observations and interpretations taking place today ([1], pp. 233–235). Ways to measure macroscopic features of complex agent-based systems, such as emergence, were already presented in the literature [2, 3]. However, complexity phenomena and emergence, when subjectively observed, thus far have mostly been described qualitatively in publications on multiagent systems. Yet, emergence measures provide an elegant and significant opportunity to verify accurately the notion of emergence taking place in a multiagent simulation, for example, in self-organization processes. With the measure of Granger-Emergence [3], researchers can even quantify on a metric scale, the intensity of emergence within a process. The manual effort, that is, the number of manual calculations or human–computer interactions in the form of separate commands, necessary to measure emergence may make it difficult to include this dimension in one's research without being supported by an easy-to-use computer-aided process. Software libraries to measure Granger-Emergence via the measure of Granger-causality exist [8], however, up until now only as a program library for the software suite Matlab and with an extensive interface. Thus, our objective is to provide the scientific community with a publicly available IT-based tool to measure emergence in agent-based simulations. Besides broader access to such software libraries, the automation of emergence measurements and its quick integration with multiagent simulation frameworks are our further goals in this endeavor. A large part of the scientific community works with free simulation and analysis programs such as NetLogo [9], Repast Simphony [10], and R [11]. Guides on integrating these tools have been published, for example, in Ref. [12] and [13]. Consequently, the easy-to-use toolbox to accurately measure emergence, we aim to provide uses of the R framework. The integration of our library in experiments with broadly used multiagent simulation frameworks, such as Netlogo, will be demonstrated in this chapter. Here, we will use a standard model of bird flocking behavior to demonstrate the use of the toolbox toward the quantitative analysis of emergent systems.

2. Research method and structure

A toolbox represents an artifact as defined by Hevner et al. [14]. Therefore, the design science research (DSR) approach information systems science provides an adequate methodology for our project. Using design science research, one is able to systematically create IT artifacts in order to find solutions to practical problems. Particularly, we are guided by the well-known DSR process model by Peffers et al. ([15], p. 54), which organizes the design process iteratively and structures it in phases as shown in **Figure 1** and briefly described below.

The artifact we wish to create is an IT-based toolbox that enables researchers to easily measure emergence within their multiagent simulations. It therefore provides an opportunity to extract more quantitative information about properties such as emergence within multiagent systems. We will explain the designed artifact and demonstrate its application to an exemplary multiagent system. We conclude with an initial discussion of the results of applying the artifact as a starting point for its evaluation. This publication represents our attempt to communicate our findings to the scientific community.

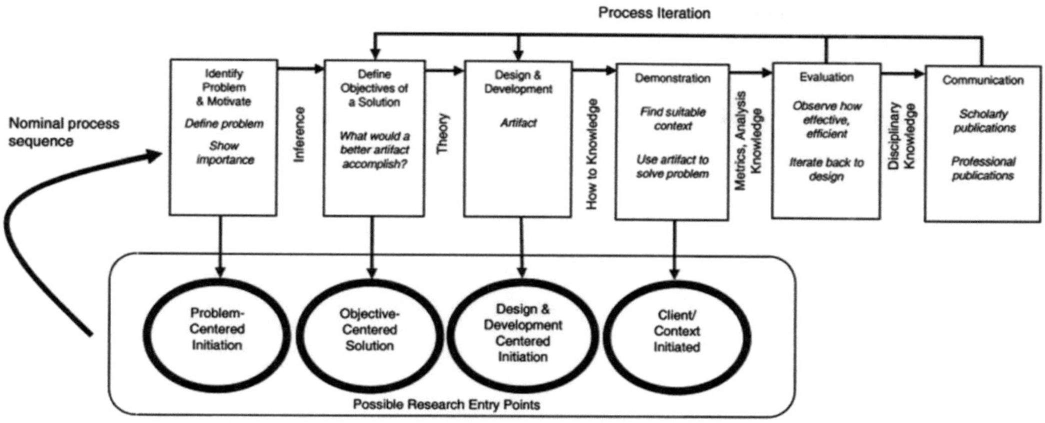

Figure 1. Design science research process model by Peffers et al. ([15], p. 54).

Hence, the structure of our book chapter is as follows: We first present the problem and the objective for a possible solution as shown in the introductory segment. By explaining the fundamentals of Granger-Emergence as a measure for weak emergence, we provide the foundation to understand the usability and benefits of the tool we design and develop. Then, we will design and present the artifact in the form of an R toolbox and its integrated utilization from typical NetLogo simulation results. The applicability and use of this tool is demonstrated with an exemplary simulation of flocks of birds (boids), measuring the emergence of flocks on the macrolevel of the simulation over the movements of each boid on the microlevel of the simulation. The measurements will be taken under different environmental parameter settings and emergence will be analyzed for each setting. Finally, we discuss positive and negative insights gained by applying the toolbox to the simulation model and conclude with some ideas for future research and tool extensions.

3. Foundations: measuring Granger-Emergence

Emergence is a phenomenon that occurs in complex systems when macroscopic processes of the system arise from the concurrence of microscopic processes, while at the same time, the macroscopic process cannot be reduced to just the sum of its constituent microprocesses. Each particular macroprocess can be seen to emerge only by simulation/full calculation and not be simply deduced prior to the simulation of all microinteractions. Notably, the occurrence of synchronous weak emergence [16] is of particular interest to the research community. Seth transformed [3] Bedaus approach to weak emergence [17] into a measure for weak synchronous emergence, the so-called Granger-Emergence. Hence, emergence can be measured via a time series analysis of a macrovariable in (Granger-causal) relation to its microvariables. This picks up Bedaus notion [17] that a weakly emergent process is both dependent upon its microcausal influences and at the same time autonomous from them. Seth's approach to this notion is to find out whether "(i) past observations of [the macrovariable] help predict future observations of [the macrovariable] with greater accuracy than predictions based on past observations of [the underlying set of microvariables] alone, and (ii) past observations of [the microvariables] help predict future observations of [the macrovariable] with greater accuracy than predictions based on past observations of [the macrovariable] alone.". This means that in order to find out whether synchronous weak emergence is present in a particular time step of a multiagent simulation, researchers need to answer the following questions:

a. Does the knowledge about a (more precise: each) single *agent's* parameter in *past* time-steps in the simulation give an advantage in (statistically) deriving the *current* measurement of the observed macroparameter thought to represent an *emergent phenomenon?*

b. Does the knowledge about *past* observations of the macroparameter representing the *emergent phenomenon* also help to predict the *current* value of the said parameter?

To answer these questions, researchers first need to capture the microlevel observations (i.e., parameters of each agent) as well as a quantified measure for the macrolevel phenomenon in a matrix of time series for each observed parameter. When simulating a boids model, this would imply recording the position of each simulated bird in each time step as well as recording a measure of the degree of flocking. Simple measures could be the standard deviation of positions, or the mean of squared numbers of other boids in the field of sight of the bird. More sophisticated and performance-demanding measures would be numbers of clusters found by a cluster analysis on the positions of each boid in the current time step of the simulation or other metrics of clustering and segregation derived from distance measures. Examples of this step will be explained in Section 5.

After recording the necessary data, question (*a*) from above can be quantitatively answered by calculating the so-called *Granger-causality* for the recorded macrolevel observations over the microlevel observations. To this end, one builds a (multivariate) statistical model for the explanation of the current macrovariable by the past observations. Seth [3] explains this by employing a demonstration example of a two-variable autoregressive process (Eqs. (1a) and (1b)). Here, we assume $X_1(t)$ is the time series for the macrovariable and $X_2(t)$ is the time series for a single microvariable parameter of the simulation; with t denoting the time-step of the simulation for which the values were recorded.

$$X_1(t) = \sum_{j=1}^{p} A_{11,j}X_1(t-j) + \sum_{j=1}^{p} A_{12,j}X_2(t-j) + \varepsilon_1(t) \tag{1a}$$

$$X_2(t) = \sum_{j=1}^{p} A_{21,j}X_1(t-j) + \sum_{j=1}^{p} A_{22,j}X_2(t-j) + \varepsilon_2(t) \tag{1b}$$

Here, p is the maximum number of lags of the variables, that is, the number of time-steps in the past of the simulation, for which observations of each variable are taken into consideration for the calculation of the current value of the parameter, thus denoting the duration for which the past observations are thought to influence the present observations. A_{ab} represents a matrix for each term that contains the coefficients for each current output variable $X_a(t)$ explained by lagged observations $X_b(t-j)$. ε_a represents the residual error term of each time series process and will be of particular interest in answering the questions posed above.

To clarify further, using a short example, assume we observe only two variables and know the last two values of these variables (i.e., lag 2). The autoregressive process notations resulting from this example would equate to

$$X_1(t) = c_{111}X_1(t-1) + c_{112}X_1(t-2) + c_{121}X_2(t-1) + c_{122}X_2(t-2) + \varepsilon_1(t), \tag{2}$$

representing a hypothetical "macrolevel observation" X_1 and

$$X_2(t) = c_{211}X_1(t-1) + c_{212}X_1(t-2) + c_{221}X_2(t-1) + c_{222}X_2(t-2) + \varepsilon_2(t), \tag{3}$$

representing a hypothetical single microlevel observation X_2.[1]

In this case, we assume we want to test whether $X_1(t)$, that is, the observed values of the macrovariable, are Granger-caused by the past (here: two) observations of the micro-variables $X_2(t-j)$. X_2 Granger-causes X_1 if the inclusion of the $X_2(t-j)$ terms in Eq. (2) leads to *better prediction* of X_1 than the exclusion does. Better prediction in turn is indicated by a lower variance of the residual term $\varepsilon_1(t)$. Hence, we first construct an autoregressive model that is *restricted* in comparison to the unrestricted model in Eq. (2):

$$X_{1R2}(t) = c_{111}X_1(t-1) + c_{112}X_1(t-2) + \varepsilon_{1R2}(t). \tag{4}$$

The model in Eq. (4) tries to predict $X_1(t)$ while leaving out information on X_2. Granger-causality is then the comparison of the variance of the residual values of the restricted model versus the unrestricted model [3]:

$$gc_{X2 \to X1} = log \frac{var(\varepsilon_{1R2})}{var(\varepsilon_1)} \; . \tag{5}$$

More details regarding the calculation of Granger-causality can be found in Ref. ([3], pp. 545–547).

Seth introduces a derivate of Granger-causality that he denotes as Granger-autonomy ([3], p. 547). This derivate is able to answer the yet unaddressed question *b* posed above in this section. Question b regards the influence of the macrovariables own past on the predictability of its current state. Modifying the example given in Eq. (4), Granger-autonomy is a calculation of Granger-causality applied to lagged observations of X_1. Accordingly, the restricted model equates to

$$X_{1R1}(t) = c_{121}X_2(t-1) + c_{122}X_2(t-2) + \varepsilon_{1R1}(t). \tag{6}$$

Granger-autonomy of process X_1, as posed by ([3], p. 547), therefore equates to

[1]Here, we initially ignore the circumstance that practical attempts to measure emergence via Granger-causality will later include more than one micro-variable. This example is just to demonstrate the step-by-step construction of the equations and calculations underlying the measurement process.

$$ga_{X1} = g_{c|X1,X1} = log\frac{var(\varepsilon_{1R1})}{var(\varepsilon_1)}. \tag{7}$$

Weak synchronous emergence can then be calculated by what Seth [3] called Granger-Emergence, by putting the Granger-autonomy value of a macroprocess (here: X_1) in relation to the average of all Granger-causalities of the microprocesses (here: only X_2) toward the macroprocess:

$$ge_{X1|X2} = ga_{X1} * \frac{1}{1}\left(\Sigma_{i=2}^{i=2} gc_{X_i \to X1}\right) = log\frac{var(\varepsilon_{1R1})}{var(\varepsilon_1)} * log\frac{var(\varepsilon_{1R2})}{var(\varepsilon_1)}. \tag{8}$$

4. Design and development of the toolbox

From the short example in Eqs. (2) and (3), it becomes apparent that while the operations are simple, the number of calculations to be performed can rise to an amount unsuitable for even just semimanual calculation of autoregressive models in multiagent simulations, where the number of observed microvariables can be large compared to just a single microvariable $X_2(t)$. Additionally, in larger agent-based models with a variety of variables to be evaluated for their link to a macrophenomenon, the determination of Granger-Emergence can be time consuming both with regard to data-preparation and separate calculation steps that are to be carried out by the researcher. Consequently, it is our goal to create an IT artifact that is capable of largely automating all calculation steps to compute the following:

- Derive a vector of Granger-causalities for each microparameter toward a given macro-variable.
- Determine the Granger-autonomy of the macrolevel observations given the simulation data.
- Calculate a Granger-Emergence value given just the simulation data and the macrovariable name.

Additionally, the following functional objectives should be accomplished:

- Easy setup and integration into existing and new models of multiagent systems.
- Flexible calculations for both the end-result sets of experimental data as well as live calculations as the simulation progresses.
- Provide researchers with quantitative measures of emergence, making it possible to compute the following:
    - Compare the amount of emergence in parameter studies of the model, finding peaks of emergent phenomena. This makes it possible to find parameter ranges for the model to promote or avoid emergence.
    - Give quantitative evidence for formerly qualitative interpretations of emergence phenomena based on a standard measure and a standard tool.
- Avoid calculation errors (quality assurance).
- It must serve as a basis for further extensions that help researchers in the field of complexity science: for example, the toolbox may be able to later automate the process of emergence

detection to a level where it is possible to just call a function with a given model and have the toolbox permute through all variables automatically to find possible emergence patterns.

- Save a significant amount of time on quantifying synchronous weak emergence for one's models.

In this section, we will first present a self-developed set of functions for the well-known statistical programming language *R*. This toolbox provides methods to analyze R dataframes for Granger-Emergence. Dataframes are a standardized structure in R that will, in our case, hold experimental results of an agent-based simulation in the form of time series values for each model variable. Given a dataframe with the simulation results and the name of the column that contain the macrolevel observations, the toolbox will be automatically capable of calculating Granger-Emergence for the simulation data. Researchers may also customize the function call to look only for emergence in specific combinations of the model variables or specific lags in the history of the simulation data that are to be considered.

Regarding the design of a toolbox, the first key feature that enables calculation of Granger-Emergence needs is an ability to construct a formula for an unrestricted model of a time-series, in which the macrovariable is explained by lagged observation of all other variables. It also needs to create a restricted model formula, which excludes a given microvariable from the unrestricted version of the formula. The R-code to derive such a model formula is given below:

```
#create a formula object using the string output of the functions inside the bracket:
formula_restricted <- as.formula(
    #concatenate the comma-separated terms inside the paste0 function:
    paste0(
     macro_variable,  #variable name of the macro-observations
    "~",               #="is to be explained by"
    paste0(            #concatenate the microvariables
       "lag(",         #Include Lags for each microvariable
         names(dataframe)[!names(dataframe) %in% restriction_variables],
#use each column except for the ones given in "restriction_variables"
         ", 1:", #create a lag sequence from 1 (first lag)
         lag_count, #to the defined lag count
       ")",
       collapse = "+" #add each lagged term to the model formula
      )
    )
  )
```

The benefit of this particular code is the utilization of Rs built-in vector-calculation routines. Apart from giving a better performance by avoiding nested for-loops, this makes the creation of the formula very flexible and elegant in that a dataframe of any size and any lag count may be given to derive a suitable formula of arbitrary length with very short, yet comprehensible, code. Moreover, the code offers adaptability for the microvariables to be tested for Granger-causality, since a vector of names can be assigned to restriction_variables. As an example for the creation of the regression formula, we can consider a dataframe with one macrovariable X1 and four microvariables X2..X5. We would like to consider the last 2 observations and calculate the Granger-causality of X4 toward X1. Given macro_variable <- "X1", lag_count <- 2 and restriction_variables <- "X4", the above code generates the following base formula for the restricted regression model:

$$X_1(t) \sim aX_1(t-1) + bX_1(t-2) + cX_2(t-1) + dX_2(t-2) + eX_3(t-1)$$

$$+fX_3(t-2) + gX_5(t-1) + hX_5(t-2). \quad (9)$$

Note that the coefficients a to h will be determined by the regression method. Because the number of regression terms directly depends on the number of microvariables, it will be important to choose the number of simulations steps in the simulation greater than the number of terms in the constructed formula, including the lagged terms. This is because otherwise the model will be able to "overfit" the time-series and create residuals of zero. Zero-valued residuals make it impossible to calculate Granger-causality and can be a hint to such an implausibility in the simulation setup. To create a simple linear regression model, one could use the R function "lm(...)". Here, we utilize the function dynlm of the dynlm package [18] for didactic reasons, because it is particularly easy to update the restricted model to an unrestricted model using this package.

```
require(dynlm)

lm_restricted <- dynlm(formula = formula_restricted, data=dataframe)

lm_unrestricted <- update.dynlm(.~.+ lag(restriction_variables, lag_count), data=dataframe)
```

The code above generates a linear model based on the restricted model formula. The update command adds the omitted variable terms to retrieve an unrestricted model.

Both models are large objects with several nested properties. One of which is the $residuals object, giving a time series with the error terms of the fitted model in comparison to the actual values of the observations (here: of X_1) in the dataframe. Using these properties, we can calculate Granger-causality in R via

```
gc <- log(var(lm_restricted$residuals)/var(lm_unrestricted$residuals))
```

Together with a number of checks and convenience conversions for readability and adaptability, the toolbox is now able to provide an easy-to-use interface for calculating Granger-causalities for given macrovariables and microvariables in a dataframe:

```
grangerCausality <- function(dataframe, macro_variable, restriction_variables, lag_count) { ... }
```

Using this interface, it is in turn easy to utilize it to calculate Granger-autonomy and Granger-Emergence:

```
grangerAutonomy <- function(dataframe, macro_variable, lag_count) {
  return(grangerCausality(dataframe, macro_variable, macro_variable, lag_count))
}
grangerEmergence <- function(dataframe, macro_variable, lag_count) {
  granger_causality_vector <- c()
  for (micro_variable in names(dataframe)) {
    if (micro_variable == macro_variable) {
     next
    }
    granger_causality_vector <- c(granger_causality_vector,
grangerCausality(dataframe, macro_variable, micro_variable, lag_count, lag_count))
  }
ga <- grangerAutonomy(dataframe, macro_variable, lag_count)
ge <- ga * 1/(ncol(dataframe) -1) * sum(granger_causality_vector)
return(ge)
}
```

Here, we calculate Granger-autonomy by applying the Granger-causality function to the macrovariable, omitting the lagged terms of the macroobservations in the restricted models. In the function Granger-Emergence, we first construct a vector of Granger-causalities for each microvariable in the dataframe to the macrovariable. Afterward, we calculate the Granger-autonomy of the macrovariable column in dataframe and return Granger-Emergence according to the formula provided in Ref. [3], applied to the particular dataframe provided as a parameter of the function call.

The complete code can be found on GitHub [19]. The codes will be updated further in upcoming versions with extensions listed in Section 6. A CRAN-package will be made available once the set of functions seems large enough.

5. Demonstrating an example

The R functions for calculating Granger-Emergence listed above provide sufficient functionality to demonstrate its general utilization and to validate the toolbox against a standard example. It is good practice to use widely known and widely available examples where possible.

We therefore build our demonstration upon the bird flocking model from the NetLogo example library.

In particular, we chose this model, due to the following reasons:

- Flocking is an apparent example of synchronous weak emergence.
- The NetLogo flocking model provides initialization parameters that make it possible to create seemingly random boid behavior or strong flocking behavior. This makes it possible to test the R code against contrasting results.
- A boid simulation was employed by Seth [3] to showcase the concept of Granger-Emergence. The general results of the demonstration in Ref. [3] should be roughly comparable to our findings.

A range of parameter instantiations of the bird flocking model were simulated. We used a population size of 15. The values for the parameter "vision" of each boid were set to 0 (no discovery of neighboring boids is possible) and to 9 (potentially leading to a strong influence by neighboring boids). Settings for the parameter "minimum separation" were cycled through the values 0.75, 1.5, 3.0, and 5.0. We simulated 1500 time steps in each run. Each simulation was performed 30 times. The settings can be automatically cycled and each combination saved to a CSV table using NetLogos integrated BehaviorSpace functions.

We modified the simulation code in NetLogo to be able to save the distance of each boid from the center and the standard deviation of the distance of all boids:

```
#BehaviorSpace value to save each boids distance and standard deviation

[distance patch 0 0] of turtles

rep_stddev

#report standard deviation of distances of boids

to-report rep_stddev

set xcorlist [distance patch 0 0] of turtles

set ycorlist [distance patch 0 0] of turtles

set stddev (0.5 * standard-deviation xcorlist) + (0.5 * standard-deviation ycorlist)

report stddev

end
```

The resulting CSV table of the BehaviorSpace experiments was read into an R dataframe omitting the first six rows and extracting only the necessary columns using the readr package [20]:

```
dataframe <- read_csv("./Flocking experiment-table_v0_ms0.75.csv", skip = 6)
```

The dataframe was transformed further to include 15 columns for the boid distance values in each step and 1 column for the macrovariable (here: standard deviation). A diff-log operation was performed on each column to reach stationary behavior of the time-series in each column. These steps are in accordance with the preparation of data taken in the original experiment in Ref. [3]. Note that using the log function and taking first-order differences does not destroy the ability to investigate the data for Granger-Emergence correctly, since all necessary information is kept by the transformation. For performance reasons, we only considered lag 1 values in our regression model construction for the recorded time series. The Granger-Emergence measurement for each run of the simulation can be retrieved by the simple interface call below:

```
grangerEmergence(dataframe_filtered_by_run, "X16", 1)
```

For each of the 30 runs in a parameter combination, the overall Granger-Emergence value was saved into a separate dataframe containing the columns Vision, Minimum Separation and Granger-Emergence. Calculation for all given parameter combinations took about 30 min on an Intel Core i7 based standard pc. **Figure 2** shows the results in a boxplot comparison.

The chart shows the factor Vision on the x-axis. For each of the two Vision instances, four boxplots were plotted, indicating the settings for the parameter Minimum Separation. The y-axis shows the Granger-Emergence results of all 30 steps for each of the combinations as a boxplot, with outliers omitted. For a Vision value of zero, the median of the Granger-Emergence is close to zero for all settings of Minimum Separation. Of the number of outliers that were produced, only one of the outliers was particularly high-valued for vision 0 and was close to 0.9. One reason for this may be pseudorandom encounters of boids over several time steps that resembled flocking. However, and importantly, these false positives are single cases clearly and easily marked as outliers even in a small batch run series. The quartiles 1–3, that is, 75% of measurements, are very close to zero for a Vision value of zero. This is in stark contrast to emergence readings for a value of nine for the parameter Vision. For this setting, compelling flocking behavior was observed in the NetLogo simulation, when combined with low settings of Minimum Separation. Consequently, the median of the Granger-Emergence over all 30 runs is significantly higher as shown in **Figure 2**. Almost no outliers were produced for Vision = 9. The box, that is, half of the measurements, stretch over a spectrum of Granger-Emergence that is both wider and higher than in simulations where no flocking was observed. In accordance with the subjective observation of the simulations in

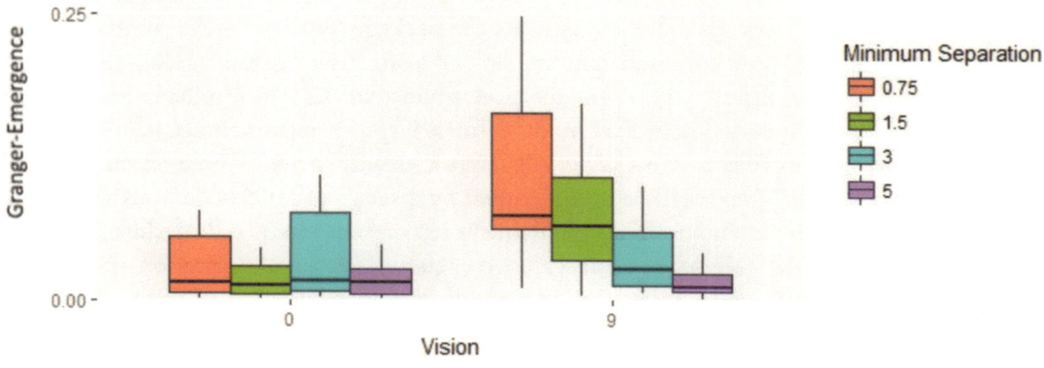

Figure 2. Boxplots of Granger-Emergence measurements over 30 runs each for parameter combinations of the NetLogo Flocking model.

NetLogo, the differences between Vision = 9 and 0 diminish when the Minimum Separation approaches approximately half of the Vision value.

6. Evaluation

The experimental results shown in this chapter are very comparable to those presented in Ref. [3]. While our specific experimental setup differs from Seth's boids simulations, we, too, obtain Granger-Emergence results that indicate the subjective observation of flocking behavior strikingly well. The methods presented above are suitable for distinguishing almost random behavior with little emergence from clearly emergent flocking behavior. Moreover, gradual differences in flocking behavior seem to leave a significant mark in the median of the measured emergence. We were able to validate our functions against the standard example of a NetLogo boids model and demonstrate its structure and usability. Very good and extensive implementations for the automated measurement of Granger-causality and Granger-autonomy exist for Matlab [8]. These implementations concentrate on a spectral perspective on Granger-causality, typically used in fields like neuroscience, and provide many interfaces for detailed tasks where this perspective fits well. Our approach successfully focused on providing a simple interface for researchers to measure directly the Granger-Emergence with a simple autoregressive modeling process according to Ref. [3]. Given the data from a simulation model, we provide a single function interface to receive immediate results in the open-source language R. This language offers direct integration with simulation tools such as Repast or NetLogo via interfaces like JRI [12]. A demonstration using this interface will be a topic for future articles of ours, building upon this publication.

The toolbox leaves room for extensions, improving convenience for researchers even further. For example, tests for significance of Granger-causality and Granger-autonomy may also be automated, saving time otherwise spent on semimanual calculation to verify the significance of the obtained results. Currently, the toolbox uses a linear regression modeling method for originally nonlinear time-series. While linear Granger-Emergence has been shown to resemble the nonlinear variants [3], we wish to provide a simple function interface to calculate nonlinear Granger-Emergence too. Furthermore, the package "dynlm" we currently employ utilizes only one processor core and may be slower to find regression models than other packages such as "speedglm" [21]. While the performance of the interface has already been optimized and is acceptable for typical models, further speed improvement is likely using GPU computation or multicore processing. All extensions will be maintained on the toolbox' GitHub project page [19] and will be accompanied by a series of articles demonstrating the particular solution. The toolbox is freely available to researchers already. With the extensions listed above, it will be able to provide extensive quantitative statements on multiagent systems and their parameter studies. We encourage further evaluation of the toolbox and discussion of improvements. Our hope is that its use will open a discussion on how to use quantification of subjectively emergent behavior in the discussion of multiagent simulations. To this end, we plan to publish a methodology for the systematic analysis of complex systems, incorporating the findings published in this chapter.

Author details

Danilo Saft* and Volker Nissen

*Address all correspondence to: danilo.saft@tu-ilmenau.de

Faculty of Economic Sciences and Media, Institute for Commercial Information Technology, Ilmenau Technical University, Ilmenau, Germany

References

[1] Miller JH, Page SE. Complex Adaptive Systems: An Introduction to Computational Models of Social Life. Princeton University Press; New Jersey; 2009

[2] Wright WA, Smith RE, Danek M, Greenway P. A generalisable measure of self-organisation and emergence. In: International Conference on Artificial Neural Networks; Springer; 2001. pp. 857–864

[3] Seth AK. Measuring emergence via nonlinear Granger causality. In: Bullock S, Watson R, Noble J, Bedau M, editors. Artificial Life XI: proceedings of the 11th international conference on the simulation and synthesis of living systems. MIT Press; Cambridge, Massachusetts; 2008. pp. 545–553

[4] Mitchell M. Complexity: A Guided Tour. Oxford University Press; New York; 2009

[5] Epstein JM, Axtell R. Growing Artificial Societies: Social Science from the Bottom Up. Brookings Institution Press; Washington; 1996

[6] Dibble C. Computational laboratories for spatial agent-based models. In: Handbook of Computational Economics. Vol. 2. Elsevier/North-Holland; Amsterdam; 2006. pp. 1511–1548

[7] Tesfatsion L. Agent-based computational economics: Modeling economies as complex adaptive systems. Information Sciences. 2003;**149**(4):262–268

[8] Barnett L, Seth AK. The MVGC multivariate Granger causality toolbox: A new approach to Granger-causal inference. Journal of Neuroscience Methods. 2014;**223**:50–68

[9] Wilensky U, Rand B. Introduction to Agent-Based Modeling: Modeling Natural, Social and Engineered Complex Systems with NetLogo. MIT Press; Cambridge, Massachusetts; 2015

[10] North MJ, Howe TR, Collier NT, Vos J. The repast Simphony runtime system. In: Agent 2005 Conference on Generative Social Processes, Models, and Mechanisms; Argonne, IL. 2005

[11] R Core Team. R: A Language and Environment for Statistical Computing. 2013

[12] JRI. JRI - Java/R Interface [Internet]. JRI; (Website); 2013. Available from: http://www.webcitation.org/6NvIpV2bn [Accessed: 2013]

[13] Nissen V, Saft D. A practical guide for the creation of random number sequences from aggregated correlation data for multi-agent simulations. Journal of Artificial Societies and Social Simulation. 2014;**17**(4):7

[14] Hevner AR, March ST, Park J, Ram S. Design science in information system research. Management Information Systems Quarterly. 2004;**28**(1):75–105

[15] Peffers K, Tuunanen T, Rothenberger MA, Chatterjee S. A design science research methodology for information systems research. Journal of Management Information Systems. 2008;**24**(3):45–77

[16] Stephan A, editors. "Emergenz." Von der Unvorhersagbarkeit zur Selbstorganisation. mentis; Dresden; 1999

[17] Bedau M. Weak emergence. Philosophical Perspectives. 1997: **11**, 375–399

[18] Zeileis A. Dynamic Linear Regression. 2016. Available from: http://CRAN.R-project.org/package=dynlm

[19] Saft D. Measure Emergence in R repository at GitHub. 2017. Available from: https://github.com/danilosaft/Measure-Emergence-in-R

[20] Hester J. Read Rectangular Text Data. 2017. Available from: https://cran.r-project.org/web/packages/readr/

[21] Enea M. Fitting Linear and Generalized Linear Models to Large Data Sets. 2017. Available from: https://cran.r-project.org/web/packages/speedglm/index.html

Chapter 9

Hybrid Architecture to Support Context-Aware Systems

Maricela Bravo, José A. Reyes-Ortiz,
Leonardo Sánchez-Martínez and
Roberto A. Alcántara-Ramírez

Additional information is available at the end of the chapter

http://dx.doi.org/10.5772/intechopen.69519

Abstract

Any system that is said to be context-aware is capable of monitoring continuously the surrounding environment, that is, capable of prompt reaction to events and changing conditions of the environment. The main objective of a context-aware system is to be continuously recognizing the state of the environment and the users present, in order to adjust the environment to an ideal state and to provide personalized information and services to users considering the user profile. In this chapter, we describe an architecture that relies on the incorporation of intelligent multi-agent systems (MAS), sensor networks, mobile sensors, actuators, Web services and ontologies. We describe the interaction of these technologies into the architecture aiming at facilitating the construction of context-aware systems.

Keywords: multi-agent system, sensor network, web services, ontologies

1. Introduction

Context-awareness is the characteristic of a system that is capable of monitoring the environment continuously aided with physical sensors and mobile sensors. The goal of a context-aware system is to obtain real data from the context (user preferences, user logs, temperature, humidity, light, etc.) in order to build a multi-valued representation of the context in a particular time, and by means of intelligent processing and reasoning of such acquired data provide relevant information in a timely manner and support for decision-making, considering the physical space conditions. An important aspect of a context-aware system is the capability of internal representation of current context, including the presence of human beings and their profiles.

Three important considerations were to be taken into account during the design of the hybrid architecture reported in this chapter:

a. *What are the tasks performed within a context-aware system?* Guermah et al. [1] described the challenges of context-aware systems: context capture, context representation, context interpretation and reasoning, service adaptation, context management and context reuse. In response to this question, the proposed hybrid architecture presented in this chapter provides technological support for these tasks to be performed.

b. *What general concepts does a context cover?* Another important design decision of the architecture was to define the general concepts that constitute a context. According with Abowd et al. [2], context is divided into four classes: location, time, activity and identity. However, in specialized literature, reported context models include more or less concepts. It is out of the scope of this chapter to present a deeper analysis of the concept coverage of context. Instead, we present an extensible and flexible model that allows the amplification or reduction of the concept coverage.

c. *What are the general functional requirements of a context-aware system?* In Ref. [3], Orsi and Tanca described an overview of the main functional requirements for context-aware systems organized in three aspects:

- Communication is the capability to adapt content presentation to different channels or devices. Communication also covers the agreement and shared reasoning between users or agents.
- Situation-awareness refers to the characteristic of modelling location and environment aspects; modelling the user personal situation, and adapting the information to the user needs. One of the most important requirements of personalized service provisioning is the ability to provide the correct information to the correct user in the correct moment.
- Managing knowledge refers to the task of determining the relevant information and services to be delivered to the users. Abowd et al. [2] also stated that a system is context-aware if it uses context to provide relevant information and/or services to the user, where relevancy depends on the user´s task.

1.1. Hybrid solution approach

In order to attend the afore-mentioned design considerations, **Table 1** shows the technological approaches that were selected to integrate the hybrid solution approach. Current advances of these technologies present significant advantages that contribute to satisfy the complex requirements of any context-aware system. In this sub-section, we briefly describe the technological approaches and their contribution for the tasks and functionalities that should be supported by any context-aware system.

The rapid development of **sensor networks** that deliver network services, enabling remote control, remote supervision and automation of buildings, offices, hospitals, etc.; together with the emergence of new smart mobile devices integrated with sensors, wireless protocols and novel applications, provide the technological foundations to design and build applications that allow continuous **context data capture or acquisition**. Context data come from various information sources: from physical sensors, mobile sensors or from virtual sources such as web pages, logs, public databases, etc. The techniques used to acquire context can vary based on responsibility,

http://dx.doi.org/10.5772/intechopen.69519

Technological approach	Task contribution	Functionality contribution
Sensor networks	Context acquisition	
Intelligent agents	Context acquisition	Communication support
	Context management	Managing knowledge
	Context interpretation	
Web services	Context acquisition	
	Service adaptation	
	Service provisioning	
Ontologies	Context representation	Situation-awareness
	Context interpretation	Managing knowledge
	Context reasoning	
	Context reuse	

Table 1. Technological approaches that integrate the hybrid solution.

frequency, context source, sensor type and acquisition process [4]. Mobile devices also represent the means by which personalized information and services can be delivered.

Web services are reusable software resources that can be shared, composed and invoked independently of the hardware, operating system and programming language used at the server and client side. In this sense, Web services allow the interoperability between hardware devices, intelligent agents and servers in order to personalize **service adaptation** and **service provisioning**.

According to Jennings and Wooldridge [5], an **intelligent agent** 'is an encapsulated computer system that is situated in some environment, and that is capable of flexible, autonomous action in that environment in order to meet its design objectives. Of particular, interest is the notion of an agent as a solver entity capable of showing flexible problem-solving behaviour. The abilities of individual agents to solve problems and communicate are fundamental to integrate a multi-agent system (MAS). Intelligent agents provide **communication** mechanisms to **control** and **monitor** the entire context-aware architecture. They are also capable of acquiring additional context data by invocation of services, maintain a shared context representation, interpret current state of the context and trigger actions that will adapt or affect the context.

Ontologies are representational models based on description logic, logic programing and frame logic that allow the formal definition of concepts and relations comprising the vocabulary of a topic area as well as the axioms and rules for combining terms and relations to define extensions to the vocabulary [6]. During the last decade, ontologies have gained popularity for context modelling due to their expressiveness and reasoning support. Ontologies allow context representation, context interpretation by explicitly defining equivalences, context reasoning and context reuse.

In order to achieve the afore-mentioned requirements and facilitate the complex interactions that occur inside a context-aware system, in this chapter, we present a **hybrid solution** approach (see **Figure 1**) that leverages current technologies by incorporating a sensor network,

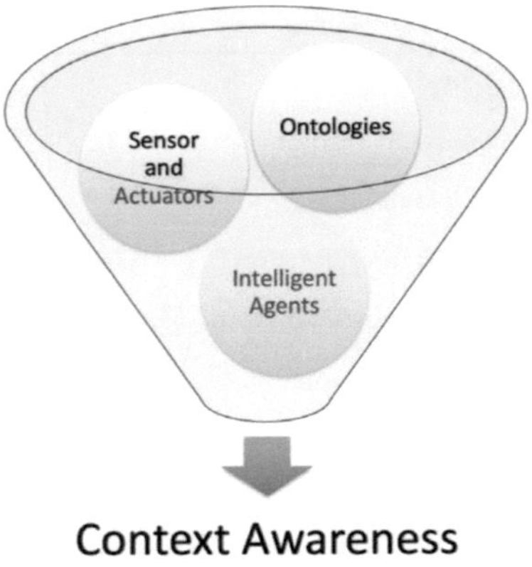

Figure 1. Integration of multiple technologies for context-awareness.

a set of specialized agents, a collection of software components deployed as Web services and context represented and reasoned by ontologies. We describe the complex interactions of these technologies facilitating the construction of context-aware systems.

The rest of the chapter is organized as follows: In Section 2, the general architecture is described; Section 3 describes the set of agents and their roles inside the architecture; Section 4 presents a multi-variable environment control system; Section 5 presents the ontological models defined for the architecture; Section 6 presents an overview of related work, and finally, in Section 7, conclusions are presented.

2. Description of the architecture

The proposed architecture is envisioned for a wireless networked **environment**, where users may be identified by their mobile device mac address or by a RFID card. Such an **environment** may be an office or laboratory into an academic institution or university, where users enter and leave the **environment** freely. The proposed architecture consists of five layers interconnected, which are described in this section. **Figure 2** shows the general description of the architecture.

2.1. Sensor network

This layer consists of a collection of physical sensors, mobile sensors and actuators. The objective of the network sensor is to obtain data from the physical context, user context and eventually activate some actuators. This layer aims at constant monitoring of environmental data such as temperature, lighting, humidity, smoke or fire and presence of humans into the environment. Another important objective of this layer is the possible identification of the users and the data generated by user interaction with the environment. The following types of sensors are considered as part of this layer:

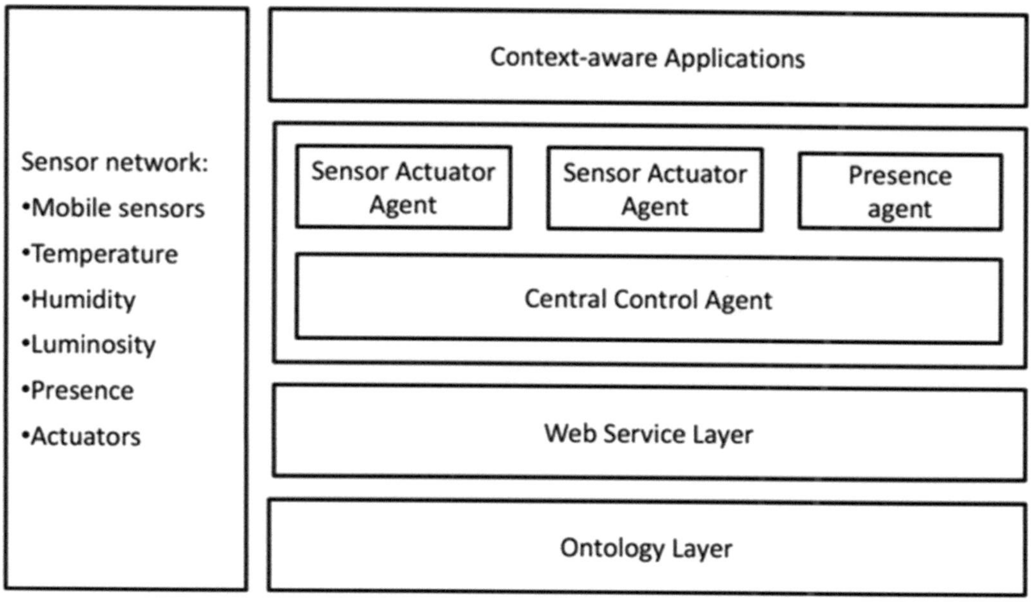

Figure 2. Hybrid architecture for context-awareness.

- Environmental sensors, which are used to obtain data of room temperature, humidity, luminosity and presence of persons.
- Mobile and wearable sensors, such as accelerometer, gyroscope, magnetometer, proximity sensor, light sensor, barometer, thermometer, pedometer, heart rate monitor, fingerprint sensors, etc.
- Automatic identification sensors carried by the user.
- Actuators represent the hardware devices through which actions are activated in order to achieve an ideal state.

2.2. Intelligent agents

Intelligent agents play an important role into the architecture. Every agent is a programme allocated into a microcontroller (Arduino or Raspberry Pi) which interacts with physical sensors and actuators to monitor and control the physical variables of the environment.

There are specialized agents performing different roles:

- Sensor and actuator agent: This kind of agent is continuously sensing the environment to detect changes and report variations that are higher than a threshold. This type of agent is capable of receiving action commands to execute over the environment by activating actuators.
- Central control agent: This agent is responsible for reading and forwarding all communication messages incoming or outgoing between agents, while recording all those communications.

- Context Server: This is the main server that computes all events and fires the actions that are executed by the environment control system, where the ontology model resides and the reasoning services execute inference about events and trigger actions to be taken by the control system.

2.3. Ontologies for context modelling

In this layer, models based on ontologies for representing contextual data, data obtained from the user, data from sensors, events and physical spaces are included. Additionally, a set of query and inference rules are included in the definitions of ontologies in order to gather more related and relevant data. Ontologies offer a formal semantic representation of data and facilitate the inference about the stored data, which helps to retrieve information relevant to the user. Moreover, being a technology based on the Web, they can be shared by multiple applications and automatically processed by computers.

2.4. Web services

Web services are incorporated for two purposes. On the one hand, Web services for data management, information extraction, storage, retrieval and updating of information in ontologies. Moreover, Web services for inference, reasoning and verifying the consistency of the data will also be created. These Web services will be supported, in full, in considering the ontological model semantic relationships between data.

2.5. Context-aware applications

In this layer, mobile applications for user interaction are developed. This interaction involves light applications for information retrieval, voice and natural language communication interfaces, mobile applications with requests in natural language and mobile applications where relevant and timely information is provided to users. All these communication applications will be focused on evaluating the usability of the context-aware environment.

3. Intelligent agents

Intelligent agents play important roles in the context-aware architecture. Intelligent agents are autonomous programmes that are responsible for the detection of changes in the state of the environment, they also do intermediation sending and receiving messages with other agents and context servers, and they are responsible for firing and executing actions that change the state of the environment. In this architecture, every agent is a programme allocated into a microcontroller (Arduino or Raspberry Pi) which interacts with physical sensors and actuators that monitor and control the physical variables of the environment. Physical agents are responsible for monitoring temperature, humidity and luminosity variables and firing the respective actuators, whereas presence agents are responsible for user recognition and if possible user identification inside the environment. All agents participating in the environment communicate with the central agent, where all data are concentrated and context-related decisions are taken. The following agent roles are defined:

a. **Sensor/actuator agent** (SAA): This kind of agent is mounted on an Arduino electronic platform, which integrates a temperature sensor, a humidity sensor, luminosity and a presence sensor. Is responsible for continuous acquisition of these environment data, and for the activation of respective actuators.

b. **Central control agent** (CCA): This agent is mounted on a Raspberry Pi card-sized computer. It is an intermediary that reads and forwards all communications from SAAs to the context server (CS) while recording all those communications.

c. **Context server** (CS): This is the main server that computes all events and fires the actions that are executed by the environment control system, where the ontology model resides and the reasoning services execute inference about events and trigger actions to be taken by the control system.

In this section, we describe the **interaction protocol** that was defined for communication purposes between all agents. A protocol specifies the rules of interaction between agents by restricting the range of allowed utterances sequences for each agent at any stage during a communication interaction [7]. According to Foundation for Intelligent Physical Agents (FIPA) specifications [8], an agent communication language (ACL) message structure contains one or more of the parameters described in **Table 2**, accordingly the only mandatory parameter is performative.

All messages defined for the interaction protocol are described in **Table 3**.

Even though agent-communicating messages were designed based on FIPA specifications, messages are translated to byte arrays packages of longitude 2 or 3. All packages were defined trying to optimize the available transmission channel. Therefore, it is sought that the size of the package is the minimum possible.

Figure 3 shows the interaction protocol implemented for communication purposes between all agents participating in the context-aware environment.

Element type	Message parameters
Type of communicative act	Performative
Participant in communication	Sender, receiver, reply-to
Content of message	Content
Description of content	Language, encoding, ontology
Control of conversation	Conversation-id, reply-with, in-reply-to

Table 2. Elements of a message according to FIPA specification.

Performative	Message format
Request	REQUEST <sender Id, receiver Id, date, time>
Info	INFO <sender Id, receiver Id, date, time, temperature, humidity, luminosity>
Presence	PRESENCE <sender Id, receiver Id, date, time, user Id>
Event	EVENT <sender Id, receiver Id, date, time, increase I decrease, temperature I humidity I luminosity, value>
Action	ACTION <sender Id, receiver Id, date, time, increase I decrease, temperature I humidity I luminosity, value>

Table 3. Description of the message format for each type of performative.

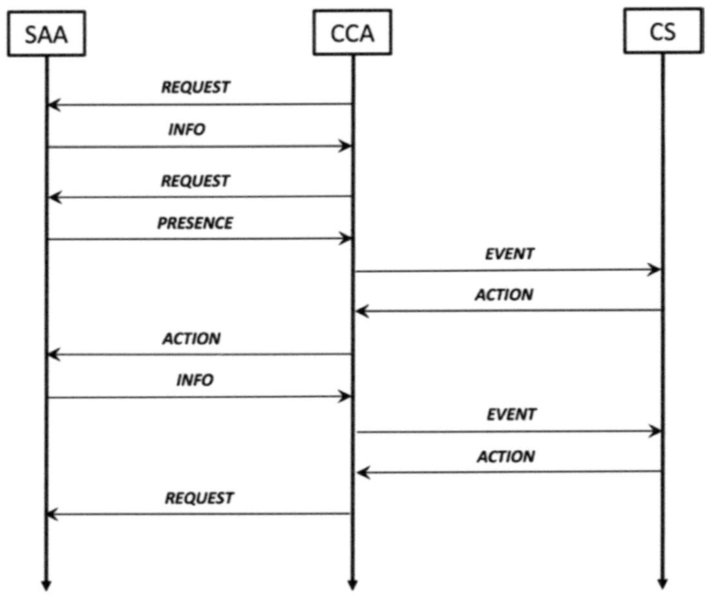

Figure 3. Agent interaction protocol.

Communication is a key requirement in any context-aware system, in this architecture, communication is carried out between agents. **Figure 3** shows that the central control agent (CCA) initiates the communication with each of the sensor/actuator agents (SAA) deployed into the environment. The CCA *requests* for information to the SAA agent, then the SAA agent delivers an *info* message with attached environmental data. In response to a *request* message, the SAA agent may deliver a *presence* message, indicating the detection of a person inside the environment, adding the unique identification of the person (RFID or MAC address). The CCA communicates with the context server (CS) using *event* messages and receiving *action* messages. An *event* message is issued whenever the value of the environmental variables changes significantly. As a response to an *event* message, an *action* message may be issued by the CS. The principal difference between an *event* and an *action* is that the former is a change in the environment that was caused by natural reasons, and *action* is a command to change the environment through an environmental control system.

3.1. Multi-variable environment control system

The set of intelligent agents deployed in the physical environment communicate with a multi-variable environment control system (MECS), which is a closed-loop system with feedback. **Figure 4** shows the components of this particular multi-variable control system.

3.2. Environment setting

Environment setting consists of a set of actions that are executed by the MECS at any moment inside the context-aware environment in order to achieve an ideal environment state. Considering a networked environment where users enter and leave the environment, the desired environment state is the set of values defined by the administrator of the environment considering mainly the activities and type of works to be carried out in the physical environment, the kind and number of possible users, and the geography where the environment is located. For the purpose of this work, the environment state is represented as a three-valued vector using the variables in **Table 4**.

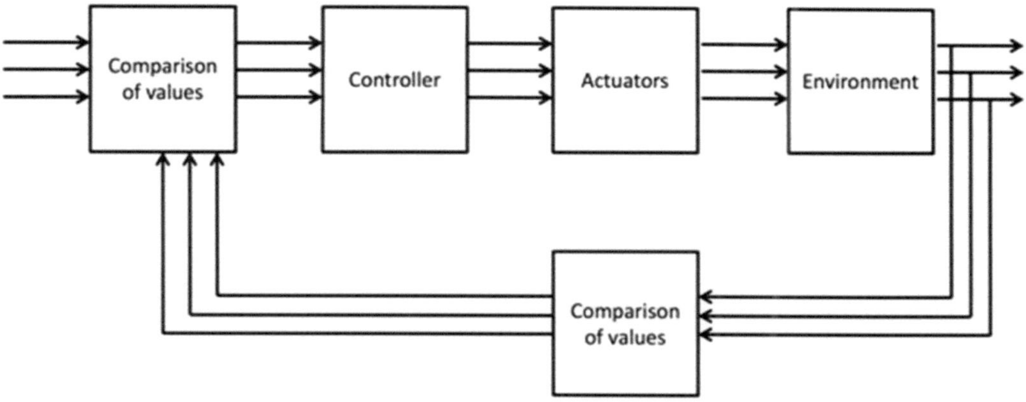

Figure 4. Multi-variable environment control system.

Variables	Humidity (%)	Temperature (°C)	Luminosity (lux)
Allowed values	30–60	−20 to 50	100–500
Desired values	45	23	200

Table 4. Environment state vector.

Activity	Types of work	Average illuminance (lux)	Minimum measured illuminance (lux)
Work requiring limited perception of detail	Kitchens, factories assembling large components, potteries	100	50
Work requiring perception of detail	Offices, sheet metal work, bookbinding	200	100
Work requiring perception of fine detail	Drawing offices, factories assembling electronic components, textile production	500	200

Table 5. Lighting recommended values.

Each of these variables defines a range of allowed values and a range of desirable values. Indoor humidity levels should be between 30 and 60%, with the ideal level being about 45%. The temperature value depends on the season of the year, the geographical location of the environment and the number of persons inside the environment. The most important aspects that influence the indoor temperature are heat from persons, heat from lights, heat from electric equipment and machines, among others. However, it is not necessary to measure all these particular data, the architecture only requires the initial specification of the ideal range of temperature to function normally and securely. Environment climate allows values ranging from the −20 to 50°C.

Lighting levels depend on various factors, such as the time of the day (morning light versus night light poses different requirements). In order to define an ideal lighting level, the administrator should consider mainly the number of persons inside the environment, the particular lighting requirements (in case that users present in the environment have sight difficulties). The amount of light falling on a surface is called 'illuminance', and it is measured in lux. This is the measurement used to optimize visual comfort because building regulations and standards use illuminance to specify the minimum light levels for specific tasks and environments. Lighting recommended values are shown in **Table 5**.

4. Ontologies for context modelling

In this section, we describe the ontologies that were designed for context modelling and reasoning. We define the design principles that guided the construction of the ontology models. Ontologies are representational models that can help to characterize and specify all of the entities needed to describe the environmental context [9] and the user profiles. A context can be composed of contextual items such as location, physical data and activity, instrumental and social context [10]. In particular, in this work, the context is divided into two general classes: **environmental context** and **user profile context**.

The logical foundation of ontologies allows the explicit specification of the user preferences and user profiles, and the reasoning facilities offer mechanisms to gather more related information in order to provide pertinent and opportune information and services to users [11, 12].

4.1. Motivating scenario

Considering a traditional academic institution in which professors are teaching subjects to students in classrooms, pre-graduate students are developing their thesis, there is a chief for each department directing and supervising administrative activities; there are academic coordinators attending student academic issues, aided with the support of administrative staff (secretaries, janitors, etc.), and visitors who come for various reasons.

The ontology model consists of three ontologies that are included into another general context ontology system. **Figure 5** shows the general ontology model.

The general ontology model consists of three ontologies:

1. The **Person** ontology was designed to represent all the information related to persons that may exist in a typical academic scenario where professors, students, staff and visitors assist. An important characteristic of this ontology was to define a unique identifier for every type of person that would be present inside the sensor-enabled context. **Figure 6** shows the general model of the **Person** ontology and **Table 6** presents some classes definitions of the **Person** ontology.
2. The **PhysicalSpace** ontology was designed to represent any kind of physical location such as cubicle, classroom, office, parking lot, plaza, green area, etc. The **PhysicalSpace** class is sub classified into **IndoorSpace** and **OutdoorSpace** subclasses. **Figure 7** shows the general class hierarchy of the **PhysicalSpace** ontology.
3. The **Device** ontology was designed to represent electronic devices located within the context-aware environment. The **Device** class is sub classified into **smartphone**, **RFID card, sensor** and **actuator** subclasses. **Figure 8** shows the general model of the **Device** ontology. An important issue of any sensor device is its capability of measuring; therefore, devices are semantically related with **physical measurement** subclasses of **light intensity**, **humidity**, **temperature** and **distance**.

The current version of the ontology was implemented in OWL 2 ontology language, and contains 35 classes, 14 object properties, 83 data type properties and has an ALCRQ(D) expressivity. **Table 7** shows the classes, object properties and data type properties defined for the ontology.

4.2. Ontology design principles

The set of ontology models reported in this chapter address particularly clarity and coherence design principles.

- **Clarity design principle**: According to Ref. [13], ontology should communicate the intended meaning of defined terms. Definitions should be objective. Definitions should be stated in formal axioms, and a complete definition (defined by necessary and sufficient conditions) is preferred over a partial definition (defined by only necessary or sufficient conditions). In order to accomplish clarity, we designed ontologies defining equalities in axiomatic class definitions.
- **Coherence design principle**: This principle is also referred as soundness or consistency. Coherence specifies that ontology definitions should be individually sound and should not contradict each other [14].

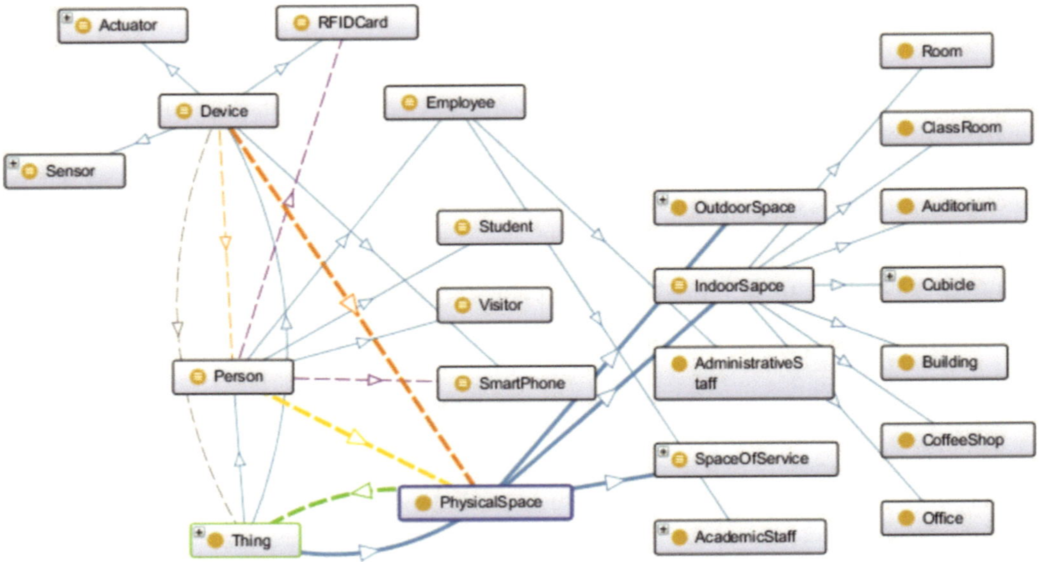

Figure 5. General context ontology model.

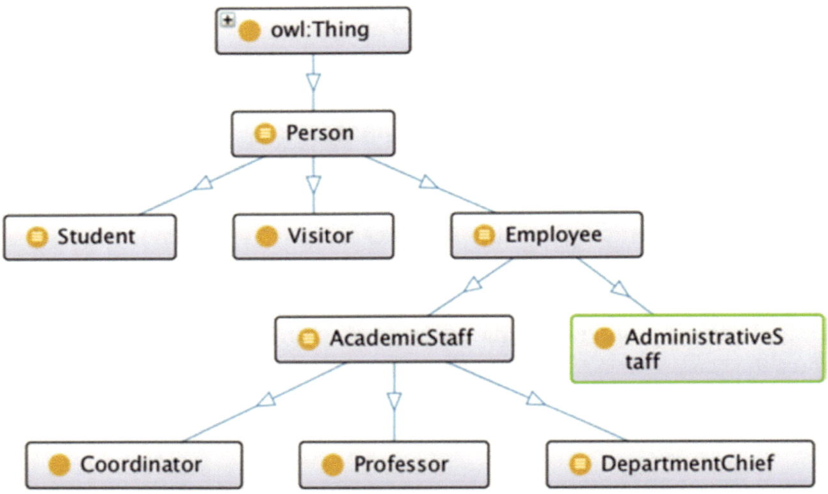

Figure 6. Class hierarchy of the Person ontology.

Ontology consistency checking was executed to verify that none of the class definitions and axioms had logical contradictions, or the individual's instantiated into the ontology. This final activity consists of executing the reasoning tasks of taxonomy classification, compute inferred types and consistency checking. The most important design principles were considered and verified through protégé tools such as Fact++ reasoner and DL-query tool. After execution of Fact++, individuals were correctly classified. For instance, Professor Ricardo Lopez was correctly classified as member of the **Professor** class. As a result, the ontology models accomplish the clarity and coherence design principles.

Concept	Axiomatic definition	Human definition
Person	(hasAge some int) and (hasGender some string) and (hasPersonName some string) and (hasWeight some float)	A **Person** is an individual that has age, has gender, has name and has weight
Employee	Person and (hasEconomicNumber some string)	Is a **Person** that has an economic number
Smartphone	Device and (hasMacAddress some string) and (hasIMEI some string)	Is a **Device** that has MAC address and has IMEI
Course	(hasCourseName some string) and (hasCredits some int) and (hasCourseKey exactly 1 string)	A course is an individual that has course name, has credits, and has primary key

Table 6. Some classes definition from the Person ontology.

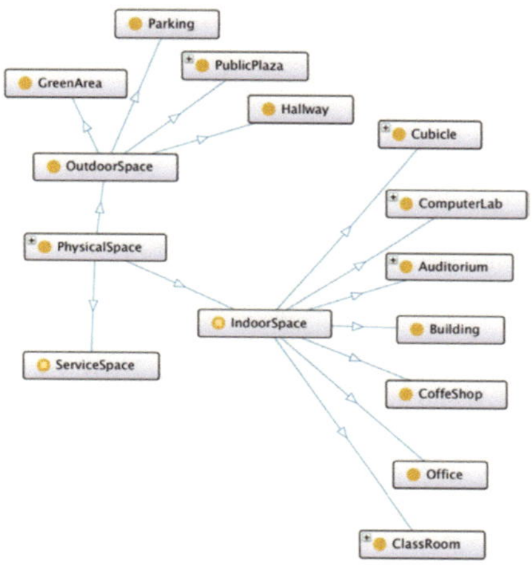

Figure 7. General model of the physical space ontology.

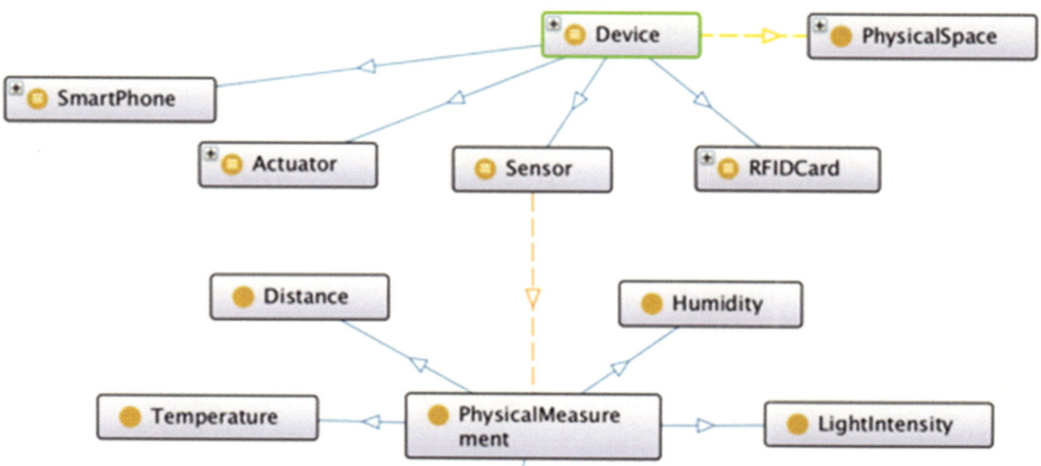

Figure 8. General model of the device ontology.

Classes	Object Properties	Data type Properties
owl:Thing	owl:topObjectProperty	owl:topDataProperty
Course	**isLocatedIn**	**activityToBePerformed**
Person	**hasDevice**	**avgHum**
Employee	**hasLoginIn**	**avgLight**
AcademicStaff	**hasOwner**	**avgTemp**
Coordinator	**isASpaceOf**	**hasAC**
DepartmentChief	**isAssociateProfessorOf**	**hasAge**
Professor	**isEnrolledIn**	hasArea
AdministrativeStaff	IsLocatedIn	**hasBirthDay**
Student	isLocatedNearOf	**hasBirthMonth**
Visitor	isPartOf	**hasBirthYear**
Device	**read**	**hasBrand**
Actuator	**requestAttention**	**hasCredits**
RFIDCard	**takeClassWith**	**hasDesignation**
Sensor		hasDoorState
SmartPhone		**hasEconomicalNumber**
PhysicalMeasurement		**hasFan**
Distance		**hasGender**
Humidity		**hasHum**
LightIntensity		**hasHumidityValue**
Temperature		**hasIDCard**
PhysicalSpace		**hasIMEI**
ServiceSpace		
IndoorSpace		
ComputerLab		
Office		
ClassRoom		
CoffeShop		
Auditorium		
Building		
Cubicle		
OutdoorSpace		
PublicPlaza		
Hallway		
GreenArea		
Parking		

Table 7. Classes, object properties and data type properties of the ontology.

5. Related work

The use of ontologies for context modelling is not a new research topic; there are many works in literature that describe the utilization of ontologies to support context-awareness or pervasive environments. In this section, a chronological overview of works reporting ontologies, architectures and frameworks for context modelling is presented, highlighting the main differences (see **Table 8**).

Chen, Finin and Joshi [15] described **CoBrA**, a context broker agent architecture that is capable of managing a shared model of the context and reasoning support for context-aware applications. The objective of CoBrA is to facilitate knowledge sharing and reasoning between agents.

Razmerita, Angehrn and Maedche [16] presented in 2003 **OntobUM**, a generic ontology-based user modelling architecture. This architecture integrates three ontologies: the user ontology, the domain ontology and the log ontology. Later in 2007 [17], authors augmented their **OntobUM** model by representing the behaviour of user's concept, such as level of activity, type of activity, level of knowledge sharing, etc. They present a conceptual layered architecture integrated with a presentation layer, a middleware layer and a storage layer. This later

	Characteristics of the architecture or framework		Context concepts represented			Context management		
	Agent oriented	Service oriented	Person or user profile	Physical context	Activities	Context representation model	Context reasoning	Context acquisition
CoBrA [15]	Yes	Yes	No	Yes	Yes	Ontologies	Flora-2	Automatically by Sensors and mobile devices
CONON [18] SOCAM [19]	No	Yes	Yes	Yes	Yes	Ontologies	DL reasoning	Manually introduced by ontology designers
OntobUM [16, [17]	Yes	Yes	Yes	No	Yes	Ontologies	No	Manually introduced by users
CoDAMoS [20]	No	Yes	Yes	Yes	Yes	Ontologies	No	Manually introduced by ontology designers
mIO! [21]	No	No	Yes	Yes	Yes	Ontologies	No	Manually introduced by ontology designers
User profile ontology [22]	No	No	Yes	No	Yes	Ontologies	No	Manually introduced by users

Table 8. Related work of ontologies for context-aware system.

architecture is similar to the architecture proposed and described in Section 2; however, the purpose of their applications differs, **OntoBUM** is intended for knowledge sharing between users inside an organization; whereas our proposed architecture is abstracted from a particular organization and it was designed to support context-aware environments and context-aware systems.

Wang et al. [18] described in 2004 **CONON**, an ontology for modelling context in pervasive computing environments. Authors propose an ontology model divided into *upper* ontology and *specific* ontology. The upper ontology model defines computational entity, location, person and activity as the most important entities of a context model. Later in 2004 [19], authors presented **SOCAM**, a service-oriented context-aware middleware architecture to support the construction of context-aware services in intelligent environments. **SOCAM** architecture incorporates CONON ontology.

Preuveneers et al. [20] presented **CoDAMoS**, an extensible context ontology for ambient intelligence, which describes four main concepts: user, environment, platform and service. Authors described the requirements for ambient intelligence: application adaptability, resource awareness, mobile services, semantic service discovery, code generation and context-aware user interfaces.

In 2010, Poveda-Villalón et al. [21] presented **mIO**! ontology network for a mobile environment. **mIO**! ontology consists of 11 modular ontologies: user, role, environment, location, time, service, provider, device, interface, source and network. This ontology covers a wide range of concepts related with context representation, however; authors do not present any reasoning results.

Skillen et al. [22] presented in 2012 a user profile model for context-aware application personalization; authors concentrated on concepts to model a dynamic context: user time, user location, user activity and user context.

6. Conclusions

The work reported in this chapter incorporates various technological paradigms, such as intelligent agents, network sensors, Web services and ontologies. The main objective of integrating these technologies was to support the development of more complex and intelligent context-aware applications.

The use of models implemented with ontologies offers significant advantages: the ability to exchange, expand, extend and maintain the individual ontologies. An example is the **Person** ontology, which can be interchanged as needed to adapt to new application needs.

The incorporation and exploitation of agents, Web services and ontological models is a clear trend that promises to improve the automatic selection and invocation of legacy and new Web services.

All these technologies together (Web services, intelligent agents and ontologies) are key facilitators for the wise management of context-based systems.

Author details

Maricela Bravo*, José A. Reyes-Ortiz, Leonardo Sánchez-Martínez and Roberto A. Alcántara-Ramírez

*Address all correspondence to: mcbc@correo.azc.uam.mx

Autonomous Metropolitan University, Delegación Azcapotzalco, Ciudad de México, México

References

[1] Guermah H, Fissaa T, Hafiddi H, Nassar M, Kriouile A. An Ontology Oriented Architecture for Context Aware Services Adaptation. arXiv preprint arXiv:1404.3280

[2] Abowd GD, Dey AK, Brown PJ, Davies N, Smith M, Steggles P. Towards a better understanding of context and context-awareness. In: International Symposium on Handheld and Ubiquitous Computing; September 1999; Berlin, Heidelberg: Springer; pp. 304-307

[3] Orsi G, Tanca L. (2011). Context Modelling and Context-Aware Querying. In Datalog Reloaded. Berlin, Heidelberg: Springer; 2011.pp. 225-244

[4] Perera C, Zaslavsky A, Christen P, Georgakopoulos D. Context aware computing for the internet of things: A survey. IEEE Communications Surveys & Tutorials. 2014; **16**(1):414-454

[5] Jennings NR, Wooldridge M. Agent-oriented software engineering. Journal of Artificial Intelligence, 2000;**117**:277-296

[6] Neches R, Fikes RE, Finin T, Gruber TR, Patil R, Senator T, Swartout WR. Enabling technology for knowledge sharing. AI Magazine. 1991;**12**(3):16-36

[7] Endriss U, Maudet N, Sadri F, Toni F. Logic-based agent communication protocols. Advances in Agent Communication Languages. 2004;**2922**:91-107

[8] FIPA ACL Message Structure Specification [Internet]. Available from: http://www.fipa.org/specs/fipa00061/SC00061G.html

[9] Devaraju A, Simon H. Ontology-based context modeling for user-centered contextaware services platform. In: Information Technology, 2008. ITSim 2008. International Symposium on. Vol. 2. New York: IEEE; 2008. pp. 1-7

[10] Paganelli F, Bianchi G, Giuli D. A context model for context-aware system design towards the ambient intelligence vision: Experiences in the eTourism domain. In: Universal Access in Ambient Intelligence Environments; Berlin, Heidelberg: Springer; 2007. pp. 173-191

[11] Chen G, Kotz D. A survey of context-aware mobile computing research. Technical Report TR2000-381, Department of Computer Science, Dartmouth College 2000;**1**(2.1)

[12] Gruber TR. A translation approach to portable ontologies. Knowledge Acquisition. 1993;**5**(2):199-220

[13] Gruber Thomas R. Toward principles for the design of ontologies used for knowledge sharing? International Journal of Human-Computer Studies **43**(51995):907-928

[14] Morbach Jan, Andreas Wiesner, Wolfgang Marquardt. OntoCAPE—A (re) usable ontology for computer-aided process engineering. Computers & Chemical Engineering 2009;**33**(10):1546-1556

[15] Chen H, Finin T, Joshi A. An ontology for context-aware pervasive computing environments. The Knowledge Engineering Review. 2003;**18**(03):197-207

[16] Razmerita L, Angehr, A, Maedche A. Ontology-based user modeling for knowledge management systems. In: International Conference on User Modeling; June 2003; Berlin, Heidelberg: Springer;pp. 213-217

[17] Razmerita L. Ontology-Based User Modeling. In Ontologies US: Springer; 2007. pp. 635-664

[18] Wang XH, Zhang DQ, Gu T, Pung HK. (2004, March). Ontology based context modelling and reasoning using OWL. In: Pervasive Computing and Communications Workshops, 2004. Proceedings of the Second IEEE Annual Conference on; March 2004; Washington, DC, USA.: IEEE; pp. 18-22

[19] Gu T, Wang XH, Pung HK, Zhang DQ. (2004,). An ontology-based context model in intelligent environments. In: Proceedings of Communication Networks and Distributed Systems Modeling and Simulation Conference; January 2004; San Diego, California, USA. 2004: pp. 270-275

[20] Preuveneers D, Van den Bergh J, Wagelaar D, Georges A, Rigole P, Clerckx T,De Bosschere K. (2004, November). Towards an extensible context ontology for ambient intelligence. In European Symposium on Ambient Intelligence; November 2004; Berlin, Heidelberg: Springer; pp. 148-159

[21] Poveda Villalon M, Suárez-Figueroa MC, García-Castro R, Gómez-Pérez A. A Context Ontology for Mobile Environments. In Proceedings of the 1st Workshop on context, information and ontologies, Heraklion, Greece. 2010

[22] Skillen KL, Chen L, Nugent CD, Donnelly MP, Burns W, Solheim I.. Ontological user profile modeling for context-aware application personalization. In: International Conference on Ubiquitous Computing and Ambient Intelligence; December 2012; Berlin, Heidelberg: Springer; pp. 261-268

Chapter 10

Resilience Enhancement in Cyber-Physical Systems: A Multiagent-Based Framework

Fábio Emanuel Pais Januário, Joaquim Leitão,
Alberto Cardoso and Paulo Gil

Additional information is available at the end of the chapter

http://dx.doi.org/10.5772/intechopen.69356

Abstract

The growing developments on networked devices, with different communication platforms and capabilities, made the cyber-physical systems an integrating part of most critical industrial infrastructures. Given their increasing integration with corporate networks, in which the industry 4.0 is the most recent driving force, new uncertainties, not only from the tangible physical world, but also from a cyber space perspective, are brought into play. In order to improve the overall resilience of a cyber-physical system, this work proposes a framework based on a distributed middleware that integrates a multiagent topology, where each agent is responsible for coordinating and executing specific tasks. In this framework, both physical and cyber vulnerabilities alike are considered, and the achievement of a correct state awareness and minimum levels of acceptable operation, in response to physical or malicious disturbances, are guaranteed. Experimental results collected with an IPv6-based simulator comprising several distributed computational devices and heterogeneous communication networks show the relevance and inherent benefits of this approach.

Keywords: cyber-physical systems, artificial cognition, context awareness, distributed middleware, heterogeneous systems

1. Introduction

Modern societies are quite dependent on efficient, stable and secure operation of critical infrastructures. As a whole, they consist of a wide range of heterogeneous devices, with several levels of resources, which are interconnected using different networking technologies [1]. These environments rely heavily on communication infrastructures, in order to take advantage of the distributed/grid or parallel computing paradigms. The migration of these systems into a cyber space that bridges the cyber world of computing and communication with the physical world is commonly referred in the literature as cyber-physical system (CPS). A CPS consists in the integration under the same umbrella of computing technologies, networking and physical processes, which aims at monitoring and controlling a given physical process [2].

This integration, however, raises a number of challenges in the context of traditional monitoring and control systems, particularly, with regard to defining a comprehensive framework for dealing with additional cyber, cognitive and human complex interdependencies, which ultimately enhance the potential for fault, malfunctions, failures or even security vulnerabilities [3]. CPSs over distributed heterogeneous environments present some vulnerabilities, which include efficient processing of information and correct assessment of the system behaviour. One main issue refers to faults and failures monitoring, being required to develop methods to identify, recover and mitigate such events. A second concern is the systems' vulnerability to cyber intrusion, where malicious actors may mask the system's degradation or relay false/fake data to higher management levels, regarding the current system's status [4]. Although the design of control systems may take into account uncertainty accommodation, namely physical disturbances, by appealing to a number of techniques such as robust control, adaptive control and stochastic control, it normally does not incorporate specific measures to deal with uncertainties associated with the cyber space.

Some previous malicious attacks on CPSs have shown that traditional protection/security mechanisms are not enough satisfactory to accommodate or mitigate such intrusions. In fact, most of the current systems have not been designed to include effective measures against cyber-attacks and have remained secured mostly through their anonymity. Anonymity, however, is no longer a guarantee of effective protection, making these systems more and more vulnerable, given the increasing likelihood of attacks. This issue is illustrated by the increasing number of incidents being reported (see [5]). In this context, cyber security gave rise to a new class of control problems, which demand a more holistic and cross-layer design approach, explicitly incorporating protection mechanisms for cyber-attacks within the overall system.

This chapter focuses on developing resilience mechanisms for such complex environments, involving a huge diversity of distributed physical devices along with a high heterogeneity of communication networks. The proposed approach makes use of agents embedded on a distributed middleware framework, where each agent is tailored for executing specific and coordinated tasks, namely, for detecting and recovering from cyber and physical malfunctions. The incorporation of these entities in the context of faults and failure diagnosis, or aiming at reducing the system vulnerability, is very appealing. They make possible the implementation of methods for resilience enhancement, including outliers detection and accommodation, as well as for maintaining the system in a safe operating state, in case of compromising events, such as communication link breakdown, or to account for security issues under the form of manipulation of data/configuration parameters by a malicious actor. For this purpose, some functionalities and attributes are provided to particular agents, so as to respond to environmental changes. To keep a permanent awareness of the overall system and react accordingly in case of compromising events, the developed mechanisms will allow to gauge the awareness of the context and the system states, including dedicated cognition functionalities.

The rest of this chapter is organized as follows. Section 2 discusses some important concepts, including that of resilience, state awareness and context awareness. Section 3 describes the proposed resilient approach and the underlying multiagent framework. Section 4 presents some results based on a simulation platform, while in Section 5, the main conclusions are drawn.

2. Resilience in cyber-physical systems

This work addresses the resilience enhancement in modern supervision systems over heterogeneous communication networks, where the physical and cyber issues are interconnected. CPSs comprise the integration of computing hardware, networking and physical processes aiming at monitoring and control a physical process, by means of feedback loops. These systems must operate dependably, safely, securely, efficiently and in real-time. A CPS roughly comprises two main layers, namely, the physical layer and cyber layer. The physical layer includes an intelligent network of actuators, sensors and additional hardware devices in order to collect information and control a physical system, while the cyber layer can be regarded as the decision-making setup, comprising information and communication devices. The cyber layer, particularly in what the industrial control systems is concerned, is typically composed of a Supervisory Control and Data Acquisition (SCADA) system [6]. The present work combines these two domains, as illustrated in **Figure 1**.

These CPSs typical consist of three main components: the control network, communication infrastructure and process network. The control network hosts all the required devices for both controlling the physical layer and providing the control interface to the process network. A typical control network can be composed of a mesh of Program Logic Controllers (PLCs), Remote Terminal Units (RTUs), as well as Wireless Sensor and Actuator Networks (WSANs). The communication infrastructure is used to interconnect different components of the system, providing a unique interface between control systems and field devices. Furthermore, the process network hosts the servers along with the Human Machine Interface (HMI) platform, which consists of servers and software packages that allow the connection to field equipment.

2.1. Resilient systems

The concept of resilience emerged, originally, associated with the fields of ecology and psychology. Nowadays, it is used in many different contexts focused on two notable areas, namely, organizational and information technology. Organizational resilience has been used to describe a movement among entities such as businesses, communities and governments to improve their ability to respond or react to and quickly recover from catastrophic events, such as natural disasters or terrorist attacks. On the other hand, the information technology resilience considers the stability and quality of service in face of threats on the computing and networking infrastructure [7].

Most researchers on information sciences define resilience purely in terms of the availability of the underlying system. Some claim that beyond availability, resiliency should include the ability to cope with threats of an unexpected and malicious nature, while others explicitly

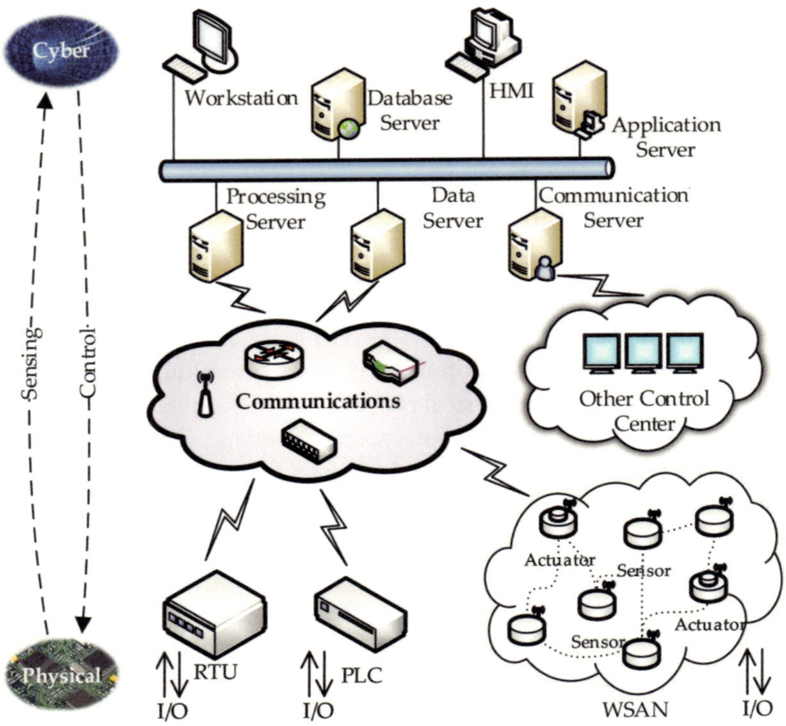

Figure 1. Example of a cyber-physical system.

include defence and recovery with respect to cyber-attacks (see [5, 8]). In the context of CPSs, resilience highlights the ability to accommodate faults or events that otherwise might compromise the stability of the system and the underlying goals.

Resilient control systems (RCSs), which are a part of CPSs, are a new control design paradigm that considers all possible threats, namely, cyber and physical aspects. In [9], it is suggested that 'Resilient control systems are those that tolerate fluctuations via their structure, design parameters, control structure and control parameters', where the presence of malicious actors is not considered. Another definition refers to as 'an effective reconstitution of control under attack from intelligent adversaries', being the resiliency only defined in terms of response to intelligent actors. In addition, in [10], it stated that 'A resilient control system is one that maintains state awareness and an accepted level of operational normalcy in response to disturbances, including threats of an unexpected and malicious nature'. This work extends the previous definition to CPSs, where threats are those events that can hamper normalcy and destabilize control system networks, including human error and malicious attacks, complex latencies and interdependencies, intermittent communication breakdown or even a network component malfunction or failure.

There are some architectures or frameworks in the literature for improving the resilience of these systems. In Ref. [11], a centralized architecture based on a fuzzy-neural data fusion engine is considered to increase the state awareness of RCSs. Its main goal is to provide real-time monitoring and analysis of complex critical control systems. Nevertheless, this approach is somewhat difficult to implement in a heterogeneous decentralized environment, where communication channels can suffer from malfunctions. In Ref. [12], an intelligent resilient control algorithm for a wireless networked control system, based on a quantification of the concept of resiliency in terms of quality of control, is proposed. The authors developed an intelligent resilient control algorithm that ensures operational normalcy in face of wireless interference incidents, such as radio frequency jamming or signal blocking. In Ref. [13], an autonomous decentralized resilient monitor system able to dynamically adapt and reconfigure, depending on current conditions, is proposed. This framework, however, requires modelling the sensors and plants, as well as metrics for data quality, which can be difficult to fulfil in a real distributed heterogeneous network. Finally, Ref. [14] defined an integrated diagnostic and control strategy, relying on an agent design to be resilient in terms of stability and efficiency. Nevertheless, it should be mentioned that the proposed intelligent techniques may be difficult to implement in some components of a heterogeneous network, namely, on wireless nodes.

2.2. State awareness

State awareness is an imprecise concept that is difficult to quantify and, in addition, can change its meaning according to the context in which it is applied. When applied in CPSs, state awareness can be divided into two related categories: the ability to know or estimate the necessary control system states to maintain a stable closed loop operation, and the provision of sufficient knowledge of operation to make reliable informed decisions [10, 15].

According the control theory fundamentals, the observability and state awareness are to some extent related. However, the main differentiation is that observability is an intrinsic system property, while state awareness is the actual measurement or estimation of the system states. This leads to the definition proposed in Ref. [15], where state awareness is considered as the availability of the internal system's states, either through direct measurement $x(t)$ or through derived estimates $\hat{x}(t)$ based on an observer/estimator. As such, in the case of a cyber-attack, if state awareness can be maintained in the presence of manipulated measurements, the effects of an attack can be mitigated. Otherwise, if state awareness is not fulfilled, the system most likely will be uncontrollable, resulting in physical damage and injury.

On the other hand, it is important that sufficient knowledge of operating parameters, which represent a basis for decision-making, is provided in CPSs. In these systems, some requirements for establishing performance depend on a number of metrics that are commonly based on the use of collected data. For this purpose, Rieger and Gertman [10] argue that it is necessary to consider everything that might affect the system's normalcy, to be able to maintain state awareness. In control systems, these measures are cyber and physical security, process efficiency and stability, and process compliancy. Moreover, it is important to note that for gaining state awareness, it is not enough having all the necessary sources of data. What is actually fundamental is the necessary information extracted from the data that allows to maintain the normal operation of the system. In the case of a cyber-attack, a spectrum of state awareness is available from the normal operating regime of the system to an attacker having complete access and knowledge of the system and dynamics. The latter is the worst scenario, because it is impossible to maintain the system under control, as being in such conditions, the shutdown of the system is the only viable option.

According to the above perspectives, in this work, state awareness is considered as the availability of the necessary information that allows to maintain an acceptable level of normal operation of the system. The required information includes that associated with the physical layer of the system with the availability of the internal system states, and that stemming from the cyber layer under the form of data regarding safety, stability and efficiency of the system.

2.3. Context awareness

Context awareness is a vital feature of modern systems, such as networked systems or monitoring and control systems. With the increase of heterogeneous systems, control and monitoring techniques are now being applied to several interconnected subsystems, including human interactions. This leads to the need for new and more intelligent and adaptive approaches, capable of understanding the system's environment and adjusting their operation, accordingly. These kinds of systems that address both the dynamisms and uncertainties are referred in the literature as context awareness systems. In order to properly define context awareness, it is necessary to first define what is meant by context.

2.3.1. Context

One of the most widely accepted definitions of the term context states that 'context is any information that can be used to characterize the situation of an entity. An entity is a person, place or object that is considered relevant to the interaction between a user and an application, including the user and applications themselves' [16]. The reader is referred to Ref. [17] and references there in, for extensions and improvements to this definition.

Currently, the notion of context can no longer be seen as a set of numerical values that characterized the situation of an entity. Recent definitions of context consider it as a collection of measured and inferred knowledge that arises from the general activity of a context awareness system. Furthermore, context is not only present when an interaction between two entities occurs, but the absence of these interactions also carries valuable information about the system itself, especially in the field of wireless networking. This motivates the development of proper mechanisms to deal with context information in the presence of imperfect, ambiguous, wrong and unknown information.

Considering this perspective, in the present work, context is a collection of measured and inferred information (potentially containing uncertain, ambiguous and unknown segments), obtained from a highly dynamic and heterogeneous environment, characterizing its current situation.

2.3.2. Context awareness system

The definition of context awareness is highly related with that of context. In 1997 and 1998, early contributions to this topic addressed the concept of context awareness in the sense of detecting, interpreting and responding to aspects of a user's environment. In Ref. [16], a system is said to be context awareness if it is able to support dynamic changes in its behaviour, as a response to perceived changes in its context. On the other hand, in Ref. [18], it is suggested that context awareness system means that one is able to extract, interpret and use context information and that can adapt its functionality to the current context of use.

Context awareness systems must cover reasoning and processing of uncertain, ambiguous and missing information [17]. The need for this support emerges with the presence of these systems in increasingly larger, dynamic, heterogeneous and less reliable environments. Concepts such as resilience and robustness can also be included in this definition.

In this work, context awareness system is a system capable of adjusting its operation based on perceived, processed and inferred context information, obtained from highly dynamic, heterogeneous and uncertain environments.

2.3.3. *Information flow in context awareness cyber-physical systems*

The field of CPSs has a wide range of areas of study and applications, resulting in the existence of a large array of context awareness CPSs proposed in the literature. Surveying the literature in this topic, it is possible to identify similarities in most approaches adopted by researchers, despite their diversity. **Figure 2** presents these similarities.

In an initial step, information from the system and environment needs to be collected, usually using sensor networks. Pre-processing tasks such as information categorization, data fusion and aggregation, imputation techniques, machine learning algorithms and inference of new information are usually applied at this point [17]. Once the information is collected and pre-processed, it must be modelled and stored. Databases and ontologies are two of the most popular and used solutions for this purpose. A context model allows a high-level description of the context by defining and characterizing entities and their relationships and can be either static or dynamic [19].

The third step is commonly referred to as context inference or reasoning. Its main goal is to deduce new information based on perceived (and stored) information, allowing for a deeper characterization of the system and its environment. Inference rules, Fuzzy Logic, Hidden

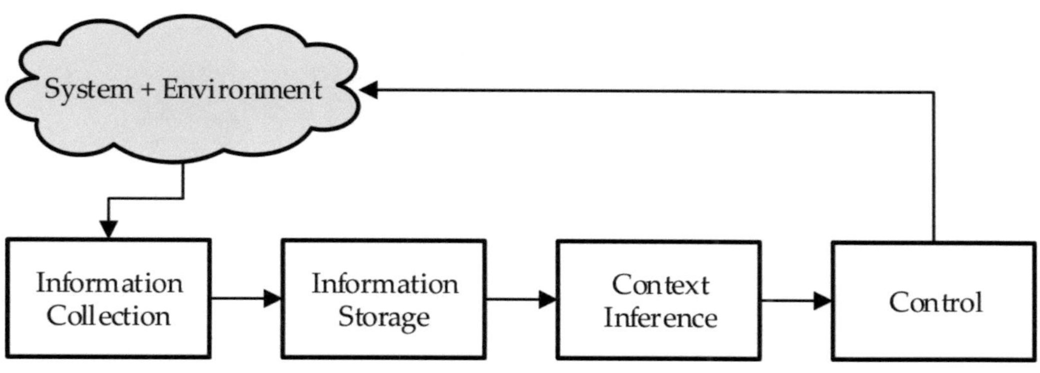

Figure 2. Information flow in context awareness CPSs.

Markov Models or Naive Bayes are some examples of context inference techniques adopted in the literature [16]. A context-aware CPS will process the output of the previously mentioned steps to identify changes in context and determine how to adapt its behaviour, in response to changes.

As CPSs usually monitor and control a given process, the fourth and final stage quite often consists in the formulation and solution of an optimization problem. Therefore, by formulating an optimization problem, a CPS can detect changes in the context and the need for adjusting its behaviour.

3. Resilient framework overview

The proposed approach for resilience enhancement is accomplished by incorporating dedicated algorithms and heuristics on a multiagent system (MAS) within a distributed middleware framework. Each agent is tailored for executing specific and coordinated tasks, namely, for detecting and recovering from physical and cyber malfunctions. The incorporation of these entities to cope with CPSs vulnerabilities is very appealing, as they provide flexibility in implementing specific functions, actions or countermeasures wherever they are needed within the network. **Figure 3** presents an overview of the proposed architecture, which comprises five layers.

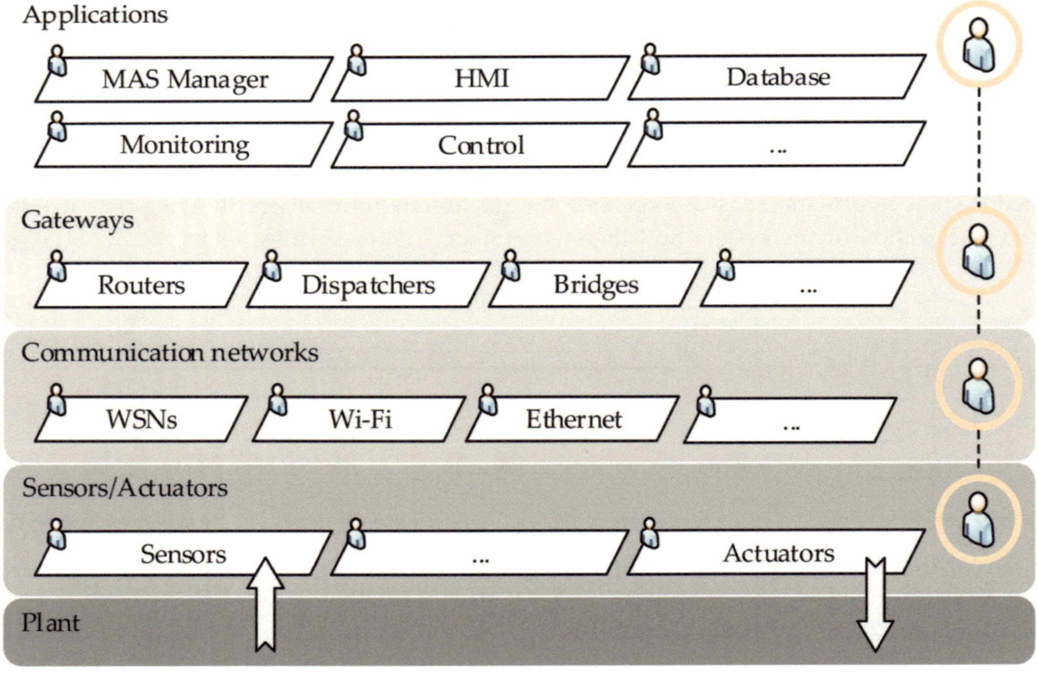

Figure 3. Resilience architecture layers.

The plant layer represents the physical infrastructure, consisting of a process under control or monitoring. This process can be a simple Single-input single-output (SISO) system or a complex system, such as a power distribution grid. To interact with the environment, it is necessary sensors and actuators that are represented in the sensors/actuators layer. Some of these devices can have computational capabilities, such as in the case of wireless nodes. The communication network layer allows the communication between the components of the system, namely, sensors, actuators and devices. These networks can be for example distributed low-power wireless networks or wired networks. The gateway layer allows the interconnection of different networks that can coexist in a CPS. This layer can have dispatchers to coordinate the communications on a WSAN or routers to relay information to the destination devices. Finally, the application layer provides a user with a number of applications, by allowing in a transparent way the interaction with networks, devices and plants.

In this approach, each layer comprises a set of agents with specific functions, which depend on where they are installed. All agents are managed by a master agent that belongs to the underlying layer and is responsible for ensuring the communication between subordinate agents and with master agents of other layers. It should be noted that in the context of CPSs, the physical system may consist of several distributed subsystems, which lead to replicating these layers for each subsystem. In this case, the master agents are responsible for ensuring the communication between these distributed layers. The proposed MAS topology implements a distributed middleware possessing the standard functions of integration, monitoring and configuration, apart from the local agents that ensure the resilience enhancement. The integration facilitates the data transfer between the process/device infrastructures and CPSs components. The monitoring function evaluates the performance of the middleware at runtime by applying some metrics. Finally, the configuration enables the definition of commands to configure data uploaded and downloaded from devices, and also the subordinate agents.

3.1. Agent features

The features of the agents proposed in this work can be aggregated into three groups (**Figure 4**): physical, cyber and multiagent system. These groups are interconnected and aim to improve the overall system resilience. It should be noted that data are collected by physical devices in the physical system, and subsequently processed by the MAS distributed over the architecture, for ensuring security, integrity and privacy to applications. Based on collected data, the MAS can assess the context and the state awareness of the system to react accordingly.

The physical system includes all physical devices, such as sensors, actuators, transductors, motors, etc. At this level, resilience is achieved by enforcing that reads/writes in the sensors/actuators are correct, not subject to any malicious attack and are not corrupted. The multiagent system aims to check the behaviour of agents and, therefore, of the entire MAS. These agents are responsible for coordinating all communications, along with the implementation of resilient mechanisms and tools. It is important to ensure in this level that the underlying agents are working properly and not suffering from any malicious attack or malfunction. The cyber system is responsible for maintaining the system security and privacy communications, and includes methods, tools and metrics implemented for improving resilience, from a cyber-security point of view.

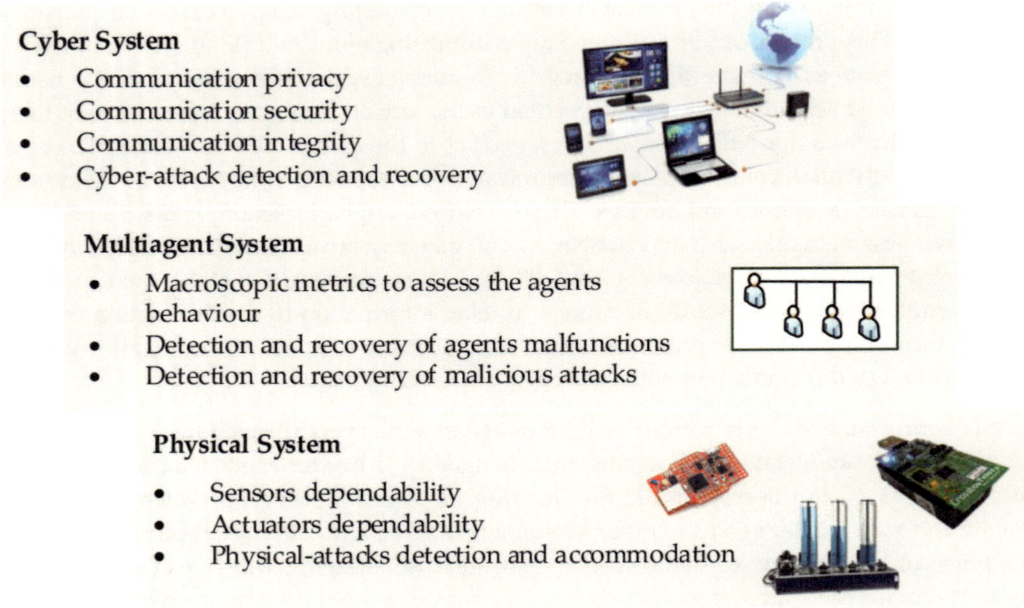

Figure 4. Agent features.

3.2. Agent behaviour

In the case of heterogeneous distributed CPSs, subsystems may all not possess the same characteristics and vulnerabilities, so the developed agents must be configured to provide the necessary functionalities to each subsystem. In the case of a detected event, the entire MAS has the ability to act accordingly in a way to provide resilience to the system, while guaranteeing the safety status of the system until the problem is completely addressed.

For this purpose, agents should adapt to the environment dynamics as illustrated in **Figure 5**. The behaviour of an agent depends on following four basic attributes:

- *State awareness*—State awareness has been described in Section 2.2. To take any action on the physical system, the agent needs to know the state of the system. Furthermore, the agent itself should contribute to keep the state awareness of the system, which is important to ensure resilience;
- *Context awareness*—The agent must act and behave in accordance with the context where it is installed/running. The agent needs to adapt, for example, to the physical platform where it is running and to problems taking place around them;
- *Agent awareness*—The awareness of an agent is important as attacks and malfunctions can also compromise the agent itself and contribute to degrading the entire system. As such, it is crucial to ensure that an agent is working properly;
- *User commands*—An agent can be configured by user commands.

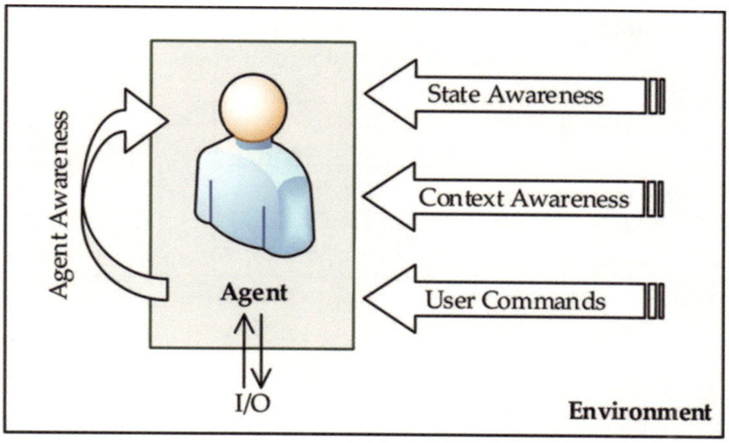

Figure 5. Agent behaviour.

4. Case study

The proposed framework for resilience enhancement is evaluated through simulations using a CPS simulator composed of a nonlinear benchmark system model, namely, a Continuous Stirred Tank Reactor (CSTR), a WSAN and additional remote devices, including a remote controller, a server where the model of the plant is running and a HMI.

4.1. Testbed simulator

The testbed simulator consists of three main components (see **Figure 6**), including a Simulink-based simulator, COntiki OS JAva Simulator [20] (COOJA) and remote devices deployed in the MATLAB environment. All of these components are distributed over five computers.

The plant, whose goal is to control or monitor, is described by a mathematical model implemented in the MATLAB-Simulink environment. In addition, ADCs and DACs associated with the sensor node and the actuator node, respectively, are included in the simulation setup to allow the interaction with the plant. To collect/send data from/to the plant and to implement the communication with remote devices, a WSAN is implemented and simulated in the COOJA environment. The COOJA simulator can emulate the operation of a real wireless device and its networking behaviour. At this level, all wireless network components are defined, by including node address, network topology, routers, along with the software that will run on each wireless node. The remote devices, namely, the controller, model-server and HMI, are considered transparently similarly as directly connected to physical hardware.

Communication and time synchronization between Simulink and COOJA is carried out using available plug-ins in the GISOO project (see [21]). GISOO is a virtual testbed for simulating wireless CPS, which integrates these two simulators and also enables users to evaluate actual embedded code for the wireless nodes in realistic experiments. Additionally, the testbed allows the communication between the WSAN and remote devices using a tunslip created in a Linux

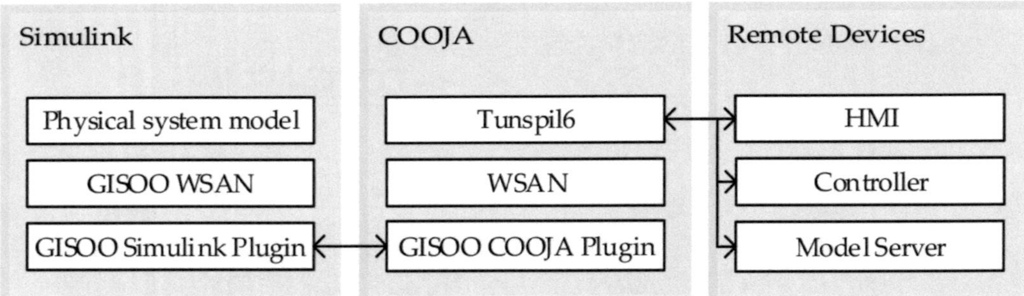

Figure 6. Testbed simulator.

environment. Finally, is should be mentioned that all the devices and nodes in this testbed have an IPv6 address, which allows the communication by User Datagram Protocol (UDP).

4.1.1. CSTR plant

The CSTR benchmark system comprises a constant volume reactor cooled by a co-current single coolant stream, as shown in **Figure 7**, where an irreversible exothermic reaction in a liquid medium takes place within reservoir (see [22]). The reactor's main purpose is to deliver the concentration of the outlet effluent C_A at a prescribed value, by manipulating the coolant flow rate q_c circulating in the reactor's jacket. The process can be described by the following differential equations:

$$\frac{dC_A}{dt} = \frac{q_A}{V}\left(C_{A,i}(t) - C_A(t)\right) - \gamma_0 C_A(t)\exp\left(-\frac{E}{R \cdot T_A(t)}\right) \tag{1}$$

$$\begin{aligned}\frac{dT_A}{dt} = \frac{q_A}{V}\left(T_{A,i}(t) - T_A(t)\right) - \gamma_1 C_A(t)\exp\left(-\frac{E}{R \cdot T_A(t)}\right) + \\ \gamma_2 q_c(t)\left(1 - \exp\left(-\frac{\gamma_3}{q_c(t)}\right)\right)\left(T_{C,i}(t) - T_A(t)\right)\end{aligned} \tag{2}$$

where C_A and T_A denote the concentration and temperature in the tank, assuming that the reactor is perfectly mixed and q_c the coolant flow rate. The remaining parameters of the system borrowed from [23] are presented in **Table 1**.

Taking into account the nominal values for the CSTR shown in **Table 1**, the operating region is constrained to:

$$\begin{aligned} 0 < C_A < 1.00 \text{ mol/l} \\ T_A > 350.00 \text{ K} \\ 0 \le q_c \le q_{c,max} \text{ l/min} \end{aligned} \tag{3}$$

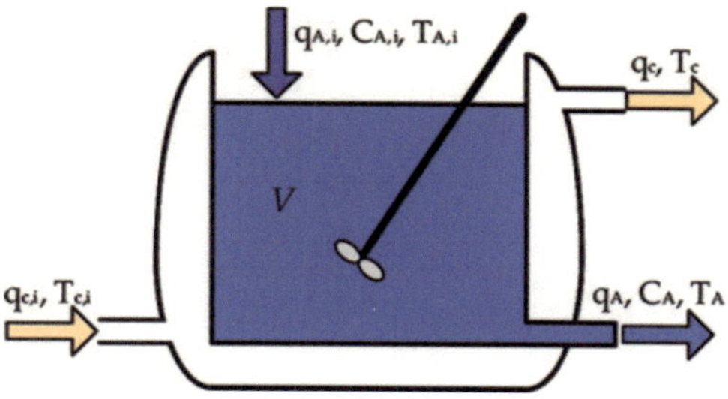

Figure 7. CSTR plant.

4.1.2. WSAN

The WSAN infrastructure includes three Crossbow TelosB nodes within the simulation environment (**Figure 8**). One of the nodes is set as a sensor and used to collect the concentration of the reactor's outlet effluent C_A, while a second node is used as actuator, associated with the coolant flow rate q_c circulating in the reactor's jacket. In addition, the remaining node is included as a sink, deploying a border router that implements the Routing Protocol for Low Power and Lossy Networks (RPL). The border router together with Tunslip allows IPv6 communication with WSAN nodes. In normal operation, the sensor node sends collected data to the applications, and the actuator node receives data from the applications through the sink node. However, all nodes have the ability to communicate directly one another, whenever necessary.

4.1.3. Remote devices

Three remote devices are used to allow the interaction with the rest of the system. Each of these devices is located on a remote computer. Through the HMI, it is possible to configure

Parameter	Description	Nominal Value
q_A	Process flow rate of component A	100 l min^{-1}
$C_{A,i}$	Feed concentration of component A	1.00 l min^{-1}
$T_{A,i}$	Feed temperature	350.00 K
$T_{C,i}$	Inlet coolant temperature	350.00 K
E/R	Activation energy	1.00 × 10^4 K
V	Volume of the tank	100.001 l
γ_0	Pre-exponential factor	7.20 × 10^{10} min^{-1}
γ_1	Constant	1.44 × 10^{13} l K min^{-1}
γ_2	Constant	0.01 l^{-1}
γ_3	Constant	7.00 × 10^2 min^{-1}

Table 1. CSTR parameters.

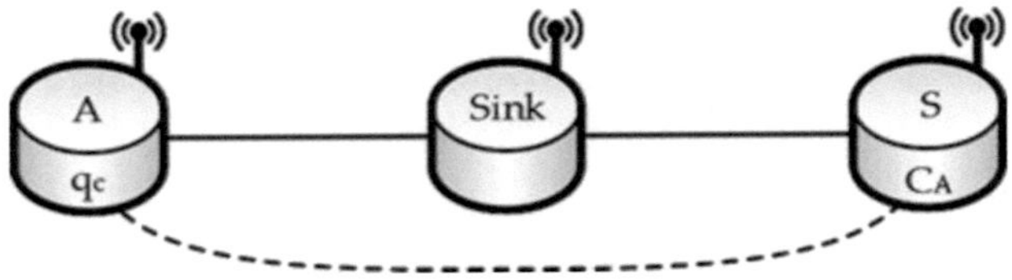

Figure 8. WSAN topology.

the entire system and observe current states, allowing the interaction with a user. The model-server is used to record historic data of the system and provide a model of the physical process to predict its response. This model is based on Eqs. (1) and (2), considering constrains in Eq. (3) and the constants in **Table 1**. Finally, the remote controller is implemented based on a Mamdani-type Fuzzy PID controller (**Figure 9**).

4.2. Multiagent system framework

The multiagent framework developed for this testbed is presented in **Figure 10**. Considering the layers presented in **Figure 3**, it is possible to observe that in this case the developed agents are distributed over the applications and the sensors/actuators layer. Each agent is responsible for a specific task and is coordinated by a master agent. Moreover, every message transmitted over the network comprises a header and a payload. The message payload contains the Message Type: the message can be originated from the systems' applications or from a node; Device ID: denoting the device address; Control ID: the command flag for local agents; Agent ID: agent's identifier; Agent MSG: data provided by an agent.

Master Agent—The master agent's main goal is to carry out extensive management routines related to subordinate local agents and to coordinate all communications. This agent is also responsible for monitoring the status of all local agents and, in case of an agent crash, to relaunch them.

Security Agent—The security agent is responsible for periodically analyzing important variables of the system for coherence, as well as the messages' structure. If any anomaly is detected, the system is switched to a safe mode operation.

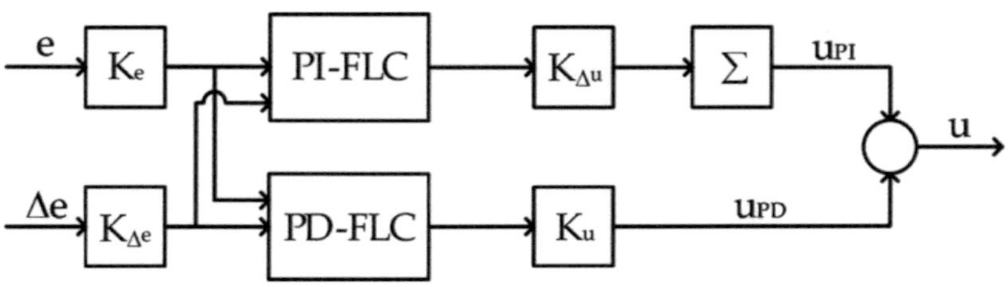

Figure 9. PID-Fuzzy logical control schematics.

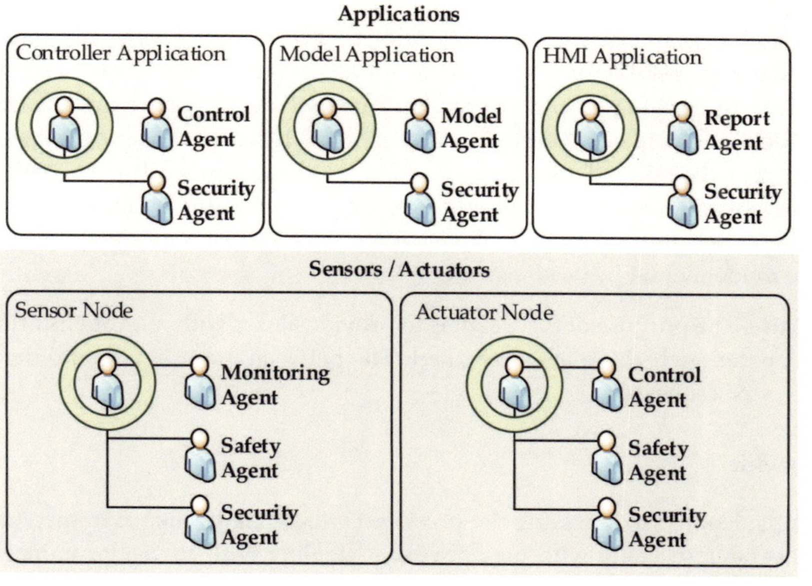

Figure 10. Multiagent framework.

Monitoring Agent—The monitoring agent is responsible for collecting data from the environment and accommodating possible outliers in raw readings. The local detection and accommodation of outliers is based on the approach suggested in [24]. It is also in charge for checking whether readings are within valid limits of operation, defined by a user.

Control Agent—In an actuator node, the control agent is responsible for sending to a digital-to-analogue converter the control actions received from the control application. This agent is also responsible for testing the periodicity of received control actions, through which communication disturbances or even a breakdown can be detected. If it is the case, the system switches to a safe mode operation. In the control application, this agent receives the sensor readings and applies a control algorithm to return the respective control action to the actuator's node. This agent is also responsible for testing the periodicity of sensor readings, and if any malfunction is detected, the system switches similarly to a safe operation mode.

Model Agent—The model agent's main goal is to predict the physical system behaviour, as well as other important components of the system. Besides, this agent receives sensor readings and control actions in order to update the underlying models. Further, this agent is crucial to ensure a safe operation mode whenever it is not possible to collect sensor readings.

Safety Agent—The safety agent is responsible for ensuring a safe operation mode, which is needed in case of communication link breakdown, remote controller's malfunction or even user induced errors/commands. In safe mode, the sensor's node safety agent, considering the context and the underlying problem or malfunction, will decide where to send readings. The actuator node's safety agent, in a similar way, decides if received control actions should be used. If they are to be rejected, local control actions based on a prescribed heuristic, such as an on-off approach, will provide the underlying control actions, and assuming the most recent available reference signal. In the case where it is not possible to have access to sensor readings, a predictive model would be used instead.

Report Agent—The purpose of this agent is to provide a user with relevant information from the system operation. It also allows the interaction between users, agents and the system, by processing users' requests.

4.3. Experiments

This section is devoted to assessing the proposed enhancing resilience framework, evaluating agent's behaviour along with the network in dealing with particular vulnerabilities on the RCS. In this context, readings are sampled from the sensors' ADCs, at a frequency of 2 Hz. To assess the effectiveness of the proposed MAS framework, in all the experiments, the control goal was to keep the concentration of the outlet effluent C_A at some prescribed values.

Two experiments were carried out, and the outcomes were discussed. In the following figures, normal operation of the system without any resilience framework is shown in blue, the operation with the MAS-proposed framework is in red, and the reference signal is presented in black. On the other hand, the flow rate refers to the underlying control actions.

4.3.1. Jamming attack

This experiment considers a jamming attack in the sink node, which prevents it from forwarding any data to other nodes and applications and receive data from the WSAN. **Figure 11** shows an attack occurring between 3.06 and 3.30 min. As can be observed, the MAS is effective in maintaining the concentration level in the neighbourhood of the most recent received reference from the server, by incorporating a safeguard approach where sensor node sends readings directly to the actuator node. When communication is restored, jamming is blocked, and the normal operation of the system is resumed.

4.3.2. Node lost

In this experiment, the communication with the sensor node is lost, due to node's malfunction. Possible causes may include power failure or congestion on the radio receptor, just to name out a few. In this case, as can be observed in **Figure 12**, the model application sends to the controller an estimation of the system output between 2.40 and 3.30 min. Once again, the MAS is effective in keeping the normal operation of the whole system until the sensor is again functional.

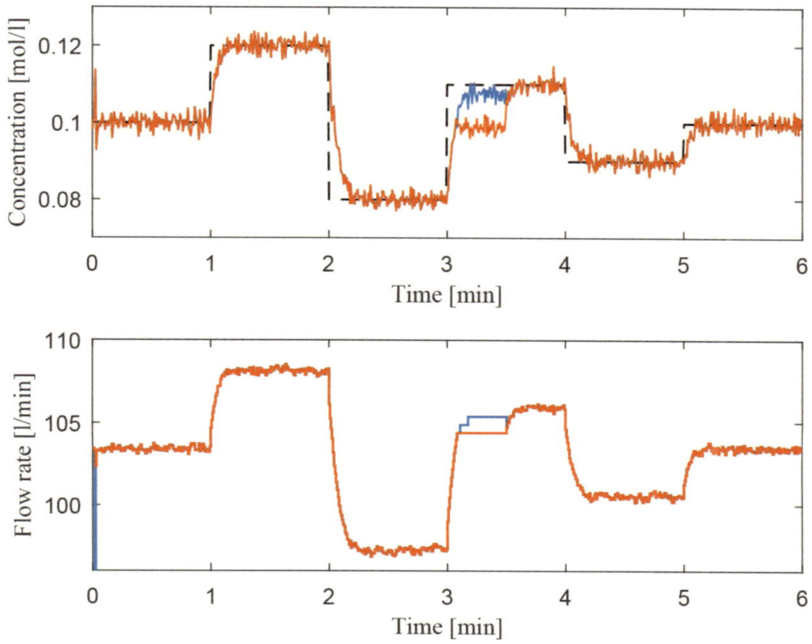

Figure 11. CSTR system: jamming attack.

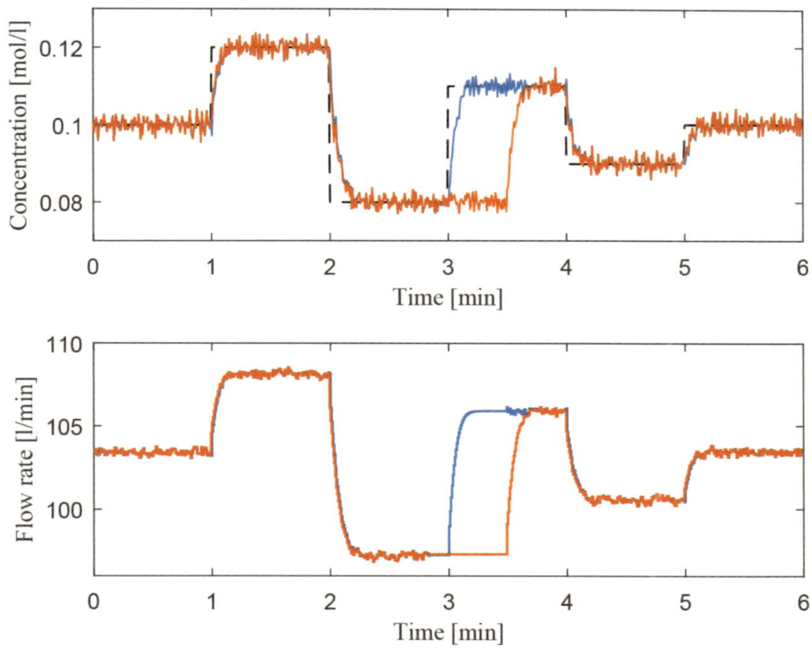

Figure 12. CSTR system: node lost.

5. Conclusions

This work dealt with a multiagent-based framework capable of improving the resilience of cyber-physical systems, as well as providing the necessary flexibility to deploy specific functions where actions or measures are needed. This allows obtaining improved responses at execution time, autonomy, services continuity and superior levels of scalability. The proposed framework focuses essentially on issues related to cyber-security and physical-security. In addition, the development of a hierarchical methodology embeds and prioritizes incoming information to ensure state awareness and context awareness, while managing and optimizing the system's response. In addition, a testbed simulator is presented, comprising a CPS with a physical process where some illustrative experiments were conducted to assess the relevance of the proposed approach. Results showed the effectiveness and pertinence of the proposed multiagent framework in the context of CPS.

Acknowledgements

Fábio Januário acknowledges Fundação para a Ciência e Tecnologia (FCT), Portugal, for the Ph.D. Grant SFRH/BD/85586/2012.

Author details

Fábio Emanuel Pais Januário[1,2]*, Joaquim Leitão[2], Alberto Cardoso[2] and Paulo Gil[1,2,3]

*Address all correspondence to: f.januario@campus.fct.unl.pt

1 Electrical Engineering Department, Faculty of Science and Technology, NOVA University of Lisbon, Campus de Caparica, Portugal

2 CISUC – Center for Informatics and Systems of the University of Coimbra, Coimbra, Portugal

3 Centre of Technology and Systems (CTS), UNINOVA, NOVA University of Lisbon, Campus de Caparica, Portugal

References

[1] Xu T, Masys A.. Critical Infrastructure Vulnerabilities: Embracing a Network Mindset. In: Masys A., editor. Exploring the Security Landscape: Non-Traditional Security Challenges. 1st ed. Cham: Springer International Publishing; 2016. p. 177-193. DOI: 10.1007/978-3-319-27914-5_9

[2] Romanovsky A., Ishikawa F., editors. Trustworthy Cyber-Physical Systems Engineering. Boca Raton: CRC Press; 2016. 462 p.

[3] Jin X., Haddad WM., Yucelen T. An Adaptive Control Architecture for Mitigating Sensor and Actuator Attacks in Cyber-Physical Systems. IEEE Transactions on Automatic Control. 2017;PP(99):1. DOI: 10.1109/TAC.2017.2652127

[4] Rieger C, Zhu Q, Basar T. Agent-based cyber control strategy design for resilient control systems: Concepts, architecture and methodologies. In: 5th International Symposium on Resilient Control Systems. IEEE; 2012. pp. 40-47. DOI: 10.1109/ISRCS.2012.6309291

[5] Yuan Y, Zhu Q, Sun F, Wang Q, Basar T. Resilient control of cyber-physical systems against Denial-of-Service attacks. In: 6th International Symposium on Resilient Control Systems (ISRCS). IEEE; 2013. pp. 54-59. DOI: 10.1109/ISRCS.2013.6623750

[6] Ali S, Qaisar S, Saeed H, Khan M, Naeem M, Anpalaga A. Network challenges for cyber physical systems with tiny wireless devices: A case study on reliable pipeline condition monitoring. Sensors. 2015;**15**(4):7172-7205. DOI: 10.3390/s150407172

[7] Hollnagel E., Nemeth C.P., editors. Resilience Engineering Perspectives, Volume 2: Preparation and Restoration. Boca Raton: CRC Press; 2016. 310 p.

[8] Arghandeh R, Meier A, Mehrmanesh L, Mili L. On the definition of cyber-physical resilience in power systems. Renewable and Sustainable Energy Reviews. 2016;**58**:1060-1069. DOI: http://dx.doi.org/10.1016/j.rser.2015.12.193

[9] Mitchel SM, Mannan MS. Designing resilient engineered systems. Chemical Engineering Progress. 2006;**102**(4):39-45

[10] Rieger C, Gertman D, McQueen M. Resilient control systems: Next generation design research. In: 2nd Conference on Human System Interactions. IEEE; 2009. pp. 632-636. DOI: 10.1109/HSI.2009.5091051

[11] Wijayasekara D, Linda O, Manic M, Rieger C. FN-DFE: Fuzzy-Neural data fusion engine for enhanced resilient State-Awareness of hybrid energy systems. IEEE Transactions on Cybernetics. 2014;**44**(11):2065-2075. DOI: 10.1109/TCYB.2014.2323891

[12] Ji K, Wei D. Resilient control for wireless networked control systems. International Journal of Control, Automation and Systems. 2011;**9**(2):285-293. DOI: 10.1007/s12555-011-0210-7

[13] Garcia H, Lin W, Meerkov S. A resilient condition assessment monitoring system. In: 5th International Symposium on Resilient Control Systems. IEEE; 2012. pp. 98-105. DOI: 10.1109/ISRCS.2012.6309301

[14] Rieger C, Villez K. Resilient control system execution agent (ReCoSEA). In: 5th International Symposium on Resilient Control Systems. IEEE; 2012. pp. 143-148. DOI: 10.1109/ISRCS.2012.6309308

[15] Melin A, Ferragut E, Laska J, Fugate D, Kisner R. A mathematical framework for the analysis of cyber-resilient control systems. In: 6th International Symposium on Resilient Control Systems (ISRCS). IEEE; 2013. pp. 13-18. DOI: 10.1109/ISRCS.2013.6623743

[16] Perera C, Zaslavsky A, Christen P, Georgakopoulos D. Context aware computing for the internet of things: A survey. IEEE Communications Surveys & Tutorials. 2014;**16**(1):414-454. DOI: 10.1109/SURV.2013.042313.00197

[17] Yürür Ö, Liu CH, Sheng Z, Leung VCM, Moreno W, Leung KK. Context-awareness for mobile sensing: A survey and future directions. IEEE Communications Surveys & Tutorials. 2016;**18**(1):68-93. DOI: 10.1109/COMST.2014.2381246

[18] Truong H, Dustdar S. A survey on context-aware web service systems. International Journal of Web Information Systems. 2009;**5**(1):5-31. DOI: http://doi.org/10.1108/17440080910947295

[19] Adomavicius G., Tuzhilin A. Context-Aware Recommender Systems. In: Ricci F., Rokach L., Shapira B., Kantor, P., editors. Recommender Systems Handbook. Boston, MA: Springer US; 2011. p. 217--253. DOI: 10.1007/978-0-387-85820-3

[20] Contiki OS. Contiki: The Open Source OS for the Internet of Things [Internet]. Available from: http://www.contiki-os.org/ [Accessed: 6 March 2017]

[21] Aminian B, Araujo J, Johansson M, Johansson K. GISOO: A virtual testbed for wireless cyber-physical systems. In: IECON 2013—39th Annual Conference of the IEEE. IEEE; 2013. pp. 5588-5593. DOI: 10.1109/IECON.2013.6700049

[22] Nguyen H-N. A benchmark problem: The non-isothermal continuous stirred tank reactor. In: Constrained Control of Uncertain, Time-Varying, Discrete-Time Systems. Cham: Springer International Publishing; 2014. pp. 181-187. DOI: 10.1007/978-3-319-02827-9_8

[23] Lightbody G, Irwin G. Direct neural model reference adaptive control. IEE Proceedings—Control Theory and Applications. 1995;**142**(1):31-43. DOI: 10.1049/ip-cta:19951613

[24] Januário F, Amâncio S, Catarina L, Luis P, Cardoso A, Gil P. Outliers accommodation in fuzzy control systems over WSAN. In: Volume 255: Intelligent Decision Technologies. Netherlands: IOS Press; 2013. pp. 334-343. DOI: 10.3233/978-1-61499-264-6-334